COUNTERFEIT GENTLEMEN

New Perspectives on the History of the South

UNIVERSITY PRESS OF FLORIDA
Florida A&M University, Tallahassee
Florida Atlantic University, Boca Raton
Florida Gulf Coast University, Ft. Myers
Florida International University, Miami
Florida State University, Tallahassee
New College of Florida, Sarasota
University of Central Florida, Orlando
University of Florida, Gainesville
University of North Florida, Jacksonville
University of South Florida, Tampa
University of West Florida, Pensacola

University Press of Florida

Gainesville · Tallahassee · Tampa · Boca Raton · Pensacola
Orlando · Miami · Jacksonville · Ft. Myers · Sarasota

Counterfeit

GENTLEMEN

 *Manhood and Humor in the Old South*

John Mayfield

Copyright 2009 by John Mayfield
Printed in the United States of America
on acid-free paper
All rights reserved
First cloth printing, 2009
First paperback printing, 2011

A record of cataloging-in-publication data is
available from the Library of Congress.
ISBN 978-0-8130-3337-2 (cloth)
ISBN 978-0-8130-3686-1 (pbk.)

The University Press of Florida is the scholarly
publishing agency for the State University System
of Florida, comprising Florida A&M University,
Florida Atlantic University, Florida Gulf Coast
University, Florida International University, Florida
State University, New College of Florida, University
of Central Florida, University of Florida, University
of North Florida, University of South Florida, and
University of West Florida.

University Press of Florida
15 Northwest 15th Street
Gainesville, FL 32611-2079
http://www.upf.com

For Sarah

Contents

Acknowledgments ix

Introduction: Negotiating Manhood in the Old South xiii

CHAPTER 1   *The Conception and Estimate of a Gentleman*   1

CHAPTER 2   *Georgia Theatrics, Georgia Yankees*   25

CHAPTER 3   *Counterfeit Presentments*   48

CHAPTER 4   *Useful Alloys*   67

CHAPTER 5   *Swamp Fevers*   83

CHAPTER 6   *Notes from the Underground*   105

Epilogue   123

Notes   129

Bibliography   141

Index   157

Acknowledgments

This book might have started in many ways. It could have begun, for example, in Mrs. Florence's English class when I was in the sixth grade. She assigned a book report but specifically outlawed anything from the Hardy Boys or Nancy Drew series, so I went rummaging through my mother's Book-of-the-Month Club selections and came up with the shortest volume on the shelf, Mac Hyman's *No Time for Sergeants*. I read it and loved it, particularly the fight in the latrine, which I reported with great detail in my best sixth-grade prose. I got an "A," but long afterwards I learned that Mrs. Florence paid my mother a visit to see where I got my research materials, so to speak. She made chit-chat with Mom while eyeballing the big bookcase in the living room. Fortunately Mom kept a lot of Bible commentaries up next to the steamers, so I passed, and Mom got another good story to tell, which she embellished in the great Southern tradition. (Mom never told anything exactly the same way twice.) Anyway, it was the first really funny book I'd ever read, and I wanted to read more. It also alerted me to the possibility that humor could be troublesome. So this could have started there.

Or it might have begun years later when I was an undergraduate history major at Columbia and took a class under the legendary James P. Shenton. He was both repulsed by and taken with the South, and one day he mentioned Joseph Glover Baldwin's *Flush Times in Alabama and Mississippi* as if it were important. I didn't know what a "flush time" was, so the title intrigued me, and besides, if Shenton thought it meant something, I took it seriously. I made a mental note to read it. Ten years later

I chanced on a copy and did just that. I could see why Shenton recommended it, so I figured that it was okay to treat humor seriously. Things sort of developed from there. Anyway, I owe Shenton a lot, and it's too bad he's not around anymore to see the fruits of his stray comment—or maybe he's lucky, time will tell.

Or it could have begun at the University of Baltimore, where faculty from English and history were putting together an interdisciplinary course on Western culture called "Arts and Ideas." No one had the slightest idea what that meant, but since I was junior faculty I got the job of teaching the first round. In the process of reading and teaching the *Iliad* I also read Bertram Wyatt-Brown's *Southern Honor*, then recently published. The connection between the two was clear, one informing the other, and I thought it might be time to dig deeper into Southern concepts of honor and manhood, which got me going into studies of Southern identity, which is what this book is ultimately about. That, plus humor, plus my own doubts that Southern men were all *that* honorable rather converged on each other, and here we are. Anyway, it could have begun that way, too.

However it began, I owe many people some serious debts. Michael O'Brien and other members of the Southern Intellectual History Circle have provided an arena in which the concept of the Southern intellectual could be treated as something more than an oxymoron. I have profited from discussions with Chaz Joyner, Chandos Brown, Joan Cashin, Dickson D. Bruce, Mitchell Snay, Michael Morrison, Susan V. Donaldson, Steve Matanle, Jonathan Bryant, and many more. At critical points I've had great commentary from Ted Ownby, Steven Stowe, and Kieran Quinlan.

I owe a special debt to John David Smith, who recruited me for this series and who was unstinting in his support, his critical acumen, and his patience. The same goes for Stephen Berry, who explains Southern history to us in the most perfect prose. Anne and Bertram Wyatt-Brown have been unfailing in their friendship and encouragement. These are people who give the profession humanity, not to mention a bit of fun.

As for Johanna Nicol Shields and David Moltke-Hansen—they are quite simply among the smartest, most acute, most knowledgeable people I've met in this profession. More than that, they are the best critics one could have: supportive yet blunt and always on target. Between the two, they *know* pretty much what needs to be known about the Old South, and I count myself fortunate that they took this project seriously.

I also thank my colleagues, both at the University of Baltimore and at Samford University, and especially Susan Murphy, who ran the office and covered for me while I wrote.

Finally, thanks to my wife, Sarah, and my daughter, Whitney. Both have put a smile on my face that had no irony to it at all.

Permissions

In preparing this volume I have drawn on certain articles I wrote and published previously. These include:

"Being Shifty in a New Country: Southern Humor and the Masculine Ideal." In *Southern Manhood: Perspectives on Masculinity in the Old South*, edited by Craig Thompson Friend and Lorri Glover, 113–35. Athens: University of Georgia Press, 2004.

"George Washington Harris: The Fool from the Hills." In *The Human Tradition in Antebellum America*, edited by Michael A. Morrison, 229–43. Wilmington, Del.: Scholarly Resources Inc., 2000.

"The Theater of Public Esteem: Ethics and Values in Longstreet's *Georgia Scenes*." In *Georgia Historical Quarterly* 75 (Fall 1991): 566–86.

I gratefully acknowledge the publishers' permissions to use extracts from these works.

Introduction
Negotiating Manhood in the Old South

This is a book about values and identity in the Old South. It uses ideas about manhood to examine those values, and it uses humor to explore manhood. It is not, strictly speaking, a book about the comic tradition in the South, a subject that has been thoroughly and skillfully explored.[1] It does not deal with yarn-spinners or tale-tellers per se, although those people were an important part of Southern history and constitute one of its enduring legacies. It is emphatically not a book about salt-river roarers, alligator-men, or bear-wrasslers either, although it uses those figures where relevant. It is, rather, a book about white Southern men and the way they regarded themselves, and if there is a common reference point here it is the alligator-man's opposite, the Southern gentleman, who appears not as a storyteller or snob but as the subject of an ambivalent expression of how antebellum Southern men defined themselves, and what that tells us about what it was, before the war, to be Southern.

Why we should study values and identity in the Old South may appear problematic, since Southern history is by definition a foray into values and identity. These days such a journey is a walk along the great divide of modernity. Falling away to one side is a view that presents the region as precapitalistic, patriarchal, honor-bound, and conservative—a perspective that stresses class and race above all else. To the other is a South modern and fluid, a partner in the evolution of capitalism and democratic institutions, but not a full partner, given the presence of slavery. Here the very issue of class is so complicated it threatens to read itself out of the picture, and even race may appear overstressed.[2] My focus is on the passage between these two idealized Souths, the area where tensions between tradition and modernity make the going interesting. Frankly, I think that the Old South was a good deal more progressive than has often been assumed, but its liberalism was nuanced and complex, defined as often as not by contradictions and doubts. These nuances are worth a hard look, and I simply wanted to get at my own answers in my own way—which led me to the study of manhood.

Why we should use manhood to explore values is only lately becoming clear. Gender is fundamental to identity, and its "work," as Anne Goodwyn Jones calls it, is to affirm, deny, or reevaluate the complex attitudes which make up a culture's "dominant fiction."[3] The dominant fiction about the antebellum South is that it was a patriarchy in which power and authority rippled outward and downward from men whose view of themselves was stable and simple. This idea has its interpretive advantages. Simplicity is the dominant trait of patriarchs. They lumber about like cultural dinosaurs, dominating things by sheer bulk, force, and a single-minded conviction that God put them on earth to rule. This perception of patriarchy has led to a curious "otherness" in Southern gender and racial studies. We know quite a bit about women by looking at how they defined themselves in relation to men. We know much about slaves and free blacks based upon how they defined themselves in relation to white men. Patriarchy serves almost as a mathematical constant here, something by which other points can be calculated.

But do we know much about white men as white men? From the sheer bulk of what has been written on the Old South it would seem obvious that we do, but our assumptions about patriarchal mastery and male solidarity are a bit tidy and, well, humorless. In a region that added over 25 million acres of prime real estate in the fifteen years after Cherokee removal began in 1830 alone, that by 1860 produced 70% of the world's cotton supply, life was anything but stable, and in changing environments like these even tough traditions like patriarchy can get fluid, be redefined, and go off on tangents. I see no evidence that white Southern men were less human or more constant or more stable than anyone else in that remarkable era. They certainly did not see themselves as static or unchallenged. Language matters, and what is remarkable to me is how seldom Southern white males used the term "patriarchy." They preferred the term "manhood." Manhood is a shifty term, not easily pinned down.

It is something that men use to define other men and themselves, and it is hardly a constant.

Manhood's driving force is the need to dominate. It may express itself through class, race, sex, violence, risk taking, or some other outlet, but always at its core it is focused on competition with other men. To paraphrase David Leverenz (who writes about Northern authors), terms like "patriarchy" may be more or less accurate in describing women's experience of men in the home or slaves' of masters on the plantation, but they do not always reflect men's experience of each other, where the competitive instinct is strong and life is an endless rivalry for dominance.[4] Here the salient term is manhood itself, and manhood has to be constantly demonstrated. To quote Anne Goodwyn Jones again, "Manhood in the south was a matter of constant creation and re-creation; the site for such creativity was typically a community of other white men."[5] The battlefield was one such community, certainly, and the Civil War gave white Southern men the opportunity to be as domineering as they liked. But so were the battlefields of home (where extended families created their own complex sets of male relationships), small towns, politics, courtrooms, manly recreations such as the hunt, and the marketplace—either local or national. Manhood there was a matter of negotiation.

This was evident to Southern men. White male Southerners had a far more textured and ambivalent sense of manhood than we generally give them credit for. Being a "man" was not a given, and they worked hard at resolving their ambivalences and fashioning new modes of manhood. Sometimes they were successful, other times not. I have chosen to call this work *Counterfeit Gentlemen*, because elite Southern male identity was a good deal more open to self-fabrication than some would admit. The term, incidentally, originates with Johnson Jones Hooper, who sat down in 1844 to write a campaign biography of Captain Simon Suggs and claimed that the best he could come up with under the circumstances was a "counterfeit presentment" (a line from *Hamlet*) of the "real" Suggs, who was of course a figment of Hooper's imagination to begin with, cooked up at a time when Hooper himself was trying to figure out what he wanted to be when he grew up, even though he was almost thirty. That's the real spirit of Southern manhood to me—confused, tentative, situational, self-fashioned, and always in search of the right pose or "presentment."

Consider the example of Daniel Hundley, who in 1860 tried to explain the South to anyone who would listen. He had good credentials. A self-made man if ever there was one, Hundley went to Harvard and studied law, then lived in Chicago before returning to Alabama, thus trading one raw environment for another. By its title, Hundley's book—*Social Relations in Our Southern States*—could have gone off in any conceivable methodological direction, but he chose to write about types of men. He listed no fewer than eight categories, from gentleman cavaliers to cotton snobs to Southern Yankees to white trash to slaves, and included not a single chapter about women, as if that would do it. Modern readers take the volume very seriously, as they should. So do I, but I also find it occasionally hilarious. Hundley has the driest of wits; his comparisons have an edge to them that Pope or Swift—or better, Will Rogers—would have appreciated. Besides, the very publication date of the book, 1860, is almost unbearably ironic. In five years it was ancient history.[6]

Hundley's book expresses two strong tendencies in the Southern male mind. One is a relentless preoccupation with the concept of manhood itself. *Social Relations* is a veritable periodic table of the many varieties of Southern men—whom Hundley types, labels, and tests like so many elements—and it stands at variance with a general urge among historians to group Southerners into dichotomies. We normally think in pairs: planters and plain folk, whites and blacks, men and women—that is, the dialectics of class, race, or gender. Hundley thought in far more complex relations, and his men compete in shifting landscapes for dominance. There may be white elite patriarchs in his South, but they are few and their power is more apparent than real.[7]

This brings us to a second inclination Hundley shared with his fellow Southern men. There is a strong streak of uncertainty in Hundley's didactic prose. He does not define manhood so much as he negotiates it, attempting to find direction through the many manhoods available to him, while assessing their true worth at the same time. He is not wholly successful at either task. He often starts a chapter with solid, unambiguous pronouncements, and then wanders off into contradictions, reservations, and asides. Occasionally he gives in to a refreshingly candid sense of despair, as if he knows that his task is futile. There is, in fact, a Shakespearian sense of loss in Hundley's work, like the bard's many characters who discover somewhere around act 4 that they have striven to be the wrong thing. Southerners loved Shakespeare, and I think that is significant, because the language of antebellum Southern men has more often than not been interpreted wholly in terms of power and assertion, and not in terms of introspection or self-doubt.

What complicated Hundley's struggle to define manhood was a tendency, stubbornly existent to this day, to arrange Southern society in strata of class and race. It is difficult to capture the tentative manhoods of Southern men because we are so conditioned to layer Southern society along such essentially horizontal lines. The quasi-feudal contours of the plantation system encourage this kind of thinking, and I know no one who would say that the Old South was *not* hierarchical. Certainly I would not. Southerners such as William Gilmore Simms often thought of social identity—manhood foremost—as an extended Great Chain of Being, with "masters," "overseers," "common folk," and such arranging themselves on a social continuum of power and influence.[8] These linguistic shortcuts, however, are heavily freighted with economic and political agendas, and they often obscure what Southerners themselves saw as a more permeable, shifting social topography.

This topography becomes a little clearer if we look to behaviors and self-images other than wealth or even race. Here the fault lines are likely to run *vertically* across classes, plain folk and gentry, and reflect in geological terms dynamic conflict and stress, not European-style sediments of authority and class. I see two overarching ethics, two competitive codes, which were not exactly antithetical but which could lead to two very different definitions of manhood. These ethics were not defined by class or wealth, although one's social status figured prominently in how the behaviors expressed themselves. To return to Jones's idea of the "dominant fiction" again: Southern men are commonly regarded as emotional, touchy about a vague thing called "honor," prone to self-indulgence punctuated by bursts of violence, and transparent as glass. Bertram Wyatt-Brown and others have described a South obsessed with honor and public reputation, "an essentially masquerade culture," as Kenneth Greenberg calls it, in which appearances were everything.[9] In the Old South, the way men confronted death or rebellious slaves, the reasons they had for hunting or gambling or cosigning notes they could not pay, the way they took offense or exercised generosity, and the way they put white women on pedestals while they slipped off to the slave quarters were all intertwined into a complex set of codes that people understood as surely as the Ten Commandments. These codes, in turn, established authority and status, and they gave a Southern man a sense of "self" that our angst-ridden modern sensibilities occasionally find shallow and even bizarre. They also produced men who were acutely sensitive to being dominated by other men and who were driven by fears of humiliation and shame, rather like Homeric warriors who would rather die than appear weak.

As pervasive as masquerade culture was, Southern men, like their Northern counterparts, felt overlapping pressures to define themselves in more modern, progressive terms. Here the terminology is less precise. "Market culture" is appropriate to an extent, as is "evangelical" or even "Victorian," depending on the context. Whatever the emphasis, Southern men felt obliged to work, provide for the family, set moral standards based on the Protestant ethic, and cultivate a cool rationalism directed toward the perfect deal. The behaviors demanded by the market and the church were not those of the clan. Manhood in the marketplace required shrewdness over fearlessness, cleverness over generosity, a tough rationalism over pride, self-discipline over conspicuous waste, and the occasional need to be downright deceptive rather than transparent. The desire to win, to dominate, remained the same, as did the fear of failure—a fear that only worsened as new lands opened to the west. Closely allied to market behaviors was an evangelical, reforming streak that added moral probity and pietism to the entrepreneur's habits of self-discipline and hard work. Ted Ownby has called these attitudes "evangelical culture" and applied them to the postwar South. To do that for the antebellum South would be a stretch, but I think the idea bears a closer look. The New South's eager embrace of business sense and evangelical morality was not born in the instant Lee surrendered, and I see its roots stretching back to the 1830s.[10]

No doubt some Southern men managed to live out one role or the other; most lived somewhere in between, which gave an edginess to Southern male culture. That brings up the issue of humiliation, or what they would have called simply "shame." These were highly competitive men, and they were keenly sensitive to humiliation. To quote Leverenz again: "Anyone preoccupied with manhood, in whatever time or culture, harbors fears of being humiliated, usually by other men. The sources of humiliation may be diverse, in parents or the loss of class position, in marketplace competition or other fears of being dominated. A preoccupation with manhood becomes a compensatory response."[11] Southern men worked to prove themselves generous, gregarious, noble, indifferent to money, physically fearless, and incapable of contradiction. They killed each other over the vaguest of slights and then treated the survivors to a round of drinks. Meanwhile they purchased land, bought slaves, and worked overtime to beat each other in the marketplace—which can be as indifferent to honor as a hangman. They went to church occasionally and grieved over their sins. They got henpecked. Is it any wonder, then, that men like Hundley were obsessed with what it meant to be manly? Defeat, shame, and humiliation—racial, sexual, social, and economic—lurked around every corner.

Not exactly a funny situation, but one ripe for humor. Southern men's preoccupation with manhood voiced itself readily through fiction, which has a capacity for nuance and speculation that expository writing often lacks. "Fiction, even bad or indifferent fiction," writes William R. Taylor, "often taps levels of the imagination which are not reached in conceptual writing and turns up reservations and contradictions which do not appear in polemics."[12] This point is particularly true of humor. Humor is of necessity alienated and detached. It can be satirical or outright farcical, as in English humor (the English have long since accepted things as crazy-in-themselves). Americans still want to improve everything, and so we have a special attraction to irony, the sense that things aren't always what they seem and don't always work out the way they are supposed to. Southern humor has been among the best and most ironic of the lot.

In the thirty years before the Civil War, white Southern men published an astonishing catalog of tales, stories, reminiscences, spoofs, and satires. Modern readers are likely to homogenize the whole lot into "frontier" or "Southwestern" humor, which is a bit misleading. Between 1830 and 1860, amateur wits in the South generated a huge body of rough, anecdotal humor for local newspapers or for publications such as William T. Porter's New York sporting journal, the *Spirit of the Times*.[13] They often used the frontier as a backdrop, but not always. Their prose was usually straightforward; they excelled in dialect. They reveled in conflict, knavery, and practical jokes, and no subject, not even sex, was taboo. Whether drawn from tall tales of the frontier or odd stories of real life, their scenes and characters have a more intensely "Southern" quality than any number of wooden cavaliers. Poe loved this sort of homespun irreverence, and if *he* found something funny it likely deserves our attention. Its influence was manifest in Mark Twain, Will Rogers, and even, farther down the line, Brother Dave Gardner.

The frontier style dominates humor studies, but it did not stand alone. By 1860 at least three distinct genres of Southern humor flourished.[14] An anecdotal style existed alongside frontier humor—the product of yarn-spinners who published odd pieces about odd characters in local newspapers or the *Spirit*. This evolved after the Civil War into "local color," a strange blend of lowbrow humor and nostalgia that sometimes verged on camp. A third style, more varied and complex, came from self-conscious artists who freely used all kinds of humor—from the frontier style to Addisonian essays, satires, genteel spoofs in the manner of Washington Irving, and humorous characters in serious novels—as part of a larger and sustained critique of Southern culture. These latter I call, for simplicity's sake, Southern humorists, not only because they used "Southern" techniques but also because they addressed peculiarly Southern issues.

They are my focus. They have particular relevance in the intellectual history of the Old South because they were not bound by the conventions of polite discourse, either fictional or didactic. They could be and were subversive, and they seemed to take delight in pricking the myths of Southern life. "With Poe, these southern writers were the first informal school to protest a growing nineteenth-century prettification of life, most absurdly realized in the South," writes Jesse Bier. "And the wellspring of their energies was more than simple irreverence, it was contempt and covert hostility for a veritable system of falsifications, of which 'moonlight and magnolias' of the old slavocracy remains the apotheosis in our history."[15] These were not mindless jokesters; they were critical, thinking men.

Only a few were artists, and we know by common consent who they were: John Pendleton Kennedy, Augustus Baldwin Longstreet, Joseph Glover Baldwin, Johnson Jones Hooper, Henry Clay Lewis, George Washington Harris, and Thomas Bangs Thorpe. Others, such as William Tappan Thompson or C.F.M. Noland, could be included; arguably, so could William Gilmore Simms. But these seven set the benchmarks for Southern humor. None conformed slavishly to the Southwestern, frontier style; most produced major, book-length works and wrote in other genres; all were artists rather than artisans. Kennedy, for example, wrote novels, a biography, and political satire. Longstreet published a pro-nullification newspaper but later turned to long essays on theology and denominational politics as well as a "serious" novel. Hooper, also a newspaper editor, wrote a compact guide to the hunt. Baldwin did character studies of great men; Harris wrote campaign material. Thorpe was an artist, essayist, and, incredibly, an antislavery novelist. Moreover, there is a chronological continuity to their writings. Kennedy and Longstreet published chiefly in the 1830s. Hooper, Lewis, and Thorpe wrote primarily in the 1840s. Baldwin's work came in the 1850s, as did Harris's, although the latter did not issue a book until 1867. They also covered the ground, literally, in an arc that ran from Atlantic South to Gulf South to mountain

South. Kennedy confined himself to Virginia. Longstreet wrote from the most settled part of Georgia (and still he is called a "frontier" wit!). Baldwin was born in Virginia and Hooper in North Carolina, but both moved to Alabama. Harris was from Knoxville and its environs, and his creation Sut Lovingood flourished (if you can call it that) nearby. Thorpe was an outsider who found his way to Louisiana and got lost there, as did Lewis. As I argue below, all shared certain common traits, yet each was unique, and each negotiated manhood in his own special way.

Manhood was central to their humor in two ways. One was audience. Humor depends on a community of readers or listeners who presumably share some common interest in the subject at hand. Southern humor was intentionally masculine. Men who told tales or wrote satires in the antebellum South did so usually for other men, specifically other white, educated men. However jaded may appear the prospect of picking over this group yet again, it should be remembered that they formed one of Jones's "communities" within which Southern men could create and recreate manhood and do so in the perfect safety of fiction.

Beyond audience was content. Southern humor centered on "manly" pursuits, whether at home, in recreation, or at work. These manly pursuits were competitive. The subjects of Southern humor can be seen politicking, opinionating, dueling, hunting, swearing, conning, arguing, horse trading, drinking, eating, lusting, and generally living at the edge or even in the middle of violent behaviors of every sort. A rivalry for dominance, physical or otherwise, is present in every form of Southern humor, and it does not matter if the style is rough and woodsy or refined and urbane. The stakes are high: manhood itself.

This interplay between audience and content is essential to understanding humor both as humor and as intellectual history. Like gender, the question becomes, What "work" does humor do? Sigmund Freud, who was privately renowned as a storyteller and jokester, saw humor as a release of aggression. Henri Bergson argued that humor must have social significance, usually as a way of isolating some perceived threat.[16] The battle of the sexes is an obvious field for this kind of psychoanalytical theory; so are bad jokes about hayseeds, city slickers, rival football teams, or any other identifiable group that doesn't happen to be your own. Content in either case is everything; that is, what the joke *says* is all-important to understanding it. Bergson's theory has had special relevance to the South. There is a long tradition in humor studies, as much neo-Marxist as it is psychoanalytical, that sets the Southern humorist up as a "self-controlled gentleman" telling jokes on the rubes down the road. Kenneth Lynn argued in 1959 that humorists were a Whiggish lot appalled by the democratization of taste and power in Jacksonian America. They used humor to draw a cordon sanitaire between themselves and the unwashed mob.[17] This point of view has not been universally accepted, especially among folklorists or literary critics who understandably focus more on the artistic merits of the genre rather than its political content. Historians, on the other hand, find its dichotomies useful.

There is another approach to humor, less classist and more humanistic, that focuses on the incongruities and ambiguities in a culture. Here, the *way* in which a joke or story is told is as important as what it says. Eliot Oring's wonderful study of the *Palmah*, a pre-independence Israeli paramilitary group active in the 1940s, is suggestive. The Palmah were an odd and not completely comfortable mix of Levantine and European Jews who told long, seemingly pointless stories about themselves which explored the boundaries where the traditions of immigrant Europeans and the customs of natives met. They poked fun at their own special combination of rubes and snobs, told stories that were so self-referential only an insider could laugh, and delighted most of all in the telling of a tale rather than its punch line. Throughout the process they explored the ambiguities and ironies of being Jewish in a new land. Identity, not class or sexual warfare, was the grist of their humor, and incongruity became its millstone. "A joke does not genuinely resolve incongruity; it displays and heightens it," writes Oring. "In choosing a humorous structure in which to cast their [internal] conflict, the Palmah not only chose to recognize and entertain the paradox of their identity, but to accept paradox as part of their identity."[18] Similarly, Southern humor has an in-house, self-deprecating quality to it, and paradox is its essence.

I think that both approaches work for understanding Southern humor. As hard as scholars have worked to refute Lynn, the fact remains that Southern humorists *were* hard on the plain folk and took particular delight in portraying them as yokels and hicks. They still do, as any recipient of endless e-mail lists of the forty-three-ways-you-know-you're-a-redneck will attest. At the same time, Bier's caution about the prettification of Victorian culture bears repeating. The antics of the rubes were no more outrageous than the attempts of the would-be elites to puff themselves up and put on airs. Both were silly in the face of the hard economic realities of the market revolution. Both displayed the uncertainties of being male in a society that posed as patriarchal yet proclaimed itself progressive. Thus did Southern humor cut both ways. The artistry of the Southern humorists was to create, like the Palmah, a medium in which these incongruities could be castigated and celebrated at the same time.

That double-edged perspective comes from the rather marginal status of the humorists themselves. Collective profiles are risky, but they give useful hints. The humorists who make it into most anthologies generally had an unfixed place in Southern society; they lived in the borderlands between seaboard South and new Southwest, or plantation South and speculative South, or settled South and mobile South.[19] Most were born shortly before or after the War of 1812 and thus shared their generation's triumphant sense of independence twice-won from the British. They grew up with the second American party system, but that does not seem to have colored their perceptions in any prescriptive way. Although Lynn claimed they were overwhelmingly Whig, the evidence suggests that many, at least a third, were Democrats. Some changed parties in mid-life. There is a generally transitive quality to their lives. "Disinherited or otherwise thrown upon borders, journeying to landscapes otherwise familiar to themselves as interiors," writes Jesse Bier, "they held desperately to old graces or values as they simultaneously joined the hurly-burly of the nation."[20]

A profile of the specific artists studied here produces some interesting commonalities. All were professionals and/or businessmen, not planters. If they owned slaves at all, they owned a few house servants, not a gang of field hands, and lived in towns rather than on plantations. One cannot call them cosmopolitan, exactly, but they weren't isolated either. Second, a surprising number had roots in the North. Either they were born there, spent part of their youth there, were educated there, or had close family connections there. Only a few could trace their Southern roots very far, and even those moved around. At the same time, most were die-hard nullifiers or secessionists. They fully subscribed to the dominant racial attitudes of their peers, and they believed unequivocally in state's rights. Their perspective, then, came from perhaps the least consciously studied group in Southern society, the middle-class Southern professional male—the ones who staffed the officers corps in the Civil War and whose children created the New South later on. If one insists on thinking in terms of class, they were petit bourgeoisie.

Most provocative, none of the major humorists of the Old South had strong relationships with their fathers. Longstreet's father, for example, was a visionary inventor who failed at everything he did; much the same might be said of the fathers of John Pendleton Kennedy and Johnson Jones Hooper. Some had, metaphorically, no fathers at all: Harris's parents parked him with a brother and simply disappeared; Thorpe's father died when Thorpe was four, leaving his mother to do the raising; Lewis's mother died and his father drifted off to the West in search of whatever widowers look for when their lives fall apart. Their family histories, in short, were chaotic, and while that doesn't prove a thing, it does make one wonder: in a supposedly patriarchal society, what happens when the patriarch is a fool, a lost soul, or a vague memory? Psychological profiles are tenuous and risky, but I will venture the rather obvious observation that fathers are key figures in patriarchal societies, stable or not. They provide role models, good or bad, for young men. Conversely, their absence or weakness may provoke more intense searches for alternate role models.

The marginality these humorists felt may have, ironically, liberated them from the easy trap of equating manhood with racial dominance. This does not mean that I am unaware of or insensitive to the primacy of race in the evolution of the South (or the whole country for that matter). It means that no one thing, race or class or any of the usual criteria for historical assessment, can fully explain what happened to the construction of Southern male identity in the run-up to civil war. Slavery, after all, was a capitalist enterprise, a form of industrial management and labor driven by profits, and the slave could be and was looked upon as a piece of machinery. Free blacks and slaves enter the stories of these humorists only occasionally, and most often only as victims of practical jokes or as avuncular stereotypes who utter something profound and then disappear. Occasionally black characters actually help set up a gag on a white man. The humorists so completely accepted the notion of white supremacy that their daily lives were *not* spent managing and humiliating men of another race (or even poor whites, for that matter). This fact cannot be overstressed. Even men who ultimately opposed slavery, such as Kennedy and Thorpe, simply *assumed* that blacks were nonstarters in the competitions of the modern world, and therefore irrelevant to a discussion of manhood. The men who wrote this humor were focused on their perceived peers, and they passed their time in a game of outperforming other white men.

The chapters that follow use the tension between masquerade culture and market/evangelical behavior as an underlying theme, but each highlights the conflict from a different perspective. The gentleman is the central figure throughout, even when the characters are louts. All Southern ideologies of manhood ultimately involve the figure of the gentleman, who in turn is present either as observer or participant in most antebellum Southern fiction, humor included. Hence, I have begun with John Pendleton Kennedy and his 1832 work, *Swallow Barn*. Neither Kennedy nor the book make it into most anthologies of Southern humor, partly because he did not write in the frontier style, partly because he was barely from the South, and partly because critics have tended either to take him too seriously or not seriously enough. *Swallow Barn* is a very serious, funny book which sets down most of the groundwork for what follows in Southern humor. Kennedy outlined the Southern country gentleman very well, and that type of manhood depended upon a certain mix of localism, familial honor, and paternalism. It was an ideal, as Kennedy described it, on the verge of extinction, yet it is an essential point of reference for understanding Southern masculinity.

The gentleman, however, was a complicated figure—noble but of questionable use in a modernizing world. The chapters that follow Kennedy may be conceived as a series of commentaries on particular aspects of the gentleman's masculine expressions. Each writer in effect took a part of the gentleman's persona and examined it under the lens of humor and with an eye to the ways the Southwestern context distorted his mythic posture. Longstreet's *Georgia Scenes* may or may not properly be labeled "Southwestern" humor. I see it as an extended commentary on the rising Southern middle class by a man whose reform impulses moved him into religion, education, and Southern nationalism all at once. Longstreet had the most potential for displaying Victorian sensibilities about the home and moral responsibility, and he is the earliest voice of an evangelical culture that would come to dominate Southern life after the war. His kind of ambition demanded a serious rethinking of republican authority and gentlemanly manhood. Longstreet's rethinking was particularly broad and ran up and down the social scale, and it was his genius to see the ways in which a single aspect of manly behavior—fighting, for example—could re-create itself across class lines.

Baldwin and Hooper, on the other hand, were old money set adrift in a world of con men and sharpers—self-conscious representatives of a South that changed dramatically as it moved west into Alabama and Mississippi. Neither man was particularly concerned with ripsnorters or alligator-men; their "frontier" was the liminal zone between traditional values and economic opportunism. Victor Turner has argued that in such liminal zones any number of transitional figures (shamans, jesters, neophytes, et cetera) appear to interpret the competing cultures to their listeners.[21] For Baldwin and Hooper, the con man was such an interpreter, and the con man's art is language. Among humorists they were the most concerned with the power of language itself—the mastery imparted through words. One found redeeming possibilities in the experience; one did not.

An essential part of masquerade culture was the controlled use of violence, yet violence on the Southern frontier was often anything but controlled. While much of the humor of the Old Southwest fairly echoes with whoops, gunshots, ear chewing, and wrassling—all exuberant escapism little different from B-movies or pulp fiction—violence supposedly had its regenerative qualities for lost manhood. As such, the gentleman laid claim to the ultimate expressions of violence: mastery over lesser men, over animals, and over nature itself. Thomas Bangs Thorpe's poignant and occasionally sad perspective came from a Yankee and an artist and an outsider looking in, and what he saw was a culture of violence and display that ran counter not only to the economic imperatives of modernization but curiously to a larger concept of stewardship of nature and self-control. The line between his bear-eaters and his gentlefolk is gray and dangerously permeable.

Henry Clay Lewis seemed to live outside all these parameters. A motherless child who ran away from what was left of home at age ten, Lewis was a strenuous, smart, supremely ambitious nobody who took advantage of a mentor's patronage to attend medical school and work his way up. His one book, *Odd Leaves from the Life of a Louisiana Swamp Doctor*, deserves real attention from both historians and literary critics alike. It is a young man's chronicle of coming of age, and in it we find the man of reason and science negotiating a masculine culture that prized impulse and romanticism. Like much Southern humor, it is cruel and maybe even sick, but its dark visions speak to the acute sense of anonymity and frustration that rootless young men must have felt on the fringes of Southern respectability. Lewis, more than any other Southern writer, shared a fundamental kinship with Edgar Allan Poe, and with Poe he moved Southern sensibilities from an exteriorized, masquerade posture to one that was interior and riven with guilt and inadequacy.

And then there was Harris, who was in some ways the last Old South humorist and the first of the New South. If Longstreet was the harbinger and early apologist for evangelical culture, Harris was its stoutest disciple and harshest critic. By the time he published his wildly anarchic Sut Lovingood stories, the country gentleman was dead on the battlefield, and new concepts of patriarchy and manly behavior were afoot. Harris can and should be taken many ways; my approach focuses on his utter rejection of masquerade culture and his metamorphosis into a Southern version of Dostoevsky's Underground Man—a confessional, interiorized, and morally tormented critic. Harris stands utterly apart from the other writers covered here, yet in his foreshadowing of the New South he summarizes them.

These stories are great fun, but what do they tell us? I began by saying that Southern humor reveals a masculine stance more interiorized and alienated than common wisdom allows. Like the Palmah, these men looked inward. A strong current of self-discipline and proto–Bible Belt moral accountability competed for masculine identity in the Old South, and the New South of the postwar era had deep roots in the earlier years. Yet this market-evangelical manliness could not break free and take command. The humorists' tales tell us rather forcefully that self-discipline and shrewdness made for "real" men, but so could masquerade culture, which was more fun, more assertive, and more Southern. It ran up and down the social scale, infecting everyone with an impulse for theatrical display. It is the tension between these ideals that furnished not only comic incongruity but a deep personal ambivalence about manhood in the lives of Southern men. In ways very similar to their Northern counterparts, they had to choose who to be.

In the end only one manly ideal triumphed. Let's return to Oring's Israelis for a moment. Their stories looked inward, celebrating paradox. They joked about themselves, and, so long as their identity was up in the air, the Palmah's stories and their sense of humor flourished. After independence, the Palmah split up and the stories vanished. It is as if these men finally found something to *be*, and the paradox of their identity vanished accordingly.

The same thing arguably happened to Southerners and their humor. All these paradoxes and manly posings largely disappeared after 1854, the publication date of Baldwin's *Flush Times*, the year Thorpe went back North, the year the Kansas-Nebraska Act was passed, and the year the Republican Party formed. Once an enemy was clearly identified and demonized, the battlefield superiority of masquerade culture—with its indifference to death and its manly postures—became the ideal, and Southern men lost their sense of ambiguity and irony. When Preston Brooks beat Charles Sumner senseless on the Senate floor in 1856, he committed an act that was impulsive, driven by honor, violent, theatrical, and clearly designed to inflict physical and emotional humiliation. It was the quintessential act of masquerade culture and its manly code, and its clarity and purity overwhelmed, for a time, any other vision of Southern manhood. The casualties were many, among them the Southern sense of humor, which for a time dried up in a suicidal fit of theatrical excess. But that is a story for another book, one not humorous at all.

COUNTERFEIT GENTLEMEN

Manhood and Humor in the Old South

1

The Conception and Estimate of a Gentleman

BEFORE THERE WAS Sut Lovingood or Ransy Sniffle or Simon Suggs or the Big Bear of Arkansas, there was the Virginia gentleman. All models of Southern manhood and masculinity had their reference point, their high ground, in this single figure, which went by several names: squire, the quality, country republican, aristocrat, Washington, Lee. Even his more impulsive kinsman, the Carolina cavalier, stood in his shadow. Why that was the case had roots deep in the colonial era and the peculiar authority that came with possession of slaves and profits from an international crop. Tobacco culture had merged seamlessly with plantation life, which in turn had joined to itself the ideal of the English squire, all of which had allowed the planter to evolve gloriously into a defender of the people and a protector of their rights. He became an icon, the general contours of which were known to any schoolboy. All agreed that the gentleman was republican—which meant that he was independent, served his people selflessly but with authority, and wore power like a familiar coat—that he was solid, civic-minded, related by blood to the whole county and half the state, that his generosity and sociability were as vast as his sense of pride and honor, that he was learned and pious but not to the point of being a twit or a prig, and—most visibly—that he did not actually work for a living, no matter how thin his margins were shaved.[1]

A sturdy icon, but a flawed one. There was always something slightly pretentious about the Virginia gentleman. His was a homegrown breed with often shallow family roots, and he had an unsettling habit of socializing with common folk and talking legalese rather than philosophy. There is considerable evidence that the Virginia planter worked hard despite his claim to leisure; he measured himself more by his tobacco output than he was willing to admit—indeed, he was obsessed with it.[2] He was materialistic, market-oriented, and extremely competitive, and his chief interest in land was acquisitive and exploitative. Even Washington—maybe even especially Washington—had devoted much of his life to surveying western lands, picking out choice bits, and speculating away. There was little time for creative writing in all this; during his heyday, the eighteenth-century gentleman's literary output was chiefly directed to legal parsing and reflections on politics—a good thing, considering the Revolution, but not particularly productive of the kind of imaginative self-study that literature and humor might have provided. In fact, humor seems to have been in short supply, especially self-mocking satire. Outside the racetrack, they were a fairly serious lot.

This situation began to change with the onset of postcolonialism, but with two ironic twists. Left to himself, no longer in direct competition with the English country squire, the Virginia gentleman might reasonably have expected in, say, 1820, to have settled in to unchallenged mastery—over slaves, women, lessers, anybody not of "the quality." With a near-perfect succession of presidents from Washington through Monroe, there was some political justification for this conceit. But the ground was moving under him, a fact early perceived by John Taylor of Caroline and John Randolph of Roanoke, who pinned the blame on outside forces of modernization and a general collapse of good taste. (Taylor retreated into long treatises on Arcadian insularity while Randolph adopted the role of eccentric.) The real trouble lay within: cotton displaced tobacco, money moved west, and the population went with it. Importantly, it was not just the hoi polloi who were moving. From Virginia on down the coast to South Carolina, planters themselves were catching the Alabama Fever, packing up, slaves and all, and heading west.[3] At the very moment of his triumph, so to speak, the Virginia gentleman found himself on the defensive, abandoned and driven to make a hard choice: join the postcolonial market revolution with gusto, or retreat into decay and marginalization. This was a "master class" in terms of its relation to slaves alone. Among the white population, the gentleman increasingly lacked either mastery or a stable class system, and so depended for his authority on tradition and appearances.

That proved a fragile platform at best, and here is the first of the ironic twists: before the slavery issue began to drive the South into an artificial coherence and cohesiveness, the Virginia aristocrat's usefulness as a masculine ideal in literature was wobbly at best. Such literature was virtually nonexistent in the 18th century, but by the 1820s Southern writers began to find a voice, and their first efforts homed in on the gentleman like birds of prey. Early works tended to record his indulgences and the legacy of waste thereof (George Tucker's *Valley of Shenandoah* is unflattering by any measure) or exile him to the past where he could be made heroic but not real (William Alexander Caruthers' treatment of Alexander Spotswood in *Knights of the Golden Horseshoe* comes to mind). Others treated him obliquely, as in William Wirt's biography of Patrick Henry, which was forced to emphasize Henry's yeoman roots and his oratory at the expense of his breeding and good taste.

All these works were written by outsiders of one stripe or another, and all saw flaws in the Virginia gentleman's arrogance and leisurely dissolution. Tucker was too much an economist to write humor, but Wirt, a sharp lawyer with a taste for Cervantes and Laurence Sterne, could not resist a light nudge at the people who paid his fees. Trying to set up a context in which Henry, one of the slipperiest of the Founders, could be made to look good, Wirt was compelled to deal with the internal contradictions of Virginia society early on in his book. Quoting an unnamed FFV (in fact Jefferson himself), Wirt described Virginia as a land of "classes," but—and the language is important—poorly defined ones. Said Wirt's source: "in a country insulated from the European world, insulated from its sister colonies, . . . little visited by foreigners, and having little matter to act upon within itself, certain families had risen to splendour by wealth," birthed "a series of men of talents," and settled in for more isolation, "*stationary* on the grounds of their forefathers." The rest is worth quoting at some length: "In such a state of things," said Wirt's observer,

> society would settle itself down into several *strata*, separated by no marked lines, but shading off imperceptibly from top to bottom, nothing disturb-

ing the order of their repose. There were, then, first, aristocrats, composed of the great landholders, who had seated themselves below tidewater on the main rivers, and lived in a style of luxury and extravagance insupportable by the other inhabitants, and which indeed, ended in several instances in the ruin of their own fortunes. Next to these were what might be called *half-breeds*; the descendants of the younger sons and daughters of the aristocrats, who inherited the pride of their ancestor, without their wealth.

Then came the pretenders, men, who, from vanity or the impulse of growing wealth, or from that enterprise which is natural to talents, sought to detach themselves from the plebeian ranks, to which they properly belonged, and imitated, at some distance, the manners and habits of the great. Next to these were a solid and independent yeomanry, looking askance at those above, yet not venturing to jostle them. And last and lowest, a *feculum* of beings, called overseers, the most abject, degraded, unprincipled race; always cap in hand to the dons who employed them, and furnishing materials for the exercise of their pride, insolence, and spirit of domination.[4]

This was written in 1817, and it is notable for several things. One is the rather contemptuous juxtaposition of wealth and breeding, money creating lineage and ending up in "pride, insolence, and spirit of domination," and, worst of all, "*half-breeds*," a corruption of the very essence of a landed gentry. The second is the insertion, right after "half-breeds," of the "pretenders"—the up'n'comers who knew how to mime a system that was itself a mime. This was a group to be watched closely and with suspicion. Also noteworthy is the utter absence of slaves in Wirt's narrative of classes. They were, in the early Virginian's estimation of himself and his evaluation of his peers, invisible. This is worth mentioning because, although slavery preoccupied later generations to the point of an idée fixe, it was not always present in Southern estimations of self.

Which leads to the other ironic twist: after slavery became *the* defining issue of what it was to be Southern, the hapless Virginia aristocrat found himself once again the model of Southern manliness. He became the reference point for an elaborate code of honor, mastery, and masculinity, and by the time Lee had surrendered with such courtliness at Appomattox, the ruling class Lee supposedly embodied was embedded permanently in the national consciousness.

But that was later. For a time, the Virginia gentleman was not the two-dimensional wall hanging he was later to become. He was open to interpretation, even caustic satire. More than that, his impact as a masculine image became the subject of a deep division in the Southerner's conception of self. Men began to take hard looks at the gentleman's effectiveness as a model for emulation, and Wirt's probing, acerbic estimation turned into outright satire. As cotton supplanted tobacco and created instant aristocrats in the new lands to the west, this satire worked its way naturally down from the real gentlemen to take in the "half-breeds" and the "pretenders" below, men who were borrowing and corrupting bits and pieces of the gentleman's culture of manhood. First, however, the humor centered on the gentleman himself. The process began with Wirt's disciple, John Pendleton Kennedy, and one of the most misunderstood books in Southern literature.

One of the remarkable things about Kennedy's *Swallow Barn* is that its author never made up his mind as to what kind of book it was.[5] When Kennedy set out to write in late 1829, he planned to produce a whimsical set of portraits of Virginia life after the fashion of Washington Irving's *Bracebridge Hall*, something in the "comic and satirical line." His narrator, Mark Littleton, was supposed to be a painter idly passing through and, as painters will do, simply observing the "odd and crotchetty people" of the Shenandoah Valley. By the time the book was published in 1832, Kennedy had complicated matters considerably. He changed Littleton into a Yankee relative, moved the scene east to a Tidewater plantation, introduced two plots about a spurious lawsuit and a budding romance, soared off into reflections on slavery, and ended with a remembrance of Captain John Smith. Along the way he inserted a street brawl, instructions on falconry, a story about the devil and a blacksmith, some fairly sophisticated observations on horses and lawyers, and a tale of heroism at sea featuring a ghost ship and a slave. Even Kennedy could not describe it, though he had gone through several drafts and was a meticulous reviser. "There is a rivulet of a story wandering through a broad meadow of episode," he explained in the preface, and promptly changed his mind. "Or, I might truly say, it is a book of episodes, with an occasional digression into the plot."

The double messages in *Swallow Barn* have made it a durable little book. In some ways it is a "plantation novel"—one of the first of a long line stretching across the decades to *Gone with the Wind*. It tends to the pastoral side of this tradition rather than the adventurous—there is an air of serenity and crystalline indifference to time in it—and it is seductively light and fanciful. English readers liked it even though it was an

American book, and Southern newspapers found it quaint and enjoyable. One went so far as to praise its "accuracy" and "the tone of healthful and moral feeling which pervades the whole work."[6] Kennedy depicted the way plantations should have been, if only all the myths about benevolent masters and happy slaves were true.

Even so, there is an unsettled quality to it, something that suggests internal decay and a slow slide into irrelevance. The book was a sad chronicle of the idle rich, a reviewer in the *New England Magazine* wrote. "His principal characters are humorously conceited, pompous, ignorant and dogmatic . . . the most ordinary, trifling, useless generation the world ever saw. . . . The whole book is a picture of the stillest of still life."[7] As Joseph Ridgely observed over a century later, *Swallow Barn* "is at cross-purposes in the treatment of its subject matter, that underneath the surface of a story which is often celebratory of recent Virginia life . . . there runs a disturbing counter-current of seriously intended satire."[8]

The "trifling, useless generation" Kennedy described was the planter elite, and what sets *Swallow Barn* apart from other plantation novels of the time is its sheer but understated irreverence and audacity. Its English comedy-of-manners humor is so quaint and adorable that it is easy to forget that *Swallow Barn* is one of the very few antebellum Southern novels that treat the planter as a figure of irony or comic incongruity. Most of the rest—including Kennedy's own later fiction—were deadly serious, as if a generation's identity hinged on importing the English country gentleman to the Tidewater unspoiled. The effort was more than an idle search for a Platonic form. In the intensely patriarchal world of the South, any masculine ideal was an ideology, a complex and powerful statement about the ruling class's claims to legitimacy and authority. To be "manly" asked certain questions. Who should leaders be? What should be their goals? How should they deal with others? How should others measure them and hold them accountable? What are their characteristics?

In the generation before war and devastation redefined everything, Southern intellectuals of every stamp tried their best to provide definitive answers to these questions, and virtually all Southern fiction of the time, humorous or serious, was a part of this response. Writers such as William Alexander Caruthers or William Gilmore Simms created fictional sociologies wherein manhood could be tried and explored. They mostly followed Simms's prescription of placing men in hard situations in order to test their manly qualities, and their heroes have a stereotypical, almost cartoon-like quality that is easy to follow and is loaded with cultural assumptions of every sort. Most set their plots in the past; some turned to the frontier. In that, they mimicked Walter Scott, certainly, but more likely Shakespeare, who had done the same thing, exiling Richard III, for example, to history and Hamlet to the boondocks of Denmark. It was a technique for safe criticism. Nonetheless, the books were essentially manuals for proper conduct, and they looked to the present and the future. In that, they are wholly different from the plantation novels of the post–Civil War era, which are largely efforts at self-justification and nostalgic denial.

Swallow Barn, however, was set in its own time, and any nostalgia it may have had was for the living and not the dead. That is suggestive, because any time a social ideal becomes sentimentalized it is already obsolete and ornamental. Beyond that, *Swallow Barn* confronted the Southern male in his sanctum sanctorum, the Virginia Tidewater plantation. If the frontier was the point of no return for the Southern male, the Tidewater was the point of origin, and Kennedy's "domestic history" (his words) was deeply absorbed in the most patriarchal, unchallenged seat of male authority the South could muster. Defining manhood there, amid slaves, plain folk, women, and dependents of every sort, was not a job to be taken lightly, and Kennedy's effort was not without ambiguity and ambivalence. "If my book be too much in the mirthful mode," he wrote, a little defensively, "it is because the ordinary actions of men, in their household intercourse, have naturally a humorous or comic character." Maybe so, but *Swallow Barn* is a *hard* look at the very epitome of Southern manhood, one that starts at the top of the pecking order and spins out implications across the social spectrum. Most astonishingly, it subverts the very concept of patrician manhood itself. In his rambling, episodic way, Kennedy took the country gentleman—the manliest of men—tamed him, domesticated him, and feminized him.

This was probably not Kennedy's conscious intent, for Kennedy ached to be a gentleman. The quest defined him, propelled him, and consumed him. "Born and educated in Baltimore," writes Vernon Parrington, "he was a son of the borderland, with strong ties of kinship and love that drew him to the Old Dominion, and even stronger ties of intellectual, social and financial interests that drew him toward Philadelphia and New York, Saratoga and Newport."[9] Rephrased, Kennedy was torn between familial nostalgia and opportunistic ambition. It was an inherited duality. Kennedy's father emigrated from northern Ireland to Philadelphia shortly after the Revolution, later set up a copper business in Baltimore, and made an impetuous marriage to a girl from western Virginia, Nancy Pendleton of Martinsburg. Kennedy's father had grand schemes and a love of display; his mother had great beauty and forceful intelligence—plus a long family tree. John Pendleton Kennedy was their firstborn, and he grew up in the mixed environments of country and city. In his youth Kennedy frequently visited his mother's kin, among them his uncle Philip Pendleton, a tie-wig Federalist who furnished him with models for the characters in *Swallow Barn*. These were genteel people in an idyllic environment, and he cherished his connections there. When the copper business went bust, however, Kennedy made a key decision. While the rest of the family joined the relatives in the Virginia countryside, Kennedy stayed in Baltimore.[10]

There, he literally created a life for himself. Kennedy's borderland nature made him an alloy of ambitions. He toyed with several careers in his life: lawyer, patron, politician, and writer. Successful at all of them, he was not *born* into any of them. Largely self-taught, Kennedy read law and hated it, but he worked his way up, ultimately becoming a corporate lawyer—a new profession for a new age. For a short time in his twenties, he and a friend, Peter Hoffman Cruse, anonymously published a light satirical journal, the *Red Book*, which was pure banditry of Irving's *Salamagundi Papers*. "The World in our opinion needs correction," Kennedy and Cruse explained, to a very small audience.[11] Their effort was short-lived, and Kennedy turned back to his first loves, politics and upward mobility. He was good at both. From fairly ordinary beginnings Kennedy became a fixture in the tonier levels of Maryland society for almost forty years. Partly this was a product of good luck. Like his father, he married into respectability and money; after his first wife died in childbirth, Kennedy wed the daughter of Edward Gray, a local factory owner. Gray was rich, Whig to the core, and wholly impatient with slackers and idlers, whom he equated with Virginia aristocrats. Gray had all the visionary ambition of Kennedy's own father, but with two enhancements. He moved decisively, and he succeeded. Kennedy adored him, emulated him, and exceeded him, and in that we have the first hint of a certain patriarchal confusion among those who came to write humor in the South. Kennedy's own father had followed the women into the countryside; the father-in-law, the adopted father, was his own master, and master of the marketplace.

The trajectory was set. In time, Kennedy came to own two houses, was a patron of the arts in every sense, and recognized Edgar Allan Poe's genius enough to promote him and lend him a little cash. He also served terms in the Maryland legislature and in Congress and was briefly secretary of the navy under Millard Fillmore. Kennedy persuaded Congress to help finance Samuel Morse's experiments with the telegraph, sent Commodore Perry to open Japan to American shipping, and along the way pumped out four novels (two of them very good), a biography of William Wirt, and some pretty fair political writings. He was in his own way a model for the American self-made man.

And yet Kennedy was never completely at ease with self-made men, whom he generally found to be a grasping, soulless lot. Kennedy was what Kenneth Lynn has called the "self-controlled gentleman," aghast at the excesses of the mob, except that his mob was the up'n'comer nouveaux riches. His only extended political satire, *Quodlibet*, was not simply a put-down of Jacksonian Democrats and wildcat banks but of "a new breed of men," what his biographer aptly termed "scrub aristocrats in the shape of [bank] presidents, cashiers, directors, and clerks. He saw in their subterfuge a scheme to entrench a political faction by arraying class against class."[12] A Whig political faction would have been fine, but Kennedy saw the country being overrun by tasteless opportunists. "What a miserable array of charlatans and make-believe statesmen and little clap-trap demagogues and mock gentlemen manufactured out of blackguards, are everywhere in the lead!" he wrote to an uncle in 1853. "We have, with very few exceptions, no man of eminent ability, none of high accomplishment, none of lofty sentiment, in any conspicuous position. How completely has the conception and estimate of a *gentleman* been obliterated from the popular mind!"[13]

If the "conception and estimate of a gentleman" was the issue, Kennedy's articulation of the ideal belied both passionate urgency and a deep ambivalence. On one hand he idealized tradition and what he called "elegancies." This strain in his thinking came to dominate his attitudes as he aged, but it was powerful even in his youth. In a letter to his wife written in 1828, Kennedy mourned the assault on taste and good breeding that seemed to affect even his mother's homeland in the Shenandoah Valley.

> One thing I should like your father to see in this country—you know his prejudice . . . against Virginia, for its loose manners and thriftless mode of life—I should like him to travel through this upper region at least to see how completely the elegancies of society and the best points of a luxurious mode of living, have been invaded by a sort of stiff, awkward, and *churchly* moral-

ity, that seems to have attacked every seal of grace in gesture, speech, 'affections of delight' (as Shakespeare calls them) with everything that made Old Virginia once the seat of noblemen, but not of pennysaving presbyterians.[14]

There is irony there. Kennedy had his own penny-saving Presbyterian qualities, and his churchly morality tended to resemble that of his father-in-law, the factory owner. He was himself nouveau riche, to the limit, and his enterprising spirit betrayed impatience with loose manners and thriftless modes of living. "The war is and shall forever be between the ignorant, the idle, the dissolute and their antagonists in the social frame," he lectured his uncle in Virginia.[15] Kennedy clearly sided with the antagonists, who were by counterdefinition smart, active, and self-controlled. His Whig politics came naturally, and his idol (in 1841 at least) was Henry Clay, a "man of *action*—eminent for his wisdom in that.... By the by, the best sort of man, after all, for posterity."[16] The operative word there is "action," for beyond that, what was cultured, refined, or elegant about Henry Clay? His sweeping nationalism aside, who more perfectly displayed a life of loose manners and thriftless extravagance?

In short, it is not certain *what* Kennedy wanted to be when he sat down in 1829 to write. Sitting literally on the border between town and country, North and South, past and present, he was attracted to the elegancies of Southern living as only an outsider could be. At the same time, the 1820s had been hard on Virginia, with tobacco prices collapsing, slaves rebelling, soils eroding, and young men leaving for new opportunities in states to the west. Besides, Baltimore was so much more fun, and the people there were more interesting. The Virginia planters, by contrast, were a slack lot, as father-in-law Gray had made clear. Kennedy was young and he wanted models, and in many ways *Swallow Barn* became a way of posing and testing manly ideals. The absence of plot in *Swallow Barn* set him free literally to make men, to create them and examine them without committing himself to any hard conclusions.

Swallow Barn is an easy book to follow, even though it goes nowhere. The narrator, Mark Littleton, is a slightly bemused but affectionate New Yorker with time on his hands who does character studies somewhat after the fashion of Laurence Sterne or even Henry Fielding. Like folksier Southern wits, Littleton assumes the role of narrator-once-removed, framing his subjects' stories with his own, more cultured perspective. The action, what there is of it, centers on Frank Meriwether, master of the plantation Swallow Barn and "a very model of the landed gentlemen," and his wife Lucretia, "a pattern of industry" and a "priestess of the American system" in her self-sufficient domesticity. Less industrious is Ned Hazard, a nephew who has been kicked out of Princeton for laziness and drinking and who has just spent a few years wandering South America in search of adventure before coming to stay at the plantation. Other characters include various children, teachers, spinsters, and hangers-on, as well as a nearby plantation family headed by another country gentleman, an old Tory named Isaac Tracy. Moving in and out of the plot are lawyers and local folk, and at the margins are the ever-present slaves—"monkey" children with their silent parents and a few old retainers who butcher the English language and make wise observations. All these people thread their way through the summer of 1829 as if tomorrow would never come.

These are the materials for a fairly traditional English comedy of manners, a genre that was amenable to Southerners because it was fashionable and because gentle comedies about the ruling class assumed that a ruling class did indeed exist. Still, Southerners were best approached obliquely, so Kennedy put distance between himself and his subjects. "Mark Littleton's" epistolary style was a variation on the technique of "framing" a story; it drew a cordon sanitaire not between a gentleman and the rabble but between a wry, culturally rich man of the world and a bunch of naive, culturally impoverished locals.[17] That these locals were the Virginia aristocracy was part of the irony and most of the audacity in Kennedy's approach. Littleton's voice is unmistakably sardonic from the start; few narrators in Southern humor set themselves up as so superior so quickly. He is also the first and last Yankee a Southern writer could send out to the Tidewater or the wiregrass without making his audience recoil defensively. After *Swallow Barn*, as tensions between North and South began to ratchet up, comic narrators became more indigenous and, in some ways, more acerbic.

Although *Swallow Barn* was modeled on the Pendletons of the Shenandoah, Kennedy moved the scene to the Tidewater, about as far back in time and tradition as one could go. As Littleton leaves the "dialectic climates of the North" for Virginia, he enters a world that is self-contained and agreeable. Traveling up the James River, Littleton floats lazily past "plain houses" and "decayed fences jutting beyond the bank into the water, as if they had come down the hill too fast to stop themselves," until he reaches the plantation called Swallow Barn. The main house "is an aristocratical old edifice which sits, like a brooding hen, on the southern bank of the James River." Originally home to the Hazards, Swallow Barn has been gifted over to Frank Meriwether, "who having married Lucretia, the eldest daughter of my late Uncle Walter Hazard, and lifted some gentlemanlike encumbrances which had been sleeping for years upon the domain, was thus inducted into the proprietary rights." Debt has invaded arcadia, the first of many signs that predators sit at the threshold of the plantation, like foxes contemplating the brooding hen. Still, the hen seems blissfully indifferent. The place "has a singularly drowsy and decrepit aspect," Littleton observes.

This is an insulated place, and the man who rules it is an insulated man. Kennedy wasted very little time getting to his man-making, and he started at the very top of the pecking order. His language is full of double entendres that can be, and have been, taken for very different things. Frank Meriwether is "a man of superfluities" (a superfluous man?), by which Kennedy meant that Meriwether had surrounded himself with dependents and hangers-on, rather like the jangle of seals that hang from his vest. "A guest is one of his daily wants," Littleton notes, and there are plenty to be had. "Frank stands related, by some tie of marriage or mixture of kin, to an infinite train of connections, spread over the state." All seem implicitly deferential toward his authority, which Meriwether exercises "from a position too distant to be reached by the sordid passions that sway the multitude." It was a lofty spot from which to view creation. This "solitary elevation of a country gentleman," observes Littleton without apparent irony,

> begets some magnificent notions. He becomes as infallible as the Pope; gradually acquires a habit of making long speeches; is apt to be impatient of contradiction, and is always very touchy on the point of honor. There is nothing more conclusive than a rich man's logic anywhere, but in the country, amongst his dependents, it flows with the smooth and unresisted course of a full stream irrigating a meadow, and depositing its mud in fertilizing luxuriance.

In that single chapter Kennedy identified three essential characteristics of the patrician masculine ideal. At the core was the patrician's essential domesticity. "Cousins count in Virginia," remarks Littleton early on, "and have great privileges," which is to say that the latchstring is always out and no one is turned away. *Swallow Barn* is built around a stable, interconnected group of dependents, an extended family that includes blood relations, poor farmers over the hill, visitors, and slaves. Strangers simply do not exist. This is a paternalistic Eden, where the man of the house is above all a nurturing figure. The theme is repeated throughout *Swallow Barn*, as seen in Meriwether's largesse, his general tolerance, and his treatment especially of slaves, horses, children, and women—all of whom tend to merge into a single object of paternal indulgence. As well as any avowedly proslavery discourse of the time, and better than most, *Swallow Barn* made the case for the organic reciprocity of plantation relations, what historian Lorri Glover has called "mutuality"—the network of siblings, cousins, et cetera, that really defined the gentry's relations with each other even as "patriarchy" defined their superiority over poor whites and blacks. All is interconnected and in its place in *Swallow Barn*, though the cost of that domestic harmony is also evident. To provide and nurture, Meriwether must be physically present in the home, a fact that has profound implications not only to those around him but, as we shall see, to his own self-conception and manhood.[18]

This domesticity encouraged a second trait: the patrician's narrow localism. It is not simply that Meriwether is a states' rights Virginian; he is "decidedly" that. Meriwether's provincialism stems from a fundamental distrust of movement or extension of any kind. His world is circumscribed and stable, and anything that introduces change is suspect. "I don't deny that the steamboat is destined to produce valuable results," he orates to no one in particular, "—but after all, I much question ... if we are not better without it." Warming to the subject, he becomes simultaneously metaphysical and political: "This annihilation of space, sir, is not to be desired. Our protection against the evils of consolidation consists in the very obstacles to our intercourse.... Virginia was never so good as when her roads were at their worst." The narrowness extends to a deeper, personal level as well. Meriwether and his ilk are simple men who cannot act in the presence of complexity or intrigue. "He thinks lightly of the mercantile interest," observes Littleton, "and, in fact, undervalues the manners of the large cities generally. He believes that those who live in them are hollow-hearted and insincere."

Meriwether's simplicity rests on what Henry Adams would later call the "habit of command."[19] No one really questions or tests him. They defer to him, and this custom of deference created a third defining characteristic of the gentleman. Not only did it give the gentleman authority and free rein to opinionate, it worked to remove him from the ordinary mill of human interests. This was an old tradition, a political and social ideal with roots deep in the colonial period and in a concept of politics where paternalism defined civic duty. Meriwether embodies the kind of "inferior and useful magistracy" who had staffed the House of Burgesses during the 18th century. It was the gentleman's obligation to act in the community's interests, to dispense "piepowder justice"; it was the community's obligation to trust him with authority.

Kennedy took the concept at face value and allowed Littleton to spin out its implications in a variety of ways. Meriwether's circle of dependents regard him as "the very guardian genius of the soil and its prerogatives," and it is an interesting choice of words. "Soil" meant home and farm, domesticity and agrarianism, and its prerogatives were that of a landed gentry, who, like Meriwether, were simply accustomed to rule. But Meriwether is the "guardian" genius, and that implied that the soil and its prerogatives were under attack. As Kennedy well knew from his visits to the Pendletons, by 1829 the weeds were taking over much of what had been productive tobacco land; Virginia's soil was in decline and so was the habit of command. The Virginia dynasty, after all, had ended with Monroe, and now a frontier cotton planter and Indian-killer was in the White House.

All these changes seem to have discombobulated Meriwether. He is "desponding" when he talks of the new democratic politics; his weighty role renders him aloof and disconnected. "In fact, he speaks like an ancient stoic," Littleton observes. This stoicism, which in time became a classical posture for certain types of Southern behaviors, rendered him politically vulnerable in a new age of Jacksonian politics—where deference to the gentleman was losing ground to obedience to the party. Even John Taylor of Caroline, who had every claim on being a patrician's patrician, had seen that agriculture's prerogatives had to be earned and advocated. If the planter was to rule, Taylor argued in *Arator*, he had to unite with other planters and act.[20]

On the other hand—and with satire there is always the other hand—stoicism could be a facade for laziness. Meriwether's political influence extends to court days and fulminations, but little else. He never ran for high office because fundamentally he is "an unambitious man." He has a law degree but obtained it by hanging around a lawyer's office in Richmond where he "smoked segars," wore "six cravats" and "yellow-topped boots," and "ate oysters" while reading a little Blackstone on the side. His days are filled with idle walks around the fields, casual perusings of political tracts, food, cigars, and the ever-present guests. Meriwether's patrician qualities have lifted him beyond not only ambition, but competition itself. He lives, in effect, in a world insulated from conflict, an organic community that must remain, as one critic notes, "motionless."[21]

For someone from the "dialectic climates of the North," Meriwether's lot is enticing, but it has its dangers. "There is a fascination in the quiet, irresponsible, and reckless nature of these country pursuits, that is apt to seize upon the imagination of a man who has felt the perplexities of business," Littleton observes halfway through the book.

> Ever since I have been at Swallow Barn, I have entertained a very philosophical longing for the calm and dignified retirement of the woods. I begin to grow moderate in my desires; that is, I only want a thousand acres of good land, an old manor-house, on a pleasant site, a hundred negroes, a large library, a host of friends, and a reserve of a few thousands a year in the stocks,—in case of bad crops,—and finally a house full of pretty, intelligent, and docile children, with some few et ceteras not worth mentioning.

The sarcasm halfway through the passage is unmistakable; the "few thousands a year in the stocks" define the whole paragraph. Meriwether is a dependent. Prerogatives of the soil and habit of command aside, he cannot exist on his own; beyond wife and friends and slaves he needs the efforts of other men—competitive ones—who will make his money for him "in case of bad crops." Meriwether's leisure and domesticity, in short, threaten to unman him. The very field of his authority was a closed system that was rapidly becoming—in the North at least—a woman's world.

This threat is carefully understated in *Swallow Barn*. No one, North or South, has ever been offended by the master of Swallow Barn, and the very humor with which Kennedy portrayed him gave him a credibility that other, more didactic variations of the gentleman lacked. What Kennedy did, rather brilliantly in his own way, was portray the most standard definition possible of the Virginia gentleman with just enough satire to make the image both lovable and outmoded.

That opened the field for other explorations in man-making. Having set down the original, Kennedy split Meriwether's patrician figure into its component parts and constructed variations on the theme. The alternate manly models are a good deal more foolish, yet they represent what a patrician gentleman like Frank Meriwether could become, given time and leisure—of which they all have too much. Each variation exaggerates some facet of the gentleman's characteristics, and each is by itself either ludicrous or juvenile or culturally irrelevant.

Two of these variations center on the gentleman as preserver of public order and as hero. Kennedy was a lawyer by trade, if not inclination, and it was probably inevitable that he would deal with his own kind in *Swallow Barn*. He was writing at a critical moment in the legal profession, when—as Robert A. Ferguson and others note—the uses of the law and the concept of the lawyer himself were changing.[22] Law had traditionally been the reserve of lettered men who had been classically trained (at least that was the ideal). Their solemn duty was to articulate moral principles in defense of a structured republican community. As Kennedy well knew, the ideal was under stress. By 1830 courts were shifting to a more instrumentalist approach wherein law was made to nurture economic competition, not republican order, and lawyers were becoming legal experts with fairly narrow specialties. Kennedy was not immune to the shift. He hated the "repulsive studies of the law," writes his biographer, and the "flinty highway of Coke and Littleton."[23] Yet he made a good living at it, representing Thomas Ellicott's Union Bank of Baltimore for years (until Jackson included it among his pet banks and Kennedy left in disgust). At the same time, he fancied himself a legal litterateur in the tradition of Blackstone or perhaps even Daniel Webster. He was particularly torn, then, by the pull of the lawyer-gentleman and the competitive tug of the lawyer-expert. Only a few years later an expatriate Virginian, Joseph Glover Baldwin, would confront the same feelings in the rough courtrooms of Alabama.

Like Baldwin, Kennedy knew that lawyering was often a matter of style and masquerade. It was theater, and in an early example of what would become a constant presence in frontier humor, Kennedy introduced the courtroom showman. One of these is Toll Hedges, a "gentleman whose pantaloons were too short for him, and whose bare legs were, consequently, visible above his stockings." He sleeps in his coat. Law, as such, simply does not interest Hedges, because it is encumbered by precedent and detail. He prefers to deal in reputations, and he gets his client Jemmy (a boozer and a rioter) off the hook by discrediting the prosecution's witness, who has dared share his liquor with the accused and yet testifies against him in court. "What credit can you attach to a cock-and-bull story told by a fellow that comes to swear against a man who has been dividing his liquor with him? For the honor of the Old Dominion, gentlemen!" he cries. The jury, overwhelmed by the evidence of conviviality and the logic of honor, dismisses the case. Hedges is a minor character in *Swallow Barn*, and Kennedy spent little time developing him. Yet his presence there, amid more proper men, has a fairly disturbing undertone.

More interesting was the gentleman lawyer. One example, Singleton Oglethorpe Swansdowne, is to the women "an elegant, refined, sweet-spoken, grave, and dignified gentleman" and, to the men, "the most preposterous ass—the most enormous humbug—the most remarkable coxcomb in Virginia." It is hard, says the narrator, "to tell the counterfeit from the real in these things." He is in the "prime of life, and still a bachelor," which sets off certain bells. In some ways, Swansdowne is reminiscent of John Taylor of Caroline, with a piping voice and a fastidious attention to clothes; he lacks, however, Taylor's abrasiveness or his ability to command attention. Littleton regards him as "effeminate," a nonstarter among competitive men. "It can be nothing but his modesty that keeps him in the background now," says one female admirer with unintended irony. "He never would have been beaten three times for Congress, if he had not been so diffident."

More assertive is Philpot Wart, who is in many ways the most interesting character in *Swallow Barn*. He is a legal Squire Western who troops around the countryside with law books and dogs and approaches all life—especially legal affairs—like a fox hunt. Wart has the character of the seasoned lawyer: tolerant, fussy, simple, solid, and possessing a "sly, quick good nature, susceptible, however, of great severity." Kennedy clearly likes him. Wart is in most respects the perfect fusion of old-style manners and more modern, competitive shrewdness. He works hard and knows his material, especially "land titles, courses and distances." He can manipulate a jury with his "insinuating address" and serves in the state assembly as a kind of deal-maker. "He is extremely secret in his operations," yet at the same time he cultivates a reputation for quoting the classics, tending to the yeomen in a "brotherly and companionable relation," and cultivating his various eccentricities, such as quoting Virgil in the flush of a fox hunt. Mostly he has Kennedy's sense of the absurdity of it all; witness his self-effacing manner of dealing with his own military glory. During the War of 1812 he commanded a company of men, the Invincible Blues, who stayed resolutely upstream a hundred miles from the British and guarded the "hen-roosts along the river from the attacks of the enemy." "Did you see hard service?" asks a dinner companion. "Tolerably severe, while it lasted," replies Philly, taking sly aim at himself: "It rained upon us nearly the whole way from here to Norfolk, and there was a good deal of ague and fever in the country at that time, which we ran a great risk of taking."

Wart combines the gentleman's credibility and ironic sense of self with a salesman's guile, and he is the ideal person to negotiate the frivolities of the country republican's narrow world. At issue is a pointless lawsuit which has preoccupied Meriwether's neighbor for decades. The neighbor, Isaac Tracy, is an old Tory trying to reclaim from Meriwether a shred of land, a piece of swampy bog "not worth a groat." Meriwether puts up with it all because Tracy's single-mindedness (he surrounds himself with legal cases, maps, and plats) has a certain republican solidity. It "looked well to see a gentleman inclined to stand by his rights: it was what every man of property ought to do!" Despite this sentiment, Meriwether is tired of fooling with the affair and hires Wart to put an end to it. Wart drags the whole lot off through the swampy land, "a great Sirbonian bog," outmaneuvers Swansdowne with ease, and expertly and intentionally loses the case for Meriwether. At that point Tracy, having planned and plotted and platted for years, seems to lose all purpose in life. "The exterminated lawsuit disturbed him," Littleton observes. "A favorite fancy had been annihilated, untimely cropped, as a flower of the field. He could not realize the idea. The privation had left him no substitute."

There are two larger points to be made from this little diversion. One concerns the changing concept of the lawyer himself. It is fitting, perhaps, that an antiquated old Tory, Tracy, hires a lawyer whose defining merits have nothing to do with the law at all. Swansdowne is a fop, easily manipulated by Wart, the dealmaker. Two decades later, when Baldwin issued *Flush Times in Alabama and Mississippi*, the mock battles over Tracy's swamp would be transformed into real battles over Cherokee lands, and the same unequal pairing of lawyerly types would provide the entertainment. Second (and this point Kennedy would surely have felt keenly), the parcel in question was at one time the site of a mill—an actual enterprise, an attempt at development and expansion—which failed and fell into disuse. Tracy does not want it back to exploit it; his sole purpose is to assert the principle of ownership. As Morton Horwitz has argued, the very concept of property was shifting *away* from Tracy's static principle of "ownership" and toward one of "development," as the Charles River Bridge case and a host of state cases made clear (almost at the moment Kennedy was writing). Kennedy's satire, in this case, drew energy from his Baltimore side and from his proto-Whig tendencies, which inclined him to see law as a means of making things happen, not preserving them as they were.[24]

The mock battle over the swamp is a courtroom parallel to the Southern male's romantic obsession with chivalry and its particular need for conquest. Manhood, particularly the chivalrous kind, was after all an outgrowth of battlefield codes of survival paired with the responsibility of defending the fief, and it required competition and struggle. By 1830 there was literary and rhetorical evidence that the chivalric code was displacing the agrarian (Walter Scott over John Taylor) in the Southern estimation of self, but the shift posed an exquisite dilemma for Southern men. They were surely competitive, and they took their code of manhood from images of the battlefield. The battleground of work, however, was not available to a man stuck on a plantation. "Planting was a specialty without professional spirit," writes Bertram Wyatt-Brown. "Whereas Yankees were learning how to separate family from work, professional criteria from parochial values, individual preferences from community sanctions, Southern planters rejoiced in the persistence of old habits."[25] Perhaps, yet the rejoicing was tinged with a certain measure of apprehension. Meriwether was comfortable in his insularity, but men like Kennedy were not, and the growing presence of men of action was too clear to ignore and too compelling to dismiss. If the plantation became identified with domestic quaintness, the patrician ideal was in danger of the ultimate humiliation: becoming feminized.

Nowhere is this threat more evident than in the future master of Swallow Barn, Ned Hazard, Meriwether's nephew. Hazard is evidence of the effects domesticity and dependence might visit upon youth. One component of manhood is boyhood, and Ned's seems to have been protracted beyond even ordinary Southern standards—which were generous. At thirty-three, Ned has yet to do a productive day's work. As a younger man, he was educated on the plantation at an "academy" run by Mr. Crab—one of Meriwether's retainers—and then sent off to Princeton, where he drank, dueled, and fell in love with a local woman a few years older than he. On the night he was supposed to elope, Ned went falling-down drunk, passed out, and missed his own wedding. Shortly afterwards, he headed off to South America in search of revolution and a purpose in life. There he was "well bitten with fleas, and apprehended as a spy, and nearly assassinated as a heretic." The glory of it all somehow did not settle in, and so poor Ned came limping back "the most disquixotted cavalier that ever hung up his shield at the end of a scurvy crusade."

Fair enough; boys will be boys, and there is not much distance between the young Ned and the young Tom Jones. The chivalric impulse, however, takes over in Ned. Ned chases Bel Tracy, old Isaac Tracy's daughter, for a good part of the book, and she sends him on quests worthy of Capellanus' *Art of Courtly Love*. Bel "almost persuades herself that this is the fourteenth century." And so Ned composes poetry, moons about unrequited love, and at one point goes thrashing through the woods in search of Bel's half-trained pet falcon (which on close inspection looks remarkably like a chicken hawk).[26]

Ned Hazard is an early example of what would become a persistent anomaly in Southern culture, the dispossessed young male. As Joan Cashin has argued, young Southern men remained in semidependency for a long time; young women (such as Bel Tracy, perhaps) were "truly dependent" indefinitely.[27] This state of dependency had worked, more or less, during the colonial years when geographical and economic mobility were slower paced, and when the country ethic of patriarchal domesticity was the unchallenged measure of manhood. By 1830, however, the pull of the Old Southwest, the declining profits from tobacco, and the emergence of a masculine ideal based on independence and economic competition were working against the Ned Hazards of the world. The comfortable routines of domestic responsibilities and local attachments seemed, to borrow Cashin's words, "uncomfortably similar to the condition of white women, white children, and slaves."[28] Kennedy, of course, did not ridicule Ned's plight directly; no good ironist would. He did, however, set Littleton (an obvious foil of Ned) as the superior voice vis-à-vis Hazard, of whom Littleton says simply, "His mind is a fairy land."

Only once does Ned really settle down to the business of manhood, and even then he is caught between conflicting impulses. When he and Littleton stop at a country tavern, they find themselves in the home of "that industrious, thriving and reputable class of comers who laudably devote their energies to disputation, loud swearing, bets and whisky—a class which, to the glory of our land, is surprisingly rife in every country side." It is Kennedy's first venture into the world of alligator-men and no'counts, but he makes it with a twist. The inevitable fight is between Ned and a "shabby gentleman," Miles Rutherford. Littleton explains that Rutherford had once been "educated in liberal studies," but had fallen into "vicious habits. An unfortunate reputation for brilliant talents, in early life, had misled him into the belief that the care by which a good name is won and preserved is a useless virtue, and that self-control is a tax which only men of inferior parts pay for success." Rutherford insults Bel's father by calling him a "stark old English Tory," so a street fight is arranged, which Ned wins. "You have had the advantage of training," pants Rutherford, but Ned is ashamed. "I have descended from my proper elevation of character," he moans. "I wish I had a hornbook of gentility to go by!"

Oddly enough, such hornbooks were on the way. As Kennedy was finishing *Swallow Barn*, John Lyde Wilson was formulating detailed instructions on the art and etiquette of dueling, in which Ned would have picked up tips on restraint.[29] Both Ned and his opponent crossed a line between gentility and aggressiveness, and both lost a measure of self-control that was essential to the patrician ideal. Rutherford is an example of a scrub aristocrat who has lapsed into sheer laziness and dissolution. He represents what Ned might become if the latter permanently loses self-control. "Southerners devoted a good deal of effort to self-discipline and to the cultivation of well-regulated human relationships," writes Dickson David Bruce. "In both cases, the main focus was to prevent the sort of spontaneous, passionate acts which one would inevitably come to regret."[30] Ned eventually recaptures his restraint and elite consciousness and goes on to marry Bel and—presumably—take over Swallow Barn. But, as we shall see, those of his type who moved west over the next three decades had considerably fewer brakes on their passions, and correspondingly more opportunities to let go. This single episode of violence in *Swallow Barn* was a fairly bloodless indication of an edginess that was to turn much harder, both for young men and for Southern humor.

By the time Isaac Tracy wins his worthless acreage and Ned captures the chicken hawk for Bel, *Swallow Barn* has lost focus—if it ever, in fact, had any. Tracy's confusion and Ned's impetuosity mark a dead end, both in the novel and in the kind of man-making Kennedy had attempted. The circumscribed world of Swallow Barn has left literally no place for movement, either of ambition or plot. At this point *Swallow Barn* begins to change tone; it becomes more of a rambling dissertation, chiefly about horses and slaves. No one, Kennedy or his critics, seems to agree on the purpose of these chapters. Reading the book in reverse, so to speak, from a post–Civil War perspective, the material on slavery comes through as darkly ironic and foreboding. Lewis Simpson sees slavery as the unwelcome weed in the pastoral garden, a growth Meriwether calls "theoretically and morally wrong" but inescapable. Kennedy's solution is an effort to create a happy medium between exploitation and agrarian arcadia by turning the slave into a variant of the English peasant. Meriwether throws off an unusual plan for a system of graduated emancipation, with "an upper, or privileged, class of slaves.... something of a feudal character" to provide authority, matched by strict respect for slave marriages (again the reversion to the domestic ideal). Simpson has noted the tension between slavery and the unrealized pastoral ideal in the novel. In a similar vein, Jan Bakker has argued that *Swallow Barn* is a pastoral vision gone awry. It is, as the problem of slavery implies, an endangered spot rather than the happy place—the *locus amoeni*—it should be.[31]

When seen as an exploration in masculine models, on the other hand, these chapters sum up the rest. Kennedy's long essay into the nature of slavery is in fact divided into two parts—a long pontification from Frank Meriwether preceded by the observations of Mark Littleton, outsider. Meriwether's pronouncements are out of character for him; they are too nuanced, too deep, and too linear. Clearly these passages are Kennedy overtly lecturing the reader on the slavery "issue" and coming up with a plan of gradual emancipation, even if the proposal to create castes of slaves is a little unusual. Simpson is entirely right in emphasizing the pastoral context of Meriwether's remarks, for Meriwether can only address life from an agrarian, essentially premodern perspective. There is no effort on Meriwether's part to address slavery as a system of economic production per se, and thus no effort to compare it with Northern factory labor. Slaves, in fact, are allies in the project to keep machinery and commerce ("this annihilation of space") out of Virginia. Meriwether's view of slavery is paternalistic and nurturing even if he does question its morality; his remedies are paternalistic and hierarchical and imply that providing slaves with a system of structured authority is the most important legacy the enlightened master can provide.

Indeed, the central metaphor for slavery is the family, and in that respect Meriwether's passionate comments on horses are more revealing than his sermon on emancipation. The horse, he declaims, has been a servant of humankind throughout history, has shared man's bed and board, and has gotten his discipline and nurturing from men. It has reciprocated with obedience and loyalty. "The horse has a family instinct," Meriwether states. It is a model of "patience, considerateness, discretion, long-suffering, amiable obedience." It works until it drops dead. "What machinery or labor-saving inventions of man could ever compensate him for the deprivation of this faithful ally?" Meriwether asks. "I say, where is there a finer type of resignation, christian resignation, than in the trusty horse?" The language is very close to that found in his orations on the slave, and his instincts are not much removed from the generation of pro-slavery apologists who succeeded him. The major difference is one of emphasis. Where the apologists were likely to stress the master's beneficent influence on the slave, Meriwether highlights the slave's contribution to the master's own insularity. That, in turn, opens an interesting question: is there any real difference, in terms of competitive manliness, between a domesticated slave and a domesticated master? Both seem destined to labor away in small worlds, dependent on each other, with "christian resignation."

All of which makes the story of Abe, the reckless slave, even more interesting. Abe is a wild boy; like Miles Rutherford he is smart but consorts with a bad lot, "the most profligate menials." (The slave quarters, like the rest of the state, has its own loafers.) Much of the problem is that Abe, like Ned or even Isaac Tracy, is underchallenged. The blacks on the plantation fit the same description as the whites: "Being a people of simple combinations and limited faculty for speculative pleasures, they are a contented race,—not much disturbed by the desire of novelty." But this is not true for all of them. Abe is simply too much for this constricted scene, and so—after a few scrapes—he is sent off to sea. The prospect loosens him up. "His imagination was awakened by the attractions of this field of adventure; by the free roving of the sailor." Free roving serves him well. A diversity of interests invigorates him; "his former monotonous avocations" had led him into "mischievous adventures," but no more. He reforms, growing into "a sturdy manhood, invigorated by the hardy discipline of his calling." The story does not end well, in one sense at least. Abe is lost at sea while attempting the heroic rescue of a stricken brig.

Kennedy's shift in tone, however, is remarkable. "Manhood" moves directly into the vocabulary of *Swallow Barn*. Up to Abe's story, Kennedy had allowed his vagrant cavaliers and domestic patricians the benefit of humor and a whimsical touch. Abe, however, is a direct model for manliness. Abe is stout-hearted, ambitious, addicted to danger and risk—a black entrepreneur. In a more traditional reading he is a cavalier, "impelled by that love of daring which the romancers call chivalry"—a term which Kennedy had applied to Ned Hazard with very different conclusions.

Abe enjoys "the full perfection of manhood." That Kennedy lavished such praise on a black man—after some four hundred pages of withholding it from whites—indicates his ultimate frustration in man-making. There simply is no way to project the patrician ideal into the commercial world of 1832, let alone into the future. At the end of the novel, Littleton finds himself in the library, thumbing through an ancient biography of Captain John Smith, as if the only models for republican manhood belonged to history.

In that sense, then, *Swallow Barn* fails at man-making. Northern patricians could reinvent themselves as captains of industry, but Southern gentlemen were more limited. Once master of his realm, by the 1830s the country republican was a prisoner to his dependents. The very characteristics that once imparted manliness to the country gentleman were being relegated to a domesticated life of feminized passivity. The squire's leisure, his attachment to the soil, his protracted boyhood, his circle of dependents, and his highly localized, contained world—all of this was being left behind by new men. The epitome of Southern manliness was at heart a domestic animal. He demonstrated mastery over a small world, and he seldom ventured outside that world. Kennedy drove the point home in his next novel, *Horse-shoe Robinson*, in which he split the manly models in two—a clever woodsman and a dashing young aristocrat. Notably, the aristocrat spends most of the book in captivity, and the toughest strategist is his bride-to-be, the domestic manager who plots his release and must enlist the woodsman to carry it through.[32]

Though Kennedy's polite comedy was not to become the style of Southern humor, he had set down some central issues that were to reappear over and over again for the next thirty years. Kennedy had hinted at the imminent intrusion of a far more complicated world into the insular realm of the domestic patriarchy, one in which action and risk taking were measures of manliness. Within a pastoral arcadia of endless games and genteel foolishness, he had introduced a lurking suspicion that mockheroics were passé and that the Southerner's overblown sense of honor was becoming a theatrical liability. Against an organic, self-sufficient republican order, where law was a moral obligation, he had held out the possibility that the lawyer himself was a mere instrument of forces, economic and democratic, beyond his control. Within a decade, other humorists had turned his vision to blacker and more violent scenarios.

2

Georgia Theatrics, Georgia Yankees

AT ABOUT THE SAME TIME Kennedy was finishing *Swallow Barn*, a lawyer from Augusta, Georgia, decided (for no recorded reason) to write down accounts of some of the stranger characters he had met riding circuit as a judge. The stories first appeared in local newspapers, then in 1835 as a book, *Georgia Scenes*. The author, Augustus Baldwin Longstreet, wrote them off as a "literary bagatelle," a mild attempt at social history. "The leading object," of the book, he explained, was "to enable those who come after us, to see us *precisely as we are*."[1] In his later years, he seemed embarrassed to have written it.

Longstreet's little bagatelle seemed to have something for everyone. It mixed gentry and no'counts. It boasted violence, farce, masquerades, cross-dressing, duels, snooty women, blind horses, and greased ganders. It was alternately earthy and prim. It introduced characters that became fixed types in Southern literature, funny or not, including good ole boys and their fights, hoss traders putting on a show, and Ransy Sniffle, the ultimate cracker ferret and paterfamilias of the Jeeter Lesters and the Snopeses—"height, five feet nothing, average weight in blackberry sea-son, ninety-five."[2] Certainly its influence on narrative form was profound. Longstreet did not exactly invent the framing technique, whereby a cultured voice introduces the action and then turns it over to a less refined narrator, but he made it available to a rising generation of storytellers and wits. He picked his characters from among people he knew, and his stories had energy and realism. Moreover, he made it legitimate to talk about violence, both physical and verbal. When a jockey dies to the general indifference of the crowd, when an improbable winner of a gander-pull looks at his winnings (a bag of quarters) and says "Oh you little shining sons o'bitches!, walk into your Mas'Johnny's pocket," when a respectable farm wife calls another respectable farm wife a "nasty, good-for-nothing, snaggle-toothed gaub of fat"—when those things happen, the reader has left *Swallow Barn* far behind.

This was masculine humor. At a personal level, it suggested fantasies of escape. Critics David Rachels and James Kibler have noted a divided personality present in Longstreet's work: two narrators, one prissy, one more flexible, as if the author were using his humor to negotiate a position between the gentleman he wanted to be and the antic boy he had once been.[3] As a child, Longstreet wanted nothing more than to "outrun, outjump, outshoot, throw down any man in the district."[4] Yet, he admitted, "I was considered by my preceptors a dunce in several of my academic studies, and treated accordingly."[5] Perhaps humor was his way of compensating. Some argue that Longstreet wrote *Georgia Scenes* as a masculine attack against "the feminizing influences of America's more polite and refined literary productions."[6] From this point of view the violence and swearing are acts of manly affirmation, a sort of antebellum howl. Longstreet seemed to relish graphic descriptions of pain and social collapse, so much so that Jesse Bier has labeled him "not only a sadist but a nihilist."[7]

The pathology, on the other hand, may have been social, and once again the voice of the gentleman resonates unmistakably. Henri Bergson argued long ago that humor is a way of isolating one's enemies and humiliating them.[8] If so, Longstreet was a snob laying waste to the rubes, with his characterization of Ransy Sniffle providing most of the evidence. Kenneth Lynn insisted that Longstreet epitomized the humorist as "self-controlled gentleman," who used humor to draw a cordon sanitaire between his Whiggish sensibilities and those of the Democratic mob. (Interestingly, Longstreet was a lifelong Democrat and never once considered voting Whig.) Recent writers such as Scott Romine have argued, more charitably, that Longstreet's narrators are agents of the ruling elite trying to travel "the middle ground between oligarchy and populism that defined public life in the antebellum South."⁹ The narrators may make fun of the good ole boys, but they also curry their favor in order to keep the patriarchy intact. Charitable or not, these analyses rest on the idea of a stratified South, one in which paternalistic elites desperately tried to maintain dominance over poor and middling whites in a democratic, expanding world. They might ridicule the plain folk, mislead them with false propaganda, or even bond with them, but the ultimate objective was to preserve a social hierarchy and validate a coherent regime. To borrow a perspective from Eugene Genovese, *Georgia Scenes* can be interpreted as a subliterary attempt of the planter elite to assert hegemony over troublesome inferiors.

But *Georgia Scenes* is a deceptive book. Its fault lines run vertically along a moral divide rather than horizontally between classes, and the voice of the gentleman never carries the authority of the country republican's. Consider the very first tale, "Georgia Theatrics." On a fine spring day one of Longstreet's aliases, "Hall," is traveling through the woods in Lincoln County, a place of "moral darkness" slightly north of Augusta. Hall hears a ferocious fight in progress somewhere behind the brush. "You kin, kin you?" someone roars.

> "Yes, I kin, and am able to do it! Boo-oo-oo!"
> "Oh wake snakes, and walk your chalks! Brimstone and ____ fire! . . . ____ my soul if I don't jump down his throat, and gallop every chitterling out of him before you can say 'quit!' "
> "Jist let the wild-cat come, and I'll tame him. Ned'll see me a fair fight, won't you, Ned?"
> "Oh, yes; I'll see you a fair fight, blast my old shoes if I don't."

This is the sound of all hell breaking loose, a "Pandaemonian riot!," but by the time Hall can intervene it is too late. "I saw the uppermost one (for I could not see the other) make a heavy plunge with his thumbs, and at the same instant I heard a cry in the accent of keenest torture, 'Enough! My eye's out!'" This is exactly the kind of language and violence that characterized frontier humor at its roughest.

It is also a charade. Behind the brush is a single teenaged boy who rises up in a strut, then seems a little embarrassed at the sight of Hall. Hall, in turn, is "horrorstruck" and begins sermonizing about "the iniquity of his crime." Once the boy sees who is lecturing him, however, he cuts Hall off. "You needn't kick before you're spurred," the kid snorts. "There a'nt nobody there, nor ha'nt been another. I was jist seein' how I could a'*fout*." He is playacting. "All I had heard and seen," states Hall, "was nothing less than a Lincoln rehearsal; in which the youth . . . had played all the parts of all the characters in a Courthouse fight." As the boy goes back to his plow, Hall finds two thumb prints "about the distance of a man's eyes apart" jammed into the earth.

"Georgia Theatrics" is quite literally an introduction to the book. As its title flatly states, the story is about theatrics, the public postures and community dramas in which the Southern self was presented and identity established. Out of these community dramas emerge two ideologies of manhood, two codes of behavior and ethics that compete in various situations up and down the social scale all through *Georgia Scenes*. The boy's behavior is essentially theater—adolescent, showy, and geared to an audience, even if only an imaginary one. As an expression of masculinity, the boy's display is an embryonic affirmation of manhood in the making as defined by masquerade culture, and that culture was *not* confined to one class or social stratum. It is not clear, for example, that the boy really is a cracker or a rube. The narrator finds him pulling a plow, which makes it probable that his family owns the farm and, in northeast Georgia, at least half-likely that they own one or two slaves. His language is coarse, but that would hardly distinguish him from other teenaged boys. A Georgia reader in the mid-1830s would not necessarily have consigned his type to the rednecks and white trash. He is playing out a role, assuming an identity, and his imaginary audience is at the courthouse, which makes him focused on the town, not the countryside. He operates from an ethic of courage and theatrics, and how he "could a'fout" is the only important thing in establishing his reputation. By contrast, the narrator is fundamentally rational and pietistic. A lawyer or a preacher (maybe both), Hall is from the town, and he urges restraint and speaks the language of instituted authority "in a tone compelled by the sacredness of [his] office." He regards the boy's actions as "iniquity" and a "hellish deed" and he calls upon the boy to repent, to help him "in relieving your fellow mortal, whom you have ruined for ever!" For him, courage and theatrics are secondary to restraint and responsibility.

Hall is, in short, Longstreet and Longstreet's kind, and he represents the ethic of an emerging middle class—so common nowadays as to be invisible, but unformed and untested at the time Longstreet began writing.[10] To describe this alternate ethic as "market-oriented" is accurate but limiting, for it encompassed more interiorized habits of self-discipline, rational calculation, and—importantly—an evangelical outlook that would come to dominate so much of the South in decades to come. Ted Ownby has called it "evangelical culture," and while it was not fully developed in 1835, its signs were there.[11] It was the product of the towns, and the town is the locus of most of the stories in *Georgia Scenes*. The plantation myth is so overwhelming that it is easy to forget that the South, like the North, had towns, that these towns were growing, and that the first vestiges of a Southern middle class were taking root in them. For Longstreet the town was the natural crossroads of the market South and, more importantly, of the lawyers, journalists, teachers, and preachers who made the market function. These were literate, ambitious, disciplined men and their wives, and they were very likely to be evangelical and reform-minded as well. They were prototypes of the New South, before the Civil War had called such a thing into being. Not yet a conscious middle class, barely acknowledged by historians even now, Southern townsmen were expected to be gentlemen, horse traders, churchgoers, and dealmakers all at once. The construction of male identity among such men was a constant process of testing and negotiating, and the town was a place where this struggle could be displayed.

It is the incongruity between this group's nascent evangelical culture and the theatricality of masquerade culture that drives the humor in *Georgia Scenes*. Characters in *Georgia Scenes* do what market folk do: they negotiate, switch roles, and play on appearances.[12] Hierarchies dissolve, and the line between vulgarity and good taste—between common and elite—is vague. Yet all the characters are acutely aware of appearances and of what masquerade culture demands of them. As in real life, the characters in the stories are not conveniently this or that; they are amalgamations of seemingly antithetical ideals which feed off of and subvert each other. Planters must be entrepreneurs, entrepreneurs must speak the language of rednecks, and all must perform in elaborately coded displays of manhood. For every fight scene there is a duel; for every gander pull there is a fox hunt; for every redneck swearing incoherently there is a blueblood singing Italian arias off-key through her nose. There is no cordon sanitaire here because there are no fixed boundaries. It is that fluidity which makes *Georgia Scenes* so much fun, but as a piece of social satire it ultimately returns to the gentleman. Who will replace Frank Meriwether?

The answer is not clear, as "Georgia Theatrics" implies. Hall holds the high ground, but the boy rebuffs him and dismisses him "with a taunting curl of the nose." However sacred Hall's office may be, it does not command the kind of deferential behavior that real gentlemen, in Southern terms, would receive. It is hard to imagine that Frank Meriwether, for example, would have corrected the boy in such moralistic terms, and harder still to think that the boy would have dismissed the squire of Swallow Barn so easily. The humor in the story ultimately turns against Hall, who is left standing mouth agape and authority challenged, the ultimate butt of the joke. As the book unfolds, this situation gets more and more complicated.

All this came from a man who was himself on a moral journey, one that took him out of the role of country lawyer and into the forefront of the evangelical and academic traditions in the South. Metaphorically, Longstreet was moving from a social ethic that idealized the liturgical display and sense of community inherent in an Anglican upper class to one that signaled the more interiorized, self-critical stance of upwardly mobile Methodists and Baptists. There is a direct line between Longstreet's middle Georgia and the New South. The same line, incidentally, connects him to another great humorist, George Washington Harris.[13]

Longstreet wrote from a particular corner of the South, and place counts heavily in *Georgia Scenes*. He was from a settled area, as much South Carolina as Georgia, at a time when cotton culture was still fairly new. This was Augusta, a solid little town on the banks of the Savannah River that lay astride the fall line dividing coastal plain from the piedmont. To the west lay a broad sweep of the most fertile land in Georgia; to the north and east lay the Edgefield district of South Carolina, a region dominated by short-staple cotton. This was no frontier. Augusta had been settled in the late 1730s; in Longstreet's time it harbored fine houses, a fire company, an academy, and even a theater.[14] The town was a commercial center, and it served a large hinterland. Within the radius of its influence came some of the most powerful figures in antebellum Southern culture. Alexander H. Stephens and Robert Toombs both hailed from the area, as did Richard Henry Wilde, a minor poet who fled to Europe.[15] From the South Carolina side of the river came James Henry Hammond, George McDuffie, Louis T. Wigfall, and Preston Brooks, the man who caned Charles Sumner half to death on the Senate floor in 1856. Also from Edgefield, interestingly, came William Gregg, who founded the Graniteville textile works in the 1850s and who was the South's leading advocate of industry and diversification. Over them all brooded John C.

Calhoun, whose plantation in Abbeville lay only sixty miles away. Most of the people who came from the area, however, were slaves. This was, in 1835, settled cotton country, some of the best in the eastern South.[16]

It was also a place of bounding ambition and fluid social status. Cotton moved in after 1800, when Eli Whitney's gin (first introduced in this very region) made the production of short-staple plants marketable. For about twenty years the area boomed. As Longstreet was growing up and getting started, the people of Augusta's hinterlands turned over thousands of acres to cotton, which for a time they sold at good prices. The profits went mostly to buy slaves, which in turn meant more cotton production—or so the theory went. It was a fundamentally different world from the tobacco culture of Kennedy's Virginia. There was no hard divide between planters and ordinary farmers; both owned slaves, both raised cotton, and both sold to the market. Many read law or medicine and took their slaves to town, where they handled the affairs of the planters and plain folk. Collectively they formed a kind of cotton bourgeoisie, a not-quite-middle-class of self-disciplined, self-made men whose very independence stemmed, ironically, from the slaves dependent on them. For the lucky and industrious, the payoff was respectability and position. For the less successful, the reward was debt, and during the 1820s there was plenty of that to be had.

Mounting debt may or may not have contributed to the violence around Augusta. (Edgefield was known as a "District of Devils.") More likely it simply exacerbated a touchy sense of honor that ran up and down the social scale. Southern masquerade culture was especially evident in this mobile and fluid society. Every action—from tipping hats to collecting debts to dueling to sociable drinking to hunting to death itself—was coded for public display. The brittleness was collective as well as individual. (Angry patrons of Augusta's prized theater drove the famed actor Edwin Forrest from the stage in 1830. He had portrayed King Philip, the leader of a bloody Indian uprising in Massachusetts in 1676, too sympathetically and thus offended those who had warmly supported the state's move to grab Cherokee land.)[17] Combativeness was no mere *code duello* reserved for the upper class, either. The violence was direct, and the perpetrators came from every station in life. "The rich and the poor fought, were injured, and died together," observes historian Vernon Burton. Their violence was inventive: alongside guns they used "knives, rocks, clubs, axes, poison, a sharpened stick, a horse's skull, a metal-bound Bible, and the 'tip of an umbrella.'"[18]

In such an unstable atmosphere the Great Revival swept in like cold air. In the first decades of the nineteenth century, revivals and tent meetings brought an unprecedented degree of religious enthusiasm to Augusta's hinterlands. It was a religion tailor-made for the new cotton bourgeoisie, for it encouraged thrift and accountability. The "preponderance of evangelicals," writes Lacy Ford, "were neither planters nor poor whites, but were instead the small slaveholders and substantial yeomen who comprised the 'middling sort' of Upcountry society."[19] This middling sort bought farms and built churches and schools. They also bought slaves, and the antislavery inclinations of early Baptists and Methodists quietly evaporated. It was a boom-or-bust religion, perfectly suited to the entrepreneur, yet its very emphasis on accountability and responsibility put it in conflict with the leisured indifference of the country gentleman.

But reform came hard. The people of Augusta, and by extension *Georgia Scenes*, were hardly the hierarchical still lifes that romance novels made Southerners out to be. If they had been, reforming the South would have involved simply inducing a little thrift and self-discipline into the upper class, then letting their example pull everyone else along. There were two problems with that. For one, there was no "upper class" around Augusta. What passed for "the quality" were by and large newly rich, first-generation planters, with a few expatriate Virginians thrown in for style, all living in a fairly permeable social atmosphere that made any common definition of "class" relative. Second, the pull of theatrical culture was too strong. Southerners (and *Georgia Scenes* makes this point emphatically) ached to see a show, even if they occasionally drove the performers from the stage.

Augusta and its environs, then, were the South distilled. The area combined a commercial economy and a Protestant work ethic with a cavalier's sense of theater. Virginians might swoon about the old homestead, but Augustans, broadly conceived, were bringing in the money and building up the cotton South. True, times had turned bad after the Panic of 1819, and debts piled up. True also, there was a substantial underclass of poor whites who scratched out horrific lives on a few rented acres and ran whiskey to the slaves. But on the whole the distance between rich and poor was no greater there than in the free labor North, with most people of the "middling sort." George McDuffie, a poor boy from Edgefield, was emblematic of the type. Like most of his peers, he was a self-made man. McDuffie started with nothing and worked his way up, earning a good education, a little breeding, and a lot of acreage and slaves. He dressed simply and worked his crops "like a negro from the break of day until dark," sweating away with the field hands and his overseer.[20] He periodically fought duels over arcane questions of honor and identity; one of these ultimately ruined his health and shortened his life. McDuffie was a Southern nationalist and a political protégé of John C. Calhoun, and in 1835, the same year Longstreet published *Georgia Scenes*, he became governor of South Carolina.

Longstreet was McDuffie's roommate, both literally and ideologically. As representatives of the middling sort, the two were a matched set. McDuffie was a farm boy from Edgefield County who moved across the river to Augusta to work in a store and go to school. Longstreet was a town kid whose mother ran a boardinghouse. The two young men shared an attic, where McDuffie read aloud to Longstreet. It was an act that legitimated intellectual life for Longstreet. "This, to me, was at first irksome, then tolerable, then delightful," Longstreet recalled. "I observed that when we read the same books and papers he always knew twice as much of their contents as I did. I determined to watch him if possible, and I commenced reading with care and in a measure studying what I read."[21]

The habit never left him. Both Longstreet and McDuffie enrolled in Moses Waddel's academy across the Savannah River in Willington, South Carolina, and there Longstreet met the second shaping influence in his life. Waddel had been a preacher for a time before opening his school; he had also married John C. Calhoun's sister in 1794. Waddel tutored the young Calhoun, sent him off first to Yale, then to law school at Litchfield, Connecticut, and finally on to politics. Among his other pupils were James Petigru, William Crawford, and Hugh Legare. Waddel was known as a stern disciplinarian; Longstreet called him "a very severe student, and a very industrious man."[22] Waddel also encouraged his students to work independently, think about what they read, and debate substantive issues. Longstreet worshiped him and in many ways emulated his career. Waddel taught, preached, and then at age forty-nine became a college president. Longstreet taught and preached too, and he ultimately became, also at age forty-nine, the president of a college.

Before that, however, Longstreet had been a fairly typical lawyer in a fairly typical town. Longstreet's family had moved to Augusta in 1785 from Princeton on the basis of his mother's inheritance. Once there, his father, William, dabbled in real estate and unworkable inventions that always came in a lap behind. (He laid claim not only to designing the steamboat but also the cotton gin; no one paid him much attention—a fact of which he was acutely sensitive.) William Longstreet was not particularly good at anything he tried, and he died after the British burned his mill in 1814. His wife, however, had wealth and thrift, so their son received one of the most progressive educations a Southern boy could get. After studying under Waddel, Longstreet retraced Calhoun's path and went to Yale, then to law school at Litchfield, then back to the piedmont. There he married a wealthy girl and settled into the practice of law. For a few years during the 1820s he rode circuit as a judge. As a lawyer he managed the affairs of the new cotton class; he also met odd characters and collected stories. By all accounts Longstreet was eminently likable, sharply opinionated, and utterly self-disciplined. He loved to play raconteur and wit, and years on the Georgia circuit gave him ample material for his stories.

With those credentials, Longstreet might easily have settled into the ownership of a small plantation and disappeared. In 1824, however, his young son died. The event seems to have dislodged him. Depressed and restless at the same time, Longstreet began to rearrange his life. He put himself under a physician's care and then began reading the Bible—converting himself, as it were, through the same kind of critical reading he had learned from McDuffie. Shortly thereafter he joined the Methodist church; a few years after that he tried his hand at writing and eventually bought a newspaper, which he dedicated to the defense of states' rights and John C. Calhoun. He also began dealing in real estate and bought a little property near Augusta.

It was an instructive moment. Longstreet's wife had brought thirty slaves into the marriage, but he found himself unable to maintain a law practice and a plantation at the same time. "My crops barely paid the expenses of making them," he recalled; "my negroes became thieves, they stole my hogs, my corn, my bacon (by false keys), and every thing they could sell." Fed up, he asked his wife if he could sell them. She "showed a little sadness," but let him have his way. "I sold them at fair prices all around," he gloated. "This sale put me out of debt and left me a clever sum over, and relieved me of the eternal torment of negroes, overseers, and creditors. Things now brightened about me greatly."[23] That reminiscence speaks volumes. In it, he redefined republican independence from an 18th century model of benevolent paternalism (per Frank Meriwether) to a Victorian attitude of manly competitiveness, market shrewdness, and clever sums. Unlike his father, he made money off everything he took up, including academics.

But he was more than just a shrewd businessman. Longstreet combined his relentless thrift with a moral energy that made him a perpetual reformer. A fiercely proud Southerner and defender of states' rights, Longstreet was nonetheless uncomfortable with the debt-ridden gentility of the planter elite. Their idleness and pointless violence disturbed him, made him a one-man agent of reform. He headed the local temperance society and positively detested dueling to the point that, as a judge, he issued writs against persons he merely suspected of the practice. As president of the College of South Carolina, he lectured the trustees on the parents' tendency to take their sons out of class to go hunting and socializing. "I have never known a College where the regular routine of business," he wrote, spitting out the word, "was so often interrupted by parental indulgence as this."[24] He grew irate at debtors of any social class, and he never let a loan ride—which set him apart from the gentlemanly norm. Vernon Parrington saw straight to his core: "In his strong instinct of acquisitiveness, his canny thrift that never failed to seize advantage by the forelock, his desire to get on in the world while serving God, he was a Georgia Yankee, with an emotional religion that took comfort in discovering that God was always on his side of any controversy."[25]

The Georgia Yankee began to write sometime around 1830. Part of his output was a series of editorials on states' rights and the tariff; part was a group of comic stories. The conjunction of the two at that particular time is provocative. Longstreet's politics were fairly typical for a piedmont Democrat. He believed instinctively in the inferiority of blacks; he hated New England abolitionism ("this satanic puritanism, this puritanic satanism," he called it).[26] He was so suspicious of federal power that he wrote a brief, now lost, denying the validity of *McCullough v. Maryland*. When John C. Calhoun began articulating an ideology of states' rights, Longstreet signed on.[27] He scratched out a series of editorials supporting nullification for the *Augusta Chronicle* in 1832 and then bought his own newspaper, the *State Rights' Sentinel*, in 1834. Longstreet was hardly an original thinker; he lacked Calhoun's appreciation of constitutional subtleties and his capacity for disciplined argument, and he was utterly devoid of Calhoun's romantic nationalism. In some ways he was more like John Taylor of Caroline, stressing personal independence and simplicity.[28] On the other hand, he did not share Taylor's agrarian nostalgia.

Like other writers of the Atlantic South in the 1830s, Longstreet labored under a sense of regional decline and loss, but he did not look backward to an Augustan age. *His* Augusta, the town, had the potential to be a great city, he sighed in 1832, but "she has been comparatively stationary, for ten years."[29] For once he stepped beyond blaming the tariff and malignant Yankees and looked inward. Southerners had, he argued, a fatal tendency to spend and show off. They were an "ardent people."[30] Despite ten years of cheap cotton and high interest rates, Augustans simply refused to learn thrift. "All the capital of the city has gone into the fine houses," Longstreet snorted. No other place in the country was "half as much in debt"; no other place made such a fetish of ostentation. "It is true," he argued,

> that within the last three or four years, some six or eight gentlemen of wealth, have lined the centre of Broad Street with very splendid buildings. And upon these, do hundreds of our fellow-citizens, who are over head and heels in debt, look, with as much complacency, and self congratulation, as if they owned them.... And in the next moment you will hear them ... declaring that they never knew such hard times for money, in their lives.[31]

The boomer mentality extended to other villages which borrowed money to throw up cotton mills or fine houses and ended up deeper in the hole. Additionally, Longstreet complained, the state suffered from "Georgia madness"—his term for a widespread resistance to spending a dime on the foundering university at Athens. This was masquerade culture run amok, and Longstreet's Georgia Yankee responded in kind. For the rest of his long life he felt a calling—there is no other word for it—to inculcate moral responsibility and plain-sense republican simplicity among his fellow Southerners.

Hence we have a divided man and a divided place. The Georgian in Longstreet's Georgia Yankee was fiercely parochial, staunchly defensive of the South, and keenly concerned with public presentation of self. The Yankee in him, however, gravitated toward restraint, economic independence, and an evangelical's sense of personal reform. This divided self shapes both the narrative technique and the content of *Georgia Scenes*. Longstreet speaks with several voices, no one of which dominates. There are at least two dialects, that of the educated man and the common white. The two narrators, "Baldwin" and "Hall," have different spheres of concern. Hall deals with stories "in which *men* appear as the principal actors"; Baldwin tends to the women. That is suggestive. By dividing his stories into male and female realms, Longstreet signaled a fundamental shift in the ways masculine behavior and moral authority could be approached in the South. The all-inclusive authority of the tobacco planter, as John Pendleton Kennedy had sensed, was sustainable only in a world where the hearth and the workplace were one and the same. Longstreet's little towns were another matter. There, as in any market town east of the fall line from Augusta, Georgia, to Augusta, Maine, gender roles become more specialized, more defined as "separate spheres."[32]

The marketplace was clearly a central part of the man's sphere, and Longstreet viewed it as a place where masquerade culture was inherently vulnerable and weak. The stories he devoted to it all deal with identity and deception, and in each case the comic challenge lies in the "unmasking"—something that is absolutely necessary in the world of commerce (one has to know whom he is dealing with and what he is getting in return) and greatly to be feared in the world of theater and masquerade.[33] "The Character of a Native Georgian," for example, introduces Ned Brace, an alter ego modeled on one of Longstreet's friends, who uses a business trip to Savannah as an opportunity to change identities and play pranks. When he checks into an inn, for example, he does not announce himself, as any Georgia gentlemen should. Instead, he scrawls a few disconnected letters on a piece of paper, which, though puzzling to the barman and the innkeeper, must remain a mystery by the rules of Southern hospitality, which dictate that the men cannot ask Ned outright what the paper says. Brace literally negotiates identity, cuts deals as to who he is. If he had tried to make any money off his pranks, Brace could be considered a con man. But he is in the game, so to speak, purely for the show of it. "He could assume any character which his humour required," and he orchestrated his stunts "in such a way as to render it impossible for any one to call him to account without violating all the rules of decency, politeness and chivalry at once."

"Calling to account" has both commercial and religious overtones. Longstreet's fierce free-trade politics suggest that he saw the market as a self-correcting mechanism; his Methodist convictions similarly inclined him to value personal restraint and self-control. These come together splendidly in "The Horse-Swap," a tale which uses the town as a stage to display deception, market shrewdness, and theatricality all at once. On court day, the one time of the month when a Southern town could guarantee an audience, two men trade nags. What would ordinarily be a simple commercial transaction becomes—in Longstreet's skillful hands—a dissertation on market behavior. "I'm the boy," says one to the crowd, "perhaps a *leetle*, jist a *leetle*, of the best man at a horse-swap that ever trod shoe leather." The language is necessarily hyperbolic, theatrical; after all, who listens to a tight-lipped salesman? He is offering "Bullet," a spindly, skittish runt that looks like a dwarf giraffe with a double-curve tail and a case of nerves. The horse is, without a doubt, "the best piece of *hoss*flesh in the thirteen united univarsal worlds." If the trader can palm this off, he can trade anything.

He does, but not to his satisfaction. A dry old farmer takes up the challenge with an old nag named Kit. Kit is placid. Not even a rifle blast next to the ears ruffles his composure. The trader is interested, then challenged, and after an elaborate ritual he parlays Bullet and three dollars for Kit. The deal done, the saddle blanket comes off Bullet's back to reveal the source of the horse's skittish spirit: a large and sickening sore. One up for the trader. "I'm a man," he gloats, "that, when he makes a bad trade, makes the most of it until he can make a better." Fair enough, but he has just acquired a horse that is placid because it is stone deaf and blind. One up for the farmer. "You are a *leetle* the best man at a horse-swap that I ever got hold of," mocks the farmer. He pockets his money and takes his horse.

The intriguing thing about the story is the idea that anyone would want either animal in the first place. One is blistered; the other is deaf as a post. In Georgia, however, the scenario makes perfect sense if we consider that the whole scene is literally played for the public. It is a sort of folk theater. The horse trader operates from a different base of values than that of the Yankee peddler or the confidence man. The fictional peddler is a tight-lipped miser who sells junk and then moves on. The con man bilks and, having bilked, leaves town one step ahead of the sheriff. The Southern horse trader, however, operates wholly in the public light. His craft is a game that must be played to an audience or there is simply no point to it. He is not really *selling* anything; he is just performing.

That, in turn, is his weakness. When the blanket comes ripping off Bullet's back, it is a symbolic affirmation of "unmasking"—the slick trader has shown up the dumb old farmer by concealing a disgusting infirmity, then revealing it. That is masquerade accountability. The stone-deaf Kit, however, is more representative of the market ethic—quiet, taciturn, and patiently awaiting the chance to make a profit. The internal logic of the marketplace is the authority here and will call the trader to account on its own, once he runs out of money.

The same calling to account does not operate, however, in the violent dramas of sport and male aggression. Here manhood also plays for the public, but restraints are dictated by the community, not the bottom line. In some of these dramas, notably "The Gander Pulling" and "The Fox Hunt," Longstreet simply allowed the excesses of masculine sport to play themselves out to their absurd ends. They are episodes of strenuous competition for nothing, which links them to the market tales and is rather the comic point, put more violently but with flare.

Longstreet's best-known story, "The Fight," is, however, dark and complex. "The Fight" is his most direct link with the bear-eaters and rip-snorters of frontier humor. It has the necessary bluster and gore, but it is actually a town tale—almost a domestic comedy—and at its core are issues of masculine identity and moral leadership.[34] Two men, Billy Stallings and Bob Durham, "were admitted on all hands to be the very *best men*" in town. Right there Longstreet nailed the issue, in italics. In this small town, the "*best men*" are easily defined: "they could flog any other two men in the county." Despite that, or perhaps because of it, Billy and Bob are friends and men of honor and integrity. Billy is all power; Bob is agility and guile. Neither, emphatically, is a cracker or a rube, and they are certainly not gentry. They speak fairly literate English. They live on "opposite sides of the Courthouse"—a metaphor, probably, for their political affiliations—and they command "battalions" in the town militia. That they are known as mighty fighters is simply a part of the roles they must play.

Billy and Bob are also the only figures in the story that Longstreet treats with any respect; the rest he lampoons viciously. At the low end of the scale is Ransy Sniffle, a cracker leprechaun who is Longstreet's finest creation, as well as one of the nastiest clowns in Southern literature. "Long spells of the fever and ague ... had conspired with clay and blackberries to throw him quite out of the order of nature." Ransy is all knots and swollen belly, with large joints, small limbs, a flat head, and "a complexion that a corpse would have disdained to own." He is the archetypical poor white, a cadaverous little dirt-eater whose only real joy in life is stirring up trouble, and he is particularly curious about the "comparative manhood" of Billy and Bob. Longstreet clearly relished the chance to tear him and his ilk apart. Writers as diverse as Erskine Caldwell, William Faulkner, and James Dickey have been at the same task ever since.

"The Fight," however, is not about Ransy, and it is not about no'counts. It is a domestic *code duello* set in motion by women and fought by surrogates. Billy and Bob's wives initiate the whole affair when both women try to buy curtain-cloth from the same merchant at the same time. These are upstanding women (women who buy curtains usually lay claim to *some* respectability), yet they bully past each other like fishwives. "Who are you, madam?" asks Billy's wife. "Your betters, madam," replies Bob's. When Billy tries to be solicitous and take his wife home, he sets off a workingman's duel.

> "Come," said he, "Nancy, let's be going; it's getting late."
>
> "I'd a been gone half an hour ago," she replied, "if it hadn't a' been for that impudent huzzy."
>
> "Who do you call an impudent huzzy, you nasty, good-for-nothing, snaggle-toothed gaub of fat, you?" returned Mrs. D.
>
> "Look here, woman," said Billy, "have you got a husband here? If you have, I'll *lick* him till he learns to teach you better manners, you *sassy* heifer you."

It is classic Longstreet—a step at gentility followed by a quick slip into the gutter. Ransy witnesses the whole thing and tears off to tell Bob, who comes roaring back:

> "Bill Stallions," said Bob . . . "what have you been saying to my wife?"
>
> "Is that your wife?" inquired Billy, obviously much surprised and a little shaken.
>
> "Yes, she is, and no man shall abuse her, I don't care who he is."
>
> "Well," rejoined Billy, "it an't worth while to go over it; I've said enough for a fight: and, if you'll step out, we'll settle it. . . . I've heard much of your manhood, and I believe I'm a better man than you are."

There is in that exchange a finality Achilles himself would have understood, but the fight is not quite Homeric or even frontier. Within minutes Billy and Bob go to battle in the square, tearing at each other in graphic ripsnorter fashion. (Bob, the clever one, the market representative, wins.) Yet unlike the fight scene in *Swallow Barn*, where Ned Hazard thrashes his inferior in a clear contest of social opposites, Billy and Bob are equals. They even have "seconds." More importantly, they are neither gentlemen nor white trash, meaning this is not a fight to establish social position. It is a moral contest for domestic harmony. After chewing each other's noses and fingers off, Billy and Bob meet again and resume their friendship, each admitting that the women made them do it. "Bobby," says Billy, "you've licked me a fair fight; but you wouldn't have done it if I hadn't been in the wrong. I oughtn't to have treated your wife as I did; and I felt so through the whole fight; and it sort o'cowed me." In a word, he felt guilty. While Bob pulled one way, conscience tugged the other. It is the only point in the story that hints at the possibility of a moral vision turned inward, and also the only point at which conscience, not repute, influences behavior.

Yet conscience is not enough. Bob wins, after all, and he does so thanks to a far stronger motivation: the fear of humiliation. Bob felt compelled to win the battle on the street for fear of losing a tougher one at home. With Billy chewing on his finger and "pealing" him, he "thought of Betsy, and knew the house would be too hot for me if I got whipped when fighting for her, after always whipping when I fought for myself." It is an interesting twist on patriarchal authority. In *Swallow Barn* Ned Hazard fought to defend the family name. Bob, though, fights like a man running scared. Among literature's mighty heroes, he is surely among the most henpecked.

As a study in "comparative manhood," then, "The Fight" is a mess. Typically Southern fight stories hinged on the storyteller's gift for gore, and the graphic detail of Longstreet's piece presaged scores of wrassles published in William T. Porter's *Spirit of the Times*. None of Porter's contributors, however, undercut their heroes in quite so subtle a way. (An exception was Thomas Bangs Thorpe, as we shall see.) Even Longstreet's narrator Hall cannot sort it out. The story is told with obvious relish and delight, yet Hall ends on a weak, moralistic trope which gives lame thanks to "the Christian religion, to schools, colleges, and benevolent associations" for making "such scenes of barbarism and cruelty" rare. The comment is perfectly in keeping with Longstreet's evolution as a Methodist, but it raises a fundamental question: who, exactly, is at fault for "this sort of thing"?

Weak leaders, one could answer, who are so bound by community expectations that they cannot make reasoned decisions. When the match is announced, no one lifts a finger to mediate the affront or arrange an apology. Bets start flying like grapeshot; people jockey for a view like gawkers at an English hanging. Violence has to happen unless someone exercises moral leadership and defuses it. Alas, there is no Frank Meriwether to temper the moment. His equivalent, Squire Thomas Loggins, makes no move to stop the violence. Instead, he gathers the crowd like a cleric blessing the hounds and makes cryptic predictions about the probable winner in language that is pure gibberish disguised as good English. He is a gentrified version of Ransy, speaking in his own weird dialect and presiding at a solemn service in a liturgy of mayhem. Thus does the Virginia gentleman—when transplanted into a bustling Georgia town—become a clown himself.

The issue is one of leadership in decline, and it becomes even more evident in "The Turf," a story about a day at the races. The racecourse gives Longstreet the device by which he can bring all society together in a landlubber's ship of fools. Women, moreover, are not only present here, they are prominent. As the narrator walks about the course he sees a world in which the rituals of Southern sociability—specifically treating, drinking, gambling, and a general tendency simply to show off—emerge as means of ratifying status, not having fun. "I saw Major Close," he says, "who two hours before declared he had not enough to pay a poor woman for making the vest he had on, treat a large company to a dollar bowl of punch; and, ten minutes after, I saw the same man stake fifty dollars on the race."

What else, however, could Major Close do? By his title we know he is someone of repute, and because of that he must show himself worthy of his standing. Both treating the crowd and postponing commercial notes were devices by which the elite could reinforce their leadership, particularly in the relatively fluid society of the cotton South. Treating established the donor's sociability and generosity; dodging debts fixed his superiority.[35] Longstreet, moralist to the end, saw the underlying rationale, although he simply refused to approve the social bonding behind such minor, but necessary, acts. "The way these gentlemen treat their creditors," he sighs, "is 'nothing to nobody.'"

With leadership like that, gentility evaporates, classes blend into one another, and no one is made virtuous by his rank. When the horses are ready and the bets are down all social distinctions disappear, including (and this damns the lot for Longstreet) the one between black and white. "Thus it went; men, women, and children, whites and blacks, all betting," whipped into a frenzy that makes it hard to discern who leads and who follows. The day's affairs thus degenerate until children fight, men fight, and, when a rider dies, a "lady" in a carriage can only call it a "little accident" which tarnishes an otherwise fine day. "We never shall have a fine breed of horses," says a general in blissful ignorance of the irony of his statement, "until the turf is more patronised." This is the Methodist in Longstreet, striking out with barely concealed contempt at the moral chaos around him, and writing one of his preachiest and least-entertaining tales in the process.

If men could not provide restraint, then the job fell to women. Even though the all-inclusive authority of the domestic patriarch could not survive transplantation to the town and the marketplace, domesticity remained essential to the preservation of republican values. Women were in a sense assigned the role of gatekeeper. In much antebellum Southern fiction the heroine performs this function ideally and to productive ends. William Gilmore Simms and John Pendleton Kennedy, for example, created heroines of remarkable strength and self-discipline who simply overwhelm their lackluster male counterparts. Kennedy's heroine in *Horse-shoe Robinson* is a good deal better at guerilla warfare and frankly smarter than her soldier husband. She knows how to negotiate, bargain, and keep her mouth shut. Similarly, the Widow Eveleigh in Simms's *Woodcraft* and the title heroine in his *Katharine Walton* are self-controlled, tough women who manage their affairs and society despite the mess men have made of it all.[36] Idealized this way, the fictional Southern belle personifies the antipode of masculine values of competition and display. In quietly providing for the rainy day, she is to the middle class townsman what the scout is to the cavalier—his guide and his repository of common sense and natural self-discipline. Like the scout, she curbs the man's romantic emotionalism and tempers his pride. More to the point, she keeps his theatrics under control.

A nice ideal, but Longstreet sensed that the reality was different. Most of his women are not up to the job. There are domestic paragons, like the country girls in "The Dance," who are homemakers even at their own parties, which start at the sensible hour of nine in the morning. They learn home economics, at home, keep their husbands on the road to success, and entertain their guests with "perfect" renditions of Scotch-Irish ballads. But such women in *Georgia Scenes* are exiled to the countryside. The town girls, on the other hand, are emblematic of the emerging middle class. They are "weakly, sickly, delicate, useless, affected"; they go away to school, where they learn to inflict French or Italian librettos on republican Georgia ears; they treat their slaves like dirt. It is not clear whether Longstreet ever read Jane Austen, although he likely did. Certainly he shared Austen's shrewd estimate of overindulged, idle women, and he instilled in them a particular gift for inciting chaos. In "The Fight" they set the violence in motion, as they do in "The Ball." They egg on and partake of the decadence in "The Turf." None of these portrayals, however, is as essentially mean-hearted and lethal as that found in "The Charming Creature." It is Longstreet's most enigmatic tale simply because it does not seem to belong in *Georgia Scenes* at all. It is not very funny, wholly preachy, and only half complete. Still, it is in some ways an interpretive key to the whole book.[37]

"The Charming Creature" outlines the perils of upward mobility in a society torn between masquerade culture and the Protestant ethic. Longstreet's nephew George is a promising young lawyer who spends his time wisely and his money frugally until he meets a charming creature, Evelina. She is lovely; she is rich, apparently well-read, apparently talented—apparently everything to everybody. Her breeding, however, is an inch-deep cover for her moral emptiness. What she lacks is any trace of self-discipline or the ability to love anything but her own reflection. She is, in fact, the ideal representative of her kind: "the only child of a wealthy, unlettered merchant, who, rather by good luck than good management, had amassed a fortune." George is instantly taken by her, as is every other man in town.

It is George's bad luck that he actually marries her. In a scene of conjugal contracting, Longstreet sets out the ethics and counterethics of Southern domesticity fairly succinctly. Evelina "would have" George adore her, learn to love "tea-parties and balls," and spend summers in New York. He would have her "rise when I do; regulate your servants with system; see that they perform their duties in the proper way and the proper time; let all provisions go through your hands; and devote your spare time to reading valuable works, painting, music, or any other improving employment or innocent recreation."

There it is—a domestic ethic worthy of Benjamin Franklin and a Southern counterethic to masquerade culture. In a few lines Longstreet captured what William Gilmore Simms spent whole chapters doing in *Woodcraft* or what John Pendleton Kennedy could do only by inference in *Swallow Barn*. Unlike those works, however, Longstreet's tale does not end happily, nor is it nearly as funny. There are a few amusing scenes where Evelina falls on her face; she can neither cook nor make her slaves do it, so a party for George's bench and bar is a disaster of raw mutton and charred roast. When she meets George's simple country family and their simple country friends she is nicely put down by a frank old farmer. He looks over the "pretty little soft creater" with the same acute eye he might use to assess a horse and says very simply, "Georgy, my son, I'm afraid you've got yourself into bad business." Mostly, however, she and the story simply grind away until all is lost. George gets her to shape up temporarily after the debts pile too high, but she quickly reverts to form. She takes to her old ways; he takes to the bottle; the home, the sanctum sanctorum of patriarchal authority, collapses.

In the end, Longstreet's befuddled townsman has nowhere to turn. Life is all ambiguity and incongruity. Identity is uncertain. The streets are not safe; competition is fierce; the home is fractious and unsettled. What is a man to do? There is no tidy answer, but the last tale forms something of an epigram to the book. Longstreet wrote *Georgia Scenes* piecemeal for a newspaper. When he assembled the tales into a single volume, he added "The Shooting Match." Here Longstreet abandoned his perch as observer and moved directly into the action and into the role of deceiver. Like the rest of the stories, it concerns identity and leadership. Also like the rest, it is a paradox that celebrates paradox. The gentleman's confusion in "The Shooting-Match" is a turning point in the Southern humorous tradition every bit as important as Frank Meriwether's lifeless insularity is to the pastoral.[38]

The action begins simply enough with a comic effort at establishing identity. Longstreet's narrator Hall is out among the country folk, ambling his horse through Upper Hogthief, Georgia, on his way to business somewhere. He meets one of the natives, and the reader gets this exchange: Says the local, "It seems to me I ought to know you." "Well, if you *ought*," replies the narrator, "why *don't* you?" The other man digs in. "What *mout* your name be?" he asks. "It *might* be anything," says the gentleman, correcting the redneck's English, but it "*is* Hall." "Pretty digging!" comes the retort. "I find you're not the fool I took you to be."

The verbal horseplay is a particular kind based on negotiation. Longstreet's gentleman here has stepped out of his ascribed role and entered one based on haggling, hidden realities, and exchange—that is, market behavior. His wordplay, he admits, is "borrowed wit; for I knew my man, and knew what kind of conversation would please him most." He cannot distance himself from these common men; rather, he must play by their rules in order to establish his legitimacy with them. He borrows his wit from the marketplace.

The game quickly turns to a test of manhood. The redneck recognizes Hall from years back when the latter, as a youth, shot a bull's-eye in a shooting match. A "chance shot," says Hall truthfully, but the plain man insists that he join him at yet another contest. After several pages of the most wonderful theatrics on the etiquette of a country competition, Hall gets manned with a gun so heavy he can barely lift it. He "wabbles" it around, literally aimlessly, squints his eyes, and lets it go off on the downswing. Incredibly, Hall not only hits the target, he gets second place. He is both surprised and thrilled. "'Second best!' exclaimed I, with uncontrollable transports." Then shrewdness kicks in; he sees possibilities in the situation and changes tone. "'Second best!' reiterated I, with an air of despondency." Many of the crew know a charlatan when they see one, but a "decided majority . . . were clearly of opinion that I was serious; and they regarded me as one of the wonders of the world." They give him his prize (a side of beef), which he promptly gives away. Later on, they make polite inquiries about the possibility of Hall's running for office. "If you ever come out for anything," says one, "jist let the boys of Upper Hogthief know it, and they'll go for you to the hilt."

Longstreet's second-best shot fused two manly ideals. As a patrician, he has behaved impeccably and has demonstrated unassuming modesty. He retains a certain aloofness, but properly defers to his constituents' demands. He gives back his prize—gifts being a gentleman's prerogative. He is honorable and honored. Hall has also triumphed in a competition, acquired a reputation for being sharp, has used his very truthfulness as a form of deceit, and has emerged as a common man's hero. He has bargained a lucky shot and a side of beef for all the adulation he could want, and he could win office now on the strength of his competitive skills. It is unlikely that he could have done so as a mere patrician. Longstreet's Hall becomes, in a sense, a con man, capable of being all things to all people.

It was a prophetic moment. The ambiguous ending is part of *Georgia Scenes*' power and influence. No other book captured the fluid state of Southern masculinity so well or provided so many alternate models of manly behavior. For the next twenty years the varied manhoods of *Georgia Scenes* appeared and reappeared in exaggerated forms. William Tappan Thompson adapted the domestic ideal in *Major Jones's Courtship*, a sweet volume about a yokelish cotton planter come to town to woo his belle and offer sage comments about the shenanigans he encounters.[39] Thompson thus tried to blend the domesticity of *Swallow Barn* with the town culture of *Georgia Scenes* and color it with the dialect of a simple democrat. The book sold well, but its appeal was essentially nostalgic, a gauzy look backward at a domestic world that was being lost in the rush west. More exuberant and more original were alligator-men (what kind of husbands would *they* make?), sportsmen, and rootless adventurers. Longstreet's middling sort themselves went on the road, a place populated as likely by rogues as by reformers. The con man took center stage.

Longstreet himself seemed to leave it all behind. *Georgia Scenes*, with all its ambiguities and deceits, captured a particular moment in his life, after which he turned full time to the business of being a Southern professional. Except for one or two sorties, he abandoned humor to write political and religious texts that were single-minded, didactic, and stridently sectional. It was as if he had decided that being "Southern" was the way to settle what was manly and what was not. During the 1840s and 1850s his strident Southern sectionalism intensified, and by 1860 he seemed eager for war.

Yet there is a poignant story that, when the first shots were fired and war came, Longstreet—then president of the College of South Carolina—went to the boys on campus and begged them to stay at their desks. Naturally they ignored him; honor had been challenged and war was just too good—too theatrical if you will—to miss. All left, yet for a time Longstreet stubbornly refused to abandon his job. He ordered his faculty to show up for class, lecture to empty classrooms if necessary, and preserve the routine—the business of education and the moral responsibility of teaching the young—no matter what.[40]

3

Counterfeit Presentments

IN 1833 JOHNSON JONES HOOPER informed his mother that he was tired of working menial jobs "without any hope of going to college."[1] He left Charleston to join an older brother in Alabama. Four years later, up in the Shenandoah Valley, Joseph Glover Baldwin threw a few law books into his saddlebags and headed off in the same direction. They probably never met, but they were in some ways very much alike. Both had been born in 1815 to old but not necessarily prosperous families; both had fathers who started out prosperous but somehow dribbled away the family fortune. Each had older, more successful brothers who tried to get them started in a useful trade. Baldwin had tried journalism, but wound up embracing law; Hooper tried practicing law but put his heart into newspaper work. Coincidentally, both Hooper and Baldwin were Episcopalian and Whig, largely self-educated, supremely ambitious, and given to fits of moodiness. Mostly they were just restless, and going to Alabama seemed like a good idea.[2]

They might as well have traveled to another continent. The new states of the frontier South were so unlike Virginia or even eastern Georgia that men such as Hooper or Baldwin moved like Marco Polo among the Chinese. It is tempting to view the cotton South as an exuberant extrapolation of the Old Dominion, divided into a tripartite structure of planters, slaves, and common whites. The reality was more complex. In contrast to the rather homey world of the Shenandoah Valley or the Carolinas, the frontier states were lands of constant motion where tradition had been supplanted by speculation and speculation had gone wild. The phenomenon was directly connected to the availability of cheap land. In the early 1830s Andrew Jackson expelled Cherokees and Choctaws from their ancestral homes, threw the emptied lands onto the market at $1.50 an acre, and then promptly rearranged the money supply so that hundreds of banks sprang up overnight, printing bills and issuing credit based on little more than a promise and a prayer. "Under this stimulating process," Baldwin observed drily, "prices rose like smoke. Lots in obscure villages were held at city prices; lands, bought at the minimum cost of the government, were sold at from thirty to forty dollars an acre, and considered dirt cheap at that."[3] "It seemed," he added, "as if a new chapter had opened in history, and that the world had been let out of the school of common sense for a holiday of commercial insanity."[4]

It was, in short, a speculator's nirvana—a condition that played havoc with manly expectations. Those who moved there under the pretense of becoming planters were in reality venture capitalists starting up risky and volatile businesses, and they experienced all the competitive pressures and insecurities such men must endure, as well as all the attendant consequences. Virtually none of the traditional agents of social control moved west without mutation. The Virginia gentleman's domestic empire, his sense of command, the deference paid him by common folk, even his sporting instincts, were all rearranged. All of which posed particular threats to social order. "Society was wholly unorganized," Baldwin sighed, "there was no restraining public opinion: the law was well-nigh powerless—and religion was scarcely heard of except as furnishing the oaths and *technics* of profanity."

Baldwin's assessment was not fundamentally different from the kind of morally anxious opinions that Longstreet had voiced in the market towns of eastern Georgia; it had simply taken on urgency and lacked an evangelical overtone. Virtually alone, without an extended family, creating plantations out of wiregrass and towns out of wide spots in the road, the Southern male was left to fend for himself. His code of honor theoretically should have sustained him and given him the tools to forge through. Instead, it left him vulnerable and prone to extremes of behavior. "Honor" was hardly a workable ethic in the cardsharp atmosphere of the new states, but Southern male behavior was unthinkable without it, and so odd extrapolations of masquerade culture took form. Those who succeeded seemed given over to conspicuous consumption and exaggerations of the Virginia gentleman's sporting life—all hammered out through a slave system that grew more exploitative the farther west one traveled. At the low end of the social scale, the unattached white male turned into a chest-thumping hybrid: half-alligator, half-horse, all triumphant manliness.

Somewhere between the planter and the roarer was the Southern professional. Hooper and Baldwin typified a special group of young men who left their homes in the east during the 1820s and 1830s—an émigré generation of displaced youth. Neither planter-rich nor common white, these men were often the second or third sons of respectable families in Virginia or the Carolinas, some of whom had fallen on hard times after the Panic of 1819. More would come after the Panic of 1837. Like Hooper and Baldwin, they had genteel lineages but shabby cuffs. Others were upwardly mobile, and many were transplanted Yankees like Thomas Bangs Thorpe. While some became planters, a critical part settled in the boomtowns, populating the bench and bar and/or editing newspapers or running banks or tending the sick or any of the dozen other professions a middle class male might dabble in. They served the planters; they shared planter attitudes about race and patriarchy. They facilitated the planter's legal whims and helped write his laws and editorials, or, as in the case of Henry Clay Lewis, they mended his broken parts. Smart, well-read, and supremely ambitious, they were Longstreet's brothers-in-arms, the professional middle class.

For such men, language was more than a stock in trade. Language was both a means of self-definition and an agent of mastery—that sine qua non of Southern manliness. In the theatrical culture of Southern manhood, one simple and effective way to create a persona was simply to assume one and announce it. "I'm the man!" roars the mighty hunter, as if the robust assertion of self could vanquish all enemies and remove all self-doubts. Such language was competitive, argumentative, exaggerated, and violent, and it became the stuff of a rich tradition of folklore and fantasy, the tall-tale school of Southwestern humor.

More subtly, however, language was an agent of authority and social control. In the insulated world of *Swallow Barn* all relationships were assumed to be complementary and organic. Frank Meriwether literally *spoke for* the community; he gave language to its aspirations and reservations. There were no such entitlements in the Southwest, despite the presence of slavery and the efforts of cotton snobs to replicate the tobacco planter's authority. In the more fluid market culture of the developing South, relationships were essentially antagonistic and calculating. All life, not just the commercial end of it, might imbue itself with a pervasive and ongoing sense of risk, a recurrent anticipation of gain and loss that gave all social intercourse a pointed, transactional quality. Language negotiated the market, and to manipulate language, to feel and savor its power, gave a man mastery. Moreover, language in this context was not simply the spoken word. It embraced the whole range of symbols and customs that marked masquerade culture, and to manipulate that culture one had to be skilled at all the forms of communication it entailed.

This may be the reason why some such men adopted humor as their preferred mode of expression. Their perspective was neither fully gentlemanly nor genuinely frontier, although it borrowed elements of both. Like Longstreet, to whom they owed a huge debt of both content and style, they adopted the stance of the slightly astonished bystander, amused by the wretched excesses around them but nervously trying to resolve some of the incongruities in their surroundings. They experimented with dialect and "realistic" presentations of violent behavior. Most were good only for a few stories published in sporting magazines like William T. Porter's *Spirit of the Times*, where they concentrated on hunting tales and shared page space with fellow sportsmen from around the country. Others developed more enduring bodies of work centering on some central theme or stereotype. For C.F.M. Noland of Arkansas, this expressive urge gave birth to the Pete Whetstone stories—thinly disguised diatribes against the new Jacksonian politics.[5] For Thomas Bangs Thorpe, as we shall see, it occasioned long and poignant examinations of the sporting life pursued by the new leisure class. Hooper and Baldwin took on market culture directly. Whatever their focus, all explored the peculiar interstice between tradition and modernity that made identity—especially male identity—so contested on the frontier.

Who better to negotiate this unsettled manhood than the clever lawyer and his evil twin, the con man? The one operated within the law, the other outside it; both manipulated language for gain and mastery. Both were marginal characters who moved back and forth between modernity and tradition.[6] Negotiation was literally their business, for good or ill. As projections of masculine identity, they reflected the unsettling fact that, in the new states, identity was a product of self-invention, not inheritance. The difference, of course, was that the lawyer at least had some credibility as an agent of authority and social order.

While Hooper and Baldwin had very similar backgrounds, they interpreted this self-invention in diametrically opposed ways. For each, the point of reference was the gentleman. For Baldwin, whose model could have been Frank Meriwether himself, this was a starting point for growth; for Hooper—who had been raised in the Carolina sporting tradition—it was a refuge. Each saw the frontier's corrosive effect on that gentleman in a generalized lapse of manners, morals, and taste. Hooper's response was to hunker down, play bad boy, and retreat into satire. Baldwin's, by contrast, was more optimistic. Alabama was tough ground, and, granted, the place was a mess. But Baldwin took the long view, an essentially Hegelian dialectic that saw conflict as the mortar and pestle of progress.

The confidence man was hardly new; in one form or another he is the sentinel of liminal societies because he speaks so directly to the issue of changing identity. It can be argued that Benjamin Franklin set an American pattern in his autobiography, inventing and adapting himself as the needs of commerce dictated. Longstreet's Ned Brace was a version of this archetype, although more a practical joker than anything else. Simms included a Yankee trader in his first frontier novel, *Guy Rivers*, and Yankees and con artists were often synonymous among Southern audiences. In each of these instances and their countless variations, there was usually a resolution of some sort. Franklin became a gentleman and retired to gentle pursuits; Brace went back to his hometown and resumed his profession; the Yankee trader or thimblerig got expelled from the community, usually on a rail.[7]

Hooper's creation, Captain Simon Suggs, was homegrown and a professional. Suggs first appeared in a short story in Porter's *Spirit of the Times* and then, in 1845, as the subject of a full-blown book, *Adventures of Captain Simon Suggs*. Hooper presented it as a campaign biography in the fashion of those written about Jackson, Van Buren, and Clay—all of which Hooper regarded as "counterfeit presentments" of their subjects' true natures—and like those biographies, his book spent a fair amount of time exploring the visage his hero presented to the world. Suggs had a large head, wiry hair, long nose, and such, but what distinguished him were the eyes and mouth. His eyes were little pools of grey light that "dance and twinkle in an aqueous humor" beneath arched, thin brows and lids "without lashes." They glowed red whenever there was liquor at hand. The mouth was four inches across, set in a permanent sneer ("but not all malice"), and constantly dribbling tobacco juice at the corners. This grotesque head was set on a "long and skinny, but muscular neck." Remove the worn-out hat and the description could easily fit that of some kind of predatory amphibian, capable of adapting to any environment—an alligator perhaps. Hence Suggs's motto: "It is good to be shifty in a new country."

This goes beyond mere ugliness; it is a purposeful distortion of identity. In his own perverse way, Suggs is the gentleman turned on end, a reflection of Southern manhood akin in its own way to Oscar Wilde's portrait of Dorian Gray. There is almost nothing in Suggs's various cons that does not feed on the catalog of gentlemanly virtues, one of which was the coveted quality of transparency. To be open and frank, unquestioned and unquestioning, demonstrated manly refinement and an elusive quality of nobility and honor. It was a relic, essentially, of the battlefield code, the Homeric display of simple courage and fearlessness where one's inner self was evident to anyone with eyes. Ned Brace, of course, had challenged this stereotype in Longstreet's humor, but Suggs positively upended it. To offer a "counterfeit presentment" was to adapt a Shakespearean posture of deceit and double meaning—and Shakespeare had written during an age of expansion and displacement too.[8]

Where did such a visage come from? It is tempting to make Suggs a simple projection of the market revolution, and he is that. The fact that Suggs looks a bit like Hooper himself is more suggestive. In the particular culture from which Hooper originated, Suggs's amphibian identity is possible only in the absence of the extended family's restraining bonds. Before Hooper could send Suggs out into a life of manipulation and deceit, in other words, it was absolutely essential to tear the web of domesticity apart, to set the boy free to reinvent himself. Suggs's defining moment comes in a startling first chapter where he cheats his father at cards. The old man is a Calvinist and self-appointed hard-shell Baptist, and when he catches Simon playing seven-up with a slave boy, he sets out to punish both. Simon distracts his father with a card game, which appeals to the old man's vanity and manages to cheat him out of a whipping, a horse, and an obligation to stay home and farm, all at once. This is destructive in itself, but the next morning, when Suggs leaves, he stuffs his mother's pipe with gunpowder. "'Now won't it be great,' he said aloud.

'Won't the old 'oman jump, and sputter, and tear off her cap, and break her spectacles! ... And Jee-ehu!'" he continued, 'won't old Jed'diah grunt, and cuss, and pray!'"

The scene depicts a home literally blowing apart, and it invites speculation into Hooper's own family relations.[9] Hooper's father may or may not have been a strict disciplinarian; what is clear, however, is that he lacked the skills to make it in a competitive world. Archibald Hooper started parenthood with many advantages—acreage in North Carolina, a few slaves, and most of all a good family which included a signer of the Declaration. The elder Hooper owned a newspaper, but he lacked business sense, and by the time Johnson Hooper left for Alabama the family was broke, living off the meager income that Hooper's mother Charlotte DeBerniere scratched out from tutoring. Charlotte was a burden herself—alternately doting and critical, always urging Hooper to be more like his older brothers. She was a pious Episcopalian, a rather curious mix of evangelicalism and tradition, and she constantly exhorted her boys to better themselves. As Johanna Nicol Shields has observed, her "complaints were hard to bear," and anyone looking for reasons why Hoopers's character Suggs exploded a pipe in his mother's face ought first to look to Hooper's own family background.[10]

Suggs got free; Hooper did not, or at least not completely. Ironically, Hooper remained dependent for some time upon his family in ways that left him unsure of himself and frustrated. He followed his brother George to Alabama in 1833, tagging along in the wake of the older, more responsible man. The experience humiliated him. "I have been a dependent all my life and it is mortifying to have to sponge on my brother's liberality when I am twenty years old," he wrote in 1836.[11] Hooper moved around for four years, went to Texas briefly in 1837, and then returned to help open a mercantile store in Tuscaloosa and promptly went bust. His life only began to settle down after 1840, when he landed a political job taking the census (hence his first story, "Taking the Census") and took up law. He settled in Lafayette, married, and in 1842 opened the *East Alabamian*, a Whig newspaper marketed to Black Belt cotton planters and parvenus. Later, in the 1850s, he fancied himself a gentleman sportsman and began to write long celebrations of the hunt, per the aspirations of the Carolina sportsman. Thus did the boy come full circle—a gentleman/journalist's son, wastrel, entrepreneur, lawyer, and, finally, gentleman/journalist.

In short, Hooper was a man in motion and unsure of himself, as were many of the men around him. Frank Meriwether's domestic realm, where cousins counted and all life was cushioned by family ties, either did not exist on the frontier or did so only in attenuated form. This was particularly true among ambitious, younger men such as Hooper and Baldwin. The sort of idle dissipation that Ned Hazard had pursued at Swallow Barn might remain the golden ideal, but practically speaking Ned Hazard's leisurely habits were unusable. They existed outside real time—quaint relics from days past or an ideal projection into a more settled, cultivated future. Fast thinking and shrewdness—qualities Ned never claimed—were the new mark of manliness. "The competitive frontier seduced eastern sons to western freedom," writes Johanna Nicol Shields, "to the irresistible promise of a future gained by wit, not given by family."[12] If the promise was great, however, so was the risk of failure, and male behaviors became edgier, more exaggerated. "New kinds of behavior appeared among the sons and daughters of planter migrants, resulting in part from disintegration of kinship networks," writes Joan Cashin. "Many planter men adopted more aggressive, self-absorbed forms of behavior, embracing the psychological aspects of 'independence' whether or not they achieved economic autonomy."[13] Absent the restraints of family and good society, Southern men became more violent, more theatrical, and less principled. Aggression and self-absorption being part of Southern humor, Hooper began to write.

The translation of exploded families and mobile men into humor generated at least two levels of irony that run throughout *Simon Suggs*. While the con man is a liminal figure, so are the men he cons. Both victim and victimizer are geographically and upwardly mobile, caught in a sense between boyhood and manhood without strong patriarchal restraints, and thus in transition. In time this state of permanent mobility came to be a social ideal in and of itself, but in Hooper's world this shift was incomplete. Men like Suggs, his victims, and Hooper himself posed challenges to patriarchal authority and traditional notions of honor, but to what end? As Michael Oriard notes, "The code of honor rested uneasily on the Southern conscience, but the Southern social order without a code of honor would have been nearly indefensible."[14] This dilemma set up a second irony in Hooper's satire. Honor, transparency, and the gentleman's code of behavior stubbornly remained the masculine ideal even if the real world demanded shrewdness and guile. What Suggs does, ever brilliantly, is use the rules of gentlemanly behavior as instruments of the con. Only someone who knew the game could win it.

He uses language as his tactic, for language was mastery, the root of oratory and a branch of masculine expression. Suggs's comic inversion is to upend the rules; if identity is an issue here, then Suggs ingeniously lets other men define him. In a typical example of his cons, Suggs sets off for Montgomery on the mail-coach, traveling with a man who is on his way to campaign for a political appointment as a bank director. "The individual assumed, and insisted on believing," that Suggs was a Mr. Smith, a politician with some influence over the choice. This Suggs denies repeatedly, but being a con artist he can smell another con artist at work, and so he lets the other man dig himself into a trap. Suggs "let on that [he] wanted a few dollars to pay expenses down," which the man immediately translates into an opportunity to help a poor legislator with his per diems, and from there it is a short run to outright bribery and several days of free food and drink for Suggs—just long enough for the real Mr. Smith to show up, by which time Suggs is off on another conquest.

While the scam itself is fairly ordinary, given the political circumstances in Alabama at the time, Suggs's genius stems from his ability to use the Southern gentleman's code of ethics to gain mastery. Unlike the confidence men in *Huckleberry Finn*, he does not deliberately assume a counterfeit persona. "Stop!" he roars when the politico tries to call him a member of the legislature. "I never said my name was Smith; nor I never set myself up for a legislatur man!" What he does do is allow his fellow traveler to "read" his appearance—incorrectly—and dig his own pit to fall in. "There are persons so skilled in human nature, so acute in their perceptions of worth and talent, that they detect at a glance those whom the people have honored," the stranger orates in words that a Southern man would instantly comprehend as noble and honorable. Suggs's "personal appearance" is that of a "gentleman of the nicest honor, and the most unimpeachable veracity." The fact that Suggs feigns modesty only adds to the stranger's estimation of his own perceptiveness. "Southern gentlemen expected men of honor to wear masks, to display a crafted version of themselves through their voices, faces, noses, and a thousand other projections into the world," writes Kenneth Greenberg.[15] It was enough, in other words, for Suggs to *appear* to be a modest, self-effacing, humble public servant. "'Look me in the eye!'" he says "with an almost tragic air. ...'You see *honesty* thar—don't you?'" The tragic air is all it takes.

Once Suggs crafts the necessary version of himself, he can use other aspects of the gentleman's code to exploit the situation. Gift giving, for example, indicated not only wealth but power; a powerful man could be generous, a weak one could not. The Southern man was most vulnerable to ruination by the unwritten rule that required him to buy drinks, cosign notes, and demonstrate his generosity and "liberality." The diary of Thomas B. Chaplin of South Carolina, for example, was often a list of parties thrown and notes signed, which Chaplin could not actually pay but which socially he could not refuse.[16] Suggs knew this. When his travels take him to a Tuscaloosa faro hall, his white hair, red eyes, and thin, wide mouth make him a ringer for a rich old hog drover who is due in from Kentucky at any moment. Again Suggs lets others identify him and transform him into "General Thomas Witherspoon." Within minutes he has even the general's own nephew buying him treats and plying him with credit, which he repays, so to speak, by treating the whole barroom to champagne and oysters on the general's tab. He was "determined," writes Hooper, "to sustain any reputation for liberality which General Witherspoon might, perchance, possess." He also walks off with fifty dollars of the nephew's cash. If masquerade culture expected the gentleman to present himself in some dramatic, theatrical way—to wear a mask—then a man's worst horror was to be exposed, revealed as a fraud. Suggs's manly genius, in this and other scams, is his ability to maintain that facade. He never wears a coat of tar and feathers. He is never revealed. "I say nothin' about myself—other people can say what they please," he snorts. He relies on the dynamics of Southern masquerade culture to take over from there.

This is mastery, but in a new and dubious way. As a masculine projection, Suggs personifies the qualities that young men of the cotton South were adopting. He is smart but without the pretensions of a formal education. "Well, mother-wit kin beat book-larnin, at *any* game!" Suggs exclaims, "book-larnin spiles a man ef he's got mother-wit, and ef he aint got that, it don't do him no good." He is competitive, but in a dead-serious, winner-take-all sort of way. He is most certainly a risk-taker, but he is indifferent to the long-term fate of his reputation. "So he isn't taken red-handed, after-claps may go to the devil!" Most of all, he maintains his identity, even though it is a mask. By contrast, his victims are stripped, exposed, and disgraced. Only a slave—to greed, to poor breeding, to ambition—would suffer such a fate. There is little in Hooper's career to suggest that he had any respect for the crowd of up'n'comers and parvenus that populated the Old Southwest. Real gentlemen (and by that he meant men like himself) would never subject themselves to the kind of exploitation and humiliation that Suggs inflicts on his prey. In the

Counterfeit Presentments 57

highly symbolic structuring of Southern masculinity, to be manipulated and mastered was to be a slave, regardless of race.

Hence Suggs—the most famous con man of the age—voices an essentially traditional point of view, skewed though it may be. He plays upon the stances of masculine honor and mastery, and he rules. Suggs is Hooper's fictionalized encounter with all the deceits and trickeries endemic to a market economy, but he is also the moral agent of a man desperately trying to demonstrate that only some kind of hierarchy or ruling force can keep things ordered and in their place.

But what other option is there? At this point Longstreet or William Tappan Thompson might have looked to religion and personal propriety, the moral conventions of the Georgia bourgeoisie. Hooper, however, had been born into the patrician class. He was Whig to the core and—perhaps more suggestively—a high-church Episcopalian with a special contempt for those who voted Democratic and prayed with the revivalists. Suggs's first victim, his father, is an "old 'hard shell' Baptist preacher; who, though very pious and remarkably austere, was very avaricious." Thus did Hooper mate piety and greed, and he played the pairing to its limit in Suggs's most energetic tale, the camp-meeting story. With the cupboard bare and pockets empty, Suggs "sat one day, ruminating," until his wife began pecking at him. "D—n it!" he roars, "*somebody* must suffer!" and he is off to an Alabama variant of Cane Ridge: preachers riling the crowd and paying special attention to the girls ("Keep the thing warm!" says one to the girls, "come to the Lord, honey!"), "delicate" women lolling about with a case of the jerks, and a "greasy negro woman" falling "'like a thousand of brick,' across a diminutive old man in a little round hat." "Gl-o-*ree*!" she hollers; "Good Lord, have mercy!" he responds. Her chant is from the heart; his is from the Book of Common Prayer.

Religion becomes its own game, to be exploited by its own rules. "Amid all this confusion and excitement Suggs stood unmoved," Hooper writes. "He viewed the whole affair as a grand deception—a sort of 'opposition line' running against his own, and looked on with a sort of professional jealousy." Again his response is to put on a mask, to be what they wanted him to be (in this case, a sinner), and to use their own code to subvert them just as he had used the code of honor to subvert the gentlemen-pretenders at the faro hall. He shakes and hollers and weeps with his eyes firmly fixed on the collection plate, which he fattens by throwing in his last five-dollar bill, at which point he appeals to the vanity of the crowd. "'Look here, breethring,' said the Captain . . . 'In course 'taint expected that you *that aint as well off as them*, will give *as much*; let every one give *accordin'* to ther means.'" Simon "had excited the pride of purse of the congregation," Hooper notes, "and a very handsome sum was collected in a very short time." Every penny goes straight into Suggs's pockets.

A great story, possibly because Hooper threw so much of his rage into it, but it goes nowhere. Hooper unleashes Suggs to destroy society in order that it might be remade according to virtue and real talent, but this does not happen. The fact that Suggs lives off "mother-wit" suggests that Hooper used him to fashion a new ideal, one that merged the shrewdness of a Yankee with the patrician qualities of a cavalier—thus generating the combination of cunning and grace that populated antebellum novels from Cooper to Simms. But the idea was stillborn, primarily because it lacked the one essential element of patrician authority that could not be compromised—that is, the sense of domestic responsibility and family rootedness that Frank Meriwether so perfectly and ridiculously embodied, or that Longstreet tried to reformulate along middle-class lines. Suggs's nagging wife and the empty cupboard may prompt Suggs to attend to "business," and Suggs is described as "really an affectionate father." But home, ultimately, is simply a base of operations, not a part of manly identity. He can be an expert gamesman, but he offers nothing else.

And so Suggs, like Hooper, rather drifts away at the end. Hooper seemed to lose interest in Suggs during the 1850s and threw his talents into political work for Alabama Whigs—a losing enterprise that Suggs would have abandoned in an instant. He grew less happy and more conservative as he aged, and in 1856 Hooper put out a guide for aspiring hunters, *Dog and Gun*, which utterly abandoned Suggs in favor of the most traditional and least workable masculine ideal of all, the English sporting gentleman.[17] In place of "mother-wit" and the game, Hooper substituted Anglophilia, breeding (both canine and human), and toy worship. *Dog and Gun* went full force for the "manliness and innocence of Field Sports" as "The Gentleman's Amusement," and it significantly opened with a blast at the "prejudiced ignorance and under-bred and over-done morality" that dared criticize quail shoots and hunting dogs as a waste of time.[18] The book is, like Hooper's spiritual instincts, liturgical, right down to the choice of gun and shot that make up the holy vessels of gentlemanly affirmation. (Gentlemen, he asserted, used shorter barrels and small shot, and never "overcharged" their guns; the sexual subtext is doubtlessly unintentional.) As the decade of the 1850s ground on toward its dreadful conclusion, Hooper poured his passion into states' rights and an increasingly narrow conservatism. He died in Richmond, working for the Confederate bureaucracy, in 1862, but not before he had joined a Roman Catholic church.

Baldwin was more adaptable.[19] Like Hooper he had experienced a shift in family fortunes, or at least the threat of it, and had gone west. Baldwin, however, had a working experience with the market economy from birth. His family heritage was built on industry, not family connections or plantations. Baldwin's father and grandfather operated cotton and woolens mills near Winchester (it is interesting to speculate whether his and Kennedy's extended families ever crossed paths). Baldwin may even have been born at one of them, the curiously named Friendly Grove Factory. He seems to have grown up working—no college, no tours of Europe, no protracted adolescence. He was, his brother recalled, "a solemn son, who had earned the nickname 'little parson,'" which may help explain his moralistic streak.[20] He moved to Staunton and then Lexington, Virginia, while a teenager, and he worked first as a law clerk and then on various newspapers, including one run by his older brother. Somewhere in this adolescent journey he became a states' rights Whig and a serious student of the law, but he was restless. When a girl rejected him and an offer came along to go west, he left, settling first in Mississippi and then in Sumter County, Alabama—square in the middle of the finest cotton lands in the country.

For the next fifteen years Baldwin helped in his own small way to create and define the Southern middle class. He lived in town, married respectably, bought a few slaves to do the chores and display his wealth, and worked tirelessly. He served—and depended on—the planters. Baldwin carefully recruited a clientele of men who were likely to sue and be sued fairly often, particularly over boundaries and bad debts. He made their interests his own, tidying up their deeds and contracts. He voiced their politics: he was a states' rights Whig, fiercely Southern but with an eye on order and expansion, and wholly protective of the planter class. During the single term he spent in the Alabama House, he spoke out against a Democratic proposal to apportion representation solely on the basis of the white population. It was better, he argued, to stick with the federal method, which added three fifths of the slave population to the census and thus privileged the vote of the planter class. Reapportionment would strip slaveholders of a power that they had become accustomed to and give credibility to abolitionist arguments, which he called "that antichrist of southern policy and interests."[21] (Despite his efforts, the measure passed.) The cotton snobs loved him, and he prospered.

Baldwin's older brother described him as a "progressive conservative," a term that calls for some reflection.[22] Whig to the core, there was nothing in Baldwin's politics that separated him from the ordinary run of planters and lawyers who populated the Black Belt. In that sense he was no different from Hooper. But Hooper stubbornly held on to an aristocratic ideal and never really acknowledged the fact that Black Belt planters were fundamentally less polished, less honorable, and less gentlemanly than their Virginia ancestors. Baldwin, on the other hand, was both smart enough to see that the Virginian could not survive in Alabama, and optimistic enough to think that the Black Belt could be refashioned into something forward-looking and new.

This progressive conservatism manifested itself in a fascination with leadership. Running throughout Baldwin's writing is a conviction that changing times call for men of mastery—the "genius" who encounters struggle, adapts himself to the situation, and takes command. There is no direct evidence that Baldwin read Hegel, but dialectics was in the air, and he did fancy himself well rounded. "To be great, there must be a great work to be done," he argued in one of his essays. "Great abilities usually need a great stimulus." Washington's struggles "purified him and qualified him for the self-denial and self-conquest" it took to take charge and achieve great things.[23] That southwest Alabama was not Valley Forge was evident to all, but it was nonetheless a place of conflict and struggle in which new democratic forms were being tested and tried.

For this task the republican gentleman had limitations. Baldwin, for one, was mercilessly self-effacing. "Eminently social and hospitable, kind, humane, and generous is a Virginian, at home or abroad," he wrote autobiographically. A gentleman of the old school was magnanimous, "well mannered, honorable, spirited, and careful of reputation, desirous of pleasing, and skilled in the accomplishments which please." He was, in short, doomed. The speculative, credit-crazed frenzies that a market economy thrived on were toxic to the patrician, who lived by a kind of anticapitalist ethos. In the Old Dominion, Baldwin observed, a man might start "the business of free living on a capital of a plantation and fifty or sixty negroes" and hold out, with the "aid of a usurer, and the occasional sale of a negro or two, . . . until a green old age." In the new economy, no such luck could be had. "All the habits of his life, his taste, his associations, his education—every thing—the trustingness of his disposition—his want of business qualifications—his sanguine temper—all that was Virginian in him, made him the prey, if not of imposture, at least of unfortunate speculations. Where the keenest jockey was often bit, what chance had *he*?"

This is an amazing display of candor in a society that avoided candor at every turn. *Flush Times* displays an acute awareness, amounting to self-consciousness, of Baldwin's Virginia roots and the limitations thereof. Unlike Hooper, who constructed an alter ego to voice his satire, or Longstreet, who used two, Baldwin moved directly and personally into the action, making himself the butt of the joke. He became the fool—hoodwinked, shown up in court, outmaneuvered and outclassed—self-consciously mocking himself and his own kind. This deeply personal approach was completely outside the stance that Southern men, authors included, normally adopted. Baldwin literally unmasked himself, gave himself the lie, and reduced the Virginia gentleman to comic helplessness. The pose also allowed Baldwin the literary freedom to move beyond the usual prescriptions and delve into the maturation and socialization of the new middle class.

Where Longstreet approached market behavior through games and competitions, Baldwin used the law, itself an elaborate competition and, some would say, game.[24] Land speculation in the 1830s transformed the law in two important ways, both of which John Pendleton Kennedy had anticipated in *Swallow Barn*. First, it turned law away from a discipline that reflected the republican order and virtue and made it an instrument of competing interests. By 1850, argues legal historian Morton Horwitz, law had metamorphosed into a tool of commerce and development. "Law, once conceived of as protective, regulative, paternalistic and, above all, a paramount expression of the moral sense of the community, had come to be thought of as facilitative of individual desires and as simply reflective of the existing organization of economic and political power."[25] Second, speculation changed the role of the lawyers themselves. As historian Robert A. Ferguson notes, the lawyer ceased being a spokesman for the whole community and became "a narrower agent of competing concerns. As the increasingly technical representative of vested interests, he found less and less reason to function as the ideological guardian of his culture."[26] The law became a commodity, and lawyers turned into its salesmen.

Flush Times is a comic history of this transformation, one that Baldwin used industrial and marketing metaphors to detail. Newcomers to the bar were entrepreneurs, men "armed with fresh licenses which they had got gratuitously"; they hawked law like snake oil, "standing ready to supply any distressed citizen who wanted law, with their wares counterfeiting the article." Old-timers, however, formed a kind of capitalist elite. Keeping the law "as a close monopoly," they had "conned the statutes for the last fifteen years" for obscure precedents and rulings which they sprang on their younger colleagues like traps. They were "perfect in forms and ceremonies—very pharisees . . . 'but *neglecting judgment and the weightier matters of the law.*'" New or old, members of the legal profession approached their craft as an industrial process. "They seemed to think that judicature was a tanyard—clients skins to be curried—the court the mill, and the thing 'to work on their leather' with—*bark*: the idea that justice had any thing to do with trying causes, or sense had any thing to do with legal principles, never seemed to occur to them once."

Again, language becomes the instrument of manipulation and mastery. The pontifications of Frank Meriwether or the sermons of Longstreet's Hall gave way to the fabrications of Baldwin's quintessential lawyer, Ovid Bolus. Where the Virginia gentleman built his reputation on restraint and honor, Bolus made his out of exploitation and chicanery. Bolus took the qualities of a gentleman, ran them through a speculator's rose-colored glasses, and distorted them. A gentleman's strict probity and consistency—which one would ordinarily associate with truthfulness—became for Bolus an absolute consistency in lying. He never told the truth, ever. "Indeed," wrote Baldwin, "sometimes his very silence was a lie." A gentleman was generous; so was Bolus. "Bolus was no niggard. He never higgled or chaffered about small things. He was as free with his own money—if he ever had any of his own—as with yours. If he never paid borrowed money, he never asked payment of others." He was the hail-fellow par excellence, telling stories on himself and others, treating the saloon to a round of drinks and putting it all on his "account," and then using his legalese—his mastery of language—and his charm to strip the suckers of every hard-earned dollar in their pockets. He was gallant with women, provided they had rich fathers, yet never took one to the altar in order not to spoil her name. He was the con man's Homeric hero, and the only time he stepped out of character was when he went after pickings that were *too* easy, rather like "setting a trap for a pet pig." Baldwin could only speculate that this lapse was a sign of ambition. He was "on the lift for Texas, and the desire was natural to qualify himself for citizenship." Bolus was a scoundrel, but Baldwin's fascination with him displayed a certain admiration for the sheer authority and sense of command that such a man—or manly ideal—could assemble. An expanding, commercializing economy could not operate on gentlemanly poise and absolute frankness. Baldwin may have not entirely approved of the shift, but at least he had the candor to admit that the Southern gentleman was quickly becoming an anachronism.

With men like Bolus on the loose, the South took on a carnival atmosphere, a Mardi Gras of upheaving social relations in which bottom became top and vice versa. "The old rules of business and the calculations of prudence were alike disregarded, and profligacy, in all the departments of the *crimen falsi*, held riotous carnival." "Shylock himself," Baldwin added, "couldn't live in those times, so reversed was everything." The rapid intrusion of market values and the simultaneous deflation of patrician ideals unsettled identity itself. "Nobody knew who or what they were," Baldwin concluded in a point that drove straight to the Southern man's ambivalent identity, "except as they claimed, or as a surface view of their characters indicated."

So who should they have been? Two serious essays in *Flush Times* suggest an answer. A short essay on Francis Strother, who was commissioned to reorganize Alabama's chaotic state bank, portrayed a rather flinty lawyer whose personal habits would have cheered John Calvin himself. "He loved labor for its own sake the way some men love ease," wrote Baldwin, meaning it as praise. A longer piece on Seargeant S. Prentiss was more ambivalent. Prentiss, a Maine-born attorney, Whig congressman, notable orator, and frequent duelist who burned out at age forty-two, got all the loving phrases associated with the patrician ideal: he was sociable, generous, gifted at oratory, guileless, a veritable Byronic genius for those who like Romantic poetry or a Prince Hal for those who favor Shakespeare. Baldwin went on for pages like this, but stopped eventually to meditate on Prentiss's weaknesses, which were ironically his very patrician qualities. Prentiss was, in fact, *too* gifted, amiable, high-spirited, and generous. "Prentiss lacked regular, self-denying, systematic application," warned Baldwin in a straightforward lecture to his readers. "He accomplished a great deal, but not a great deal for his capital."

Manhood, then, was a capital venture: risk and investment, compounded with discipline and restraint, propelled by genius. Baldwin's humor was not enough to germinate the concept, and so he turned to serious prose, a companion piece called *Party Leaders* that he issued only a year after *Flush Times* appeared. Like Longstreet's *William Mitten* or Thorpe's *The Master's House*, this more didactic piece isn't much fun, but it suggests an author anxious to drive a point home. Baldwin surveyed American history through its great men, in this case Jefferson, Hamilton, Jackson, Clay, and—interestingly—John Randolph of Roanoke, and he did so in search of "masculine virtues."[27] The choice of subjects and title are interesting, for in idealizing partisanship Baldwin openly accepted the competitive, self-interested ethic of the new nation and the frontier.

Curiously, most of the book focused on Randolph, the least skilled party leader of them all. Baldwin was keenly aware of Randolph's faults; still, he praised the Virginian for his "constancy," "heart," and devotion to one particular idea: Virginia itself. Importantly, Randolph was a master of language, itself a tool of mastery. This was the consummate Virginia gentleman, and it seemed, at least, that Randolph would naturally have risen to the top. He missed the mark, however, and Baldwin knew why:

> He had not the coolness, the tact, the knowledge of men, the compromising disposition, the forbearance, the conciliation, the sympathy, the power of making friends of the many, of drawing to himself the confidence and respect of others, the sober gravity and weight of character which befit such a place.[28]

The passage is an idealized, almost too-perfect blending of the Protestant ethic and the con man. Coolness, tact, and a compromising disposition to elicit confidence and trust were market virtues. To combine them with sober gravity and weight of character added the critical moral dimension.

How and where was all this best developed? Baldwin idealized Henry Clay precisely because Clay was a creation of the frontier and because he moved with decisiveness. (Again, Kennedy had seen the same qualities.) Language and oratory were fine, Baldwin wrote, but real leadership came from doing something concrete. "Clay's claims to fame are not in his printed speeches. They are in his measures, which are deeds, and in his acts, which are monuments." Clay started his career in the raw state of Kentucky, where leadership could recreate itself. "A young community, unorganized and free, furnishes an open, unoccupied field for energy and intellect."[29] It was where men of authority had to fashion themselves from the ground up, through struggle.

This was not mere idle talk. By the time Baldwin wrote his two books, he had worked out a pretty good life for himself, had gained a certain stature in his adopted state, and had paid back his social debts by helping to write the civil code for Alabama, no mean act in such a chaotic place. Still, he was unhappy with Alabama, he explained in a letter to his wife, because it was small, local, and boring. He had "no business playing big cards at a picayune game."[30] Ever restless and possibly frustrated at his own success, he published *Party Leaders*, took his own advice, and moved to California. There, he wrote yet another civil code for yet another uncivil state. In the broadest sense, Baldwin took his own advice regarding masculinity and abandoned Virginia and its gentlemen forever.

4

Useful Alloys

THERE IS A MOMENT NEAR THE END OF Thomas Bangs Thorpe's only novel, *The Master's House*, when the hero, Graham Mildmay, gathers up his rifle and tries to slip away, as if going off on a hunt. His wife stops him for an awkward moment, looking at the gun. "I could not have the heart to shoot any thing," she says, "even the looks of that poor buck you brought home the other day, made me feel sad,—its glazed and liquid eyes haunt me even now." Mildmay takes her hand and starts philosophizing: "There is enough of the savage life in us, Annie, in spite of our civilization," he says, "to make the sports of the field sometimes agreeable; I think, perhaps, a dash of the wild man forms a useful alloy for even the noblest natures." With that he travels to a prearranged spot, rubs a little dirt between his fingers to steady his nerves (a hunter's trick), and kills his neighbor in a duel.[1]

This is an arresting scene, full of nuance and contradiction. Mildmay is a pure Southern aristocrat with a fine plantation, but he has a New England education, a New England wife, and New England reservations about slavery. He is sensitive and reflective, characteristics we hardly expect to find in a cotton planter from West Feliciana Parish, Louisiana.

Still, his fascination with the hunt and sports of the field is clearly masculine; her revulsion, feminine. The talk of wild men and noble natures is romantic, but its merger into the sporting imagery of the hunt and its quick evolution into ritualized, ceremonial murder are jarring. Even the innocent act of steadying his nerves becomes loathsome, a plunge literally into the dirt. Mildmay crosses a boundary into a place where he should not go, but it is a vague line, more a grey zone where the forms and ends of violence get confused.

The most incongruous thing about the scene, however, is that it was written by Thomas Bangs Thorpe. Thorpe's reputation as a writer and humorist is based almost wholly on "The Big Bear of Arkansas"—a tale so definitive of the mighty hunter school that William T. Porter made it the title piece of his first collection of rough frontier humor. "Big Bear" was crude and violent, as was much of what Thorpe wrote. His characters arm themselves to the teeth with guns, dogs, and specially equipped steamboats; they chase down creation bears, hunt buffalo, shoot topknots off of Indians, despoil the countryside, knock down 200-year-old trees, fight each other, and kill anything that moves. They are sometimes bear-eaters and alligator-men, but more often they are gentlemen on a toot—out there slumming with the bad boys like the city slickers in James Dickey's *Deliverance*.

That said, *The Master's House* is almost predictable, the parting shot of a deeply disillusioned man. To return to *Deliverance* again: if Thorpe resembles anyone in that novel it is Ed Gentry, the aptly named photographer tagging along for the fun and the chance to be a real man but altogether too serious and too sensitive to really let go. Gentry, when faced with the opportunity to kill a deer, cannot bring himself to destroy something so aesthetically pure and natural. Similarly, Thorpe's artistic instincts may have limited him. He was a painter and a New Englander and a preacher's son who aspired to be a Southern gentleman and who self-consciously adopted the gentleman's style—especially his ferocious love of tent life and manly sports. Those qualities are worth noting, for he brought an outsider's view to Southern masculinity, and his stories ultimately are not about rip-snorters but about his own adopted peers. For seventeen years he existed in the South as an exotic animal, a literary man and an artist scratching out a living doing oils, stories, and editorials for the nouveaux riches of New Orleans and upriver Louisiana. He took part in their politics, their boosterism, and their recreations; he wrote stories about the wonders of nature and the thrill of the chase for the *Spirit of the*

Times. He was hardly a whooper or a chest-beater or even an armed fop, yet his stories center on violence.

Violence is the element that gives fire to his best work, as if he somehow needed to rationalize it and deal with it, embrace it or reject it. It necessarily entered his world because he was an artist of the wild and because he voluntarily attached himself to the realm of violent men, both "natural" and "civilized." He wanted to merge the two, to use the landscape of the frontier South to fuse the purity of the savage and the nobility of the gentleman into a new creation—what his character Mildmay called a "useful alloy." What he actually found was not useful or romantic or noble at all, but rather a self-centered and even lethal compound of aristocratic pretensions and common greed. In his hands the self-assured domestic paternalism of Frank Meriwether evolved into something grotesque.

Thorpe's perspective toward Southern masculinity began forming in New England.[2] Born in Massachusetts in 1815, he was the son of a Methodist minister who died when Thorpe was four. His mother turned him over to grandparents in Albany while she went to New York to rebuild her life. There she married a bookbinder and then reclaimed her son. The boy displayed a genuine talent for art, and in his teens he apprenticed himself to John Quidor, the genre painter. Thorpe was promising enough that he planned to go to Europe to study his art and make a name for himself. Instead, his mother—ever the Methodist—shipped him off to Wesleyan College to get a good, straightforward education. There, in one of life's little ironies, Thorpe met John William Burruss of Woodville, Mississippi, and Newett Vick, son of the founder of Vicksburg. They invited him home, and Thorpe, like so many Northerners with more ambition than money, accepted. If unable to become famous in Europe, why not try Louisiana?

As Thorpe's biographer Milton Rickels has noted, the young man seemed particularly anxious to appear genteel and settled, not the upwardly mobile outsider he actually was. He begged Burruss to introduce him "as a person [in] every way worthy of the highest esteem as a gentleman."[3] He particularly wanted to avoid the impression that he was an *"inexperienced artist, an adventurer, a person patronized."* The fact was that he was all that: his portfolio was small and derivative, he was desperate to get out of town, and he was broke and in need of a patron. After a few months in Baton Rouge, Thorpe met Bennet Barrow, who seems to have taken on the role of sponsor. Barrow was a ferocious entrepreneur and a meticulous organizer, a terror to overseers and slaves alike.[4] He was also extraordinarily vain and liked the idea of having his portrait painted. For years he and Thorpe kept up an on-again, off-again relationship. Thorpe added a little cachet to the Louisiana bogs; in turn Barrow introduced Thorpe to the planter culture of the Old Southwest in its most extreme form. To all appearances, this was an easygoing, sociable group.

What Thorpe did not know—could not possibly have realized—was that he had entered a boundary zone, a no-man's-land of frontier excess. By chance, he had set foot in West Feliciana Parish, Louisiana, part of an area east of Baton Rouge which had been under various iterations of Spanish or French rule for nearly two hundred years and which had mostly been a scene of intrigue and fraud. This was where writer Walker Percy's ancestor had set up shop in the 1780s as an *alcande*, a governor, claiming blood lines all the way to the earls of Northumberland and then drowning himself with an iron pot roped to his neck when the pretension proved false.[5] It was where Spanish and French governors had regularly expected honoraria, so to speak, in their dealings with Anglo planters. It was West Florida, where in 1810 dissident American immigrants invaded the Spanish fortress at Baton Rouge, killed the commandant, and declared their independence as a republic (only to have James Madison appropriate the whole parcel two months later in the name of national security). One of the revolutionaries was Reuben Kemper, who gained a certain notoriety by beating one of his detractors so badly that the man took to sleeping in the woods for fear of his life, where he caught swamp fever and died anyway.[6] Kemper later had a county named after him.

Not a settled place, and one where the centrifugal forces that Baldwin and Hooper had encountered were evident up and down the social scale. Two kinds of Southerners took root there. On one hand were hard, mobile plain folk far tougher than the clownish Ransy Sniffle. They lived outside the pale of republican authority—outside of any authority at all, perhaps. Their spokesman, as it were, was the salt-river roarer—the sort of eye-gouging, ear-chewing mighty man that would have devoured, literally, Longstreet's Billy or Bob and which Thorpe helped turn into a frontier icon. Humorists made much of this lot in a way that was both mocking and affectionate. The roarer provided exaggerated behavior, wonderfully crude dialect, and chest-beating masculinity in an exuberantly aberrant package.

But no one, at least no one who could read, wanted to *be* half-alligator. More influential, and more unsettling to anyone in search of a viable role model, were the planters who actually ran the place. Barrow and his ilk modeled themselves partly on the idealized aristocrat of the Virginia tobacco plantation but more specifically on his variant, the sportsman/planter of the South Carolina rice fields. They built extraordinary plantations, dressed well, ran horses in New Orleans and fishing boats on the Mississippi, and drank prodigiously. Between binges, they were hard and sharp entrepreneurs. (Harriet Beecher Stowe was right to put Simon Legree in Mississippi, not Virginia.) Barrow, for one, kept a journal, and it is an impersonal ledger of crops put in, loans made and bills collected, deer shot, and slaves whipped. It has no humor, no self-reflection.

Of this Thorpe knew nothing, at least not at first. What he did know was that Louisiana seemed to hold prospects. Simply hanging out with Barrow's crowd and picking up the odd commission, however, did not pay bills, so Thorpe diversified. He discovered a talent for writing, which he turned into a career in newspaper work, and soon he was publishing a newspaper—a Whig one, naturally, in keeping with the political preferences of his patrons. He also began shipping stories to Porter's influential sporting rag, the *Spirit of the Times*, and they gained him national attention.[7] Most popular among these were the hunting tales, which Thorpe wrote with genuine feeling. The landscape painter in him appreciated the romance of nature; the genre painter liked the odd characters and quirky personalities. More practically, hunting obsessed his readers, and it was on the hunt that Thorpe connected with the kinds of people he wanted to know.

The hunt, after all, was a place where the community of gentlemen was most evident and where their power and masculinity could be arranged and codified. As Nicholas Proctor has argued, the chase provided a theater to display mastery—over nature, over animals, over other men—and its violence was an orchestrated display of moral qualities and class distinctions.[8] For the lowly, game was merely meat and the hunt a full-time job, rather like plowing. For the gentleman, though, it was an experience that transcended generations and built character. "Field sports are both innocent and manly," announced William Elliott in *Carolina Sports*, and being a South Carolina squire he knew all about innocence and manliness. The hunt inculcated qualities of sagacity and observation; it built "good morals." Beyond that, field sports were the natural domain of the natural aristocrat, and the South Carolina sportsman had extended the Virginia gentleman's rather tame obsession with fox hunting to include virtually any variant of the sporting kill, including bears and devilfish. "I am a hereditary sportsman," Elliott stated simply, "and inherit the tastes of my grandfather, as well as his lands."[9]

Elliott wrote from the stance of the South Carolina landed gentry; Thorpe's perspective was much more complicated. Thorpe had a vantage point on the edge of the frontier wherein, the theory went, men could re-create themselves. There was no question that both transplanted Yankees and displaced cavaliers meant to replicate their homelands in states to the west. The question was, could they? The frontier was intensely competitive, and the various elements of manly distinction were often at odds with each other. Hunting and its orchestrated violence were touchy things. In the right hands, the gentleman could merge himself with the wonders of nature. In the wrong hands, the innocent manliness that Elliott and his sort personified could turn into something farcical and crude. This was the issue that Thorpe unwittingly confronted as he began to write.

In Thorpe's idealized, artistic world, the thrill of the hunt and the kill had redemptive qualities, what Richard Slotkin has termed "regeneration through violence," or what William Elliott called "innocent manliness."[10] Thorpe catalogued these qualities in a story about buffalo hunting written for his first anthology.[11] In its most savage and natural incarnation, the hunt was intensely spiritual, an extension of war itself reserved primarily for the "wild Indian." The act of killing was simple and unadulterated, "the fruition of the best hopes of his existence." It opened paths to the "Great Spirit." This was the noble savage gone to excess, but not an uncommon figure for writers of the time, as Cooper or even William Gilmore Simms would attest. Indians, however, could be romanticized in ways that whites could not. Common white men (and the emphasis is on "common") brought a more exploitative, almost barbarian ethic to the kill. "To the rude white hunter," Thorpe wrote, the hunt was "the high consummation of his habit and power to destroy.... it is the very unloosing of all the rough passions of our nature," which Thorpe defined as "ambition" and "appetite." The common man kills "with the conscience entirely at rest."

Two models of masculinity are at work there—the noble savage and the mighty hunter—so we would expect the gentleman to combine the best of both and emerge as something nobler still. To his credit, Thorpe tried. "To the 'sportsman,' who is matured in the constraint of cities and the artificial modes of enlightened society," the hunt promised escape and renewal. It "stirs up the latent fires repressed by a whole life ... gratifies every animal sense possessed by the savage and the hunter, and opens a thousand other avenues of high enjoyment known only to the cultivated and refined mind." Theoretically, the gentleman's cultivation could tame the commoner's rough passions and merge them with a kind of heroic detachment that turned the act of destruction into a transcendent moment.

It didn't happen that way. Although Thorpe sprinkled his stories with requisite tropes about how the chase encouraged the "chivalrous sentiments of the soul," his better work in fact stood his ideals on end.[12] He endowed the ripsnorter tradition with a sense of tragedy and then—to compound the irony—turned the gentleman's high enjoyments into farce and burlesque. Whether the frontier was a corrupting agent itself or (more probably) the exploitative, wasteful natures of commoners and cotton snobs alike were indistinguishable, Thorpe's whoopers and his gentlemen merge into each other. If anything, Thorpe's rude white hunter has a certain elegance and nobility about him that mocks the sporting gentleman's crude excess.

This point is evident in Thorpe's "Big Bear of Arkansas," which is as fine a piece of humor and manly introspection as there is.[13] Briefly, Thorpe meets Jim Doggett, the greatest, mightiest hunter of them all, on a steamboat ride and sets him reminiscing about the ultimate bear hunt. Framing his own story around Doggett's tale, Thorpe created the perfect set-up: a gentleman telling violent stories about violent men without actually being violent himself. Doggett's tale is a good one: a long chase for a "creation bar" that evades every trick and every dog Doggett (pun intended) sets after him. Doggett hunts the beast without respite or remorse, but none of his hunter's tricks will get the bear within his sights. By sheer attrition, however, the miracle moment does come, and it finds Doggett with his pants down—his "habit" after the morning coffee kicks in—and the bear suddenly looming up like a "*black mist.*" Doggett grabs his gun and gets off a shot while tripping over his "inexpressibles." The bear collapses into a fence "like a falling tree through a cobweb."

The artistry is in the ambivalence. It is easy to see this story both as a celebration of the frontiersman and as a clever send-up of all the yokels who ever bragged that they were half-alligator and half-turtle, for in many ways Doggett is relentlessly common. He disdains sportsmen who hunt for game. "Game . . . means chippen-birds and shite-pokes," and for Jim Doggett "a bird any way is too triflin." He is only a brag or two removed from an ordinary farmer, but of course he won't farm. "I don't plant any more: natur intended Arkansaw for a hunting ground, and I go according to natur." He is a mighty hunter, but a flawed one. His failing is the plain fact that his claim to triumphant masculinity is merely a lucky shot. Underwear doesn't factor into the plots of most antebellum literature, but it is critical here and the fact that Doggett trips over his own "inexpressibles" makes him into something of a buffoon. On the other hand, Doggett does have qualities of patience, foresight, and, well, doggedness which Thorpe lauded in other stories and which have, oddly enough, more of the market ethic than the sporting about them. Doggett may be in his own way an entrepreneur, and entrepreneurs know how to stick with it, carry on, and take advantage of luck, even with their pants down.

Beyond that, the story contains an element of sadness and self-realization that sets it entirely apart from that of the usual salt-river roar. There is a connection to nature in Doggett's quest that, although not as pure as the savage's, is still transcendent. The chase, not the kill, engages Doggett's soul. The bear "*hunted me,*" Doggett admits, and in return he "loved him like a brother." This is intimacy, but it cannot last. What makes this story and others like it special is that the violence lends a sense of tragic loss to the very men who kill, as if they destroy themselves in the act. The white man is denied the transcendent moment because the creation bear, unlike Ahab's white whale, simply gives up and accepts death rather than fight any longer. "I never liked the way I hunted him, *and missed him,*" Doggett muses about the bear, which seems to have possessed a wisdom about death and fate that a mere man could not grasp. "My private opinion is, that that bar was an *unhuntable bar, and died when his time come.*" This is the inevitability of westward expansion. That said, he lapses into a moment of "grave silence," as if possessed by a "superstitious awe." Then he gets drunk. It's a deliciously ambivalent moment: the mighty man of nature confronting his own destructive waste—a point subtly reinforced by his posture at the time of the kill.

"Big Bear" was so good it eclipsed anything else Thorpe ever wrote, and it made him a celebrity of sorts among the fraternity of yarn-spinners and gentleman wits who were reshaping Southern humor during the 1840s. One didn't have to appreciate its ambivalence or its sense of tragedy to enjoy it, and most readers probably never tried. Porter used it as the lead piece and title for his first collection of humorous tales (some of which were not Southern at all, but simply western and thus part of the frontier), and Thorpe found himself with a few minutes of fame and the comfort of gentleman friends. He redoubled his energies, cranking out even more stories and outlandish tales. The optimist in him chased after deer and birds with the best society, and scattered throughout his stories are gushy celebrations of the virtues of the sporting life palmed almost verbatim from Elliott and his peers. But Thorpe remained a guest at their tables, never the host, a situation he parodied in a story where he drops in for dinner at an oyster-house and entertains the table with his wit, only to discover he has crashed a private party.[14] Alongside Thorpe's optimism lay a growing strain of disillusion and despair.

This was more than simply frustrated upward mobility. There is evidence in Thorpe's stories that he was having serious doubts about the innocent manliness of the hunt and the genteel superiority it supposedly displayed. Violence and the waste that surrounds it were comical in the "Big Bear," where the protagonist was common, but it was harder to make it work in stories about sporting gentlemen. This was the New Englander in Thorpe. He was no Thoreau, but neither was he William Elliott. There is a moment in *Carolina Sports* at which Elliott tries to justify the random killing of devilfish by an involved cost-benefit analysis based on the usefulness of its oil and liver. It is a lame effort that Elliott promptly and wisely abandoned. Thorpe, however, took the issue seriously, and running through his writings is an uneasy sense that violence—however men might extol its virtues—was not only an affront to nature but a moral corruption to the killer. In the same story in which he cataloged hunters, for example, Thorpe reported shooting a buffalo and watching it die nobly "like an old patriarch about to bid adieu to the world." The sight "cooled the warm blood of the hunt within me; the instinct of destruction was for the time overpowered by that of better feelings." "There was a waste of life" in such hunts—organized, detached, impersonal—that he likened to "an ever-present spirit of evil." Moreover, his direct use of the term "patriarch" had broader connotations. Violence, the hunt, and the hunters were killing off a more settled, organic way of life.

And yet waste, conspicuous and showy, was the very point of the gentleman's approach to sport. If the act of killing was in fact a moment of profound intimacy, then how could one explain the essentially impersonal, exploitative, and above all theatrical nature of the gentleman's approach to sport and violence? A true sportsman would never, ever stoop to hunting merely to put food on the table, as would a pothunter. He trumpeted instead his intimacy with nature and his mastery thereof. This was an ideal easily corrupted. There was no intimacy, for example, in the mechanized slaughter of "Woodcock Fire Hunting"—a tale that has more elements of common commercial farming than of gentlemanly sport. Woodcock are a slow-moving species that feed chiefly off worms, and in this story, the first following the "Big Bear," Thorpe described a gentlemanly form of pothunting that was so astonishingly *ungentlemanly* that many of his readers considered it a hoax. The sport employed a slave or two—no yappy dogs—who flushed the birds wholesale with torches, at night. Hunters simply knocked down the startled birds with mustard-shot. A "good shot," wrote Thorpe, "has only to overcome the astonishment, and we will add, *horror*, at the mode in which he sees his favorite game killed, to be a perfect master" at the game. Where Jim Doggett almost lost his prey, the woodcock fire hunter can't miss. "Heavens," said Thorpe in mock desperation, "this is murder!"

It is a light tale, but Thorpe was pushing the edge here. Writers to the New York *Spirit of the Times* objected to it in dead seriousness. Fire hunting, after all, should have been abominable to any sporting gentleman precisely because there was no *sport* to it at all. Night hunting, moreover, had no real counterpart in the English and Carolinian sporting tradition. The absence of dogs took away the feverishness of the chase, as did the facts that woodcock took a while to flap themselves aloft and were easy, slow-moving targets. Even small things, like the use of mustard-shot rather than heavier loads, indicated that expediency, not sport, set the rules (mustard-shot spreads wide and requires less skill). These were all pothunters's tricks at harvesting meat, and William Elliott's type avoided using them.[15] But Elliott was South Carolinian; this was Louisiana, where the restraints of the sportsman's ethic had been diluted by the crudeness of the new country and the runaway acquisitiveness of the capitalist ethic. Thorpe was essentially describing the mechanical routine of a cotton plantation: slaves in front, boundless nature all around, gentlemen reaping the profits.

Equally disturbing was the pure show of it all, the theatrical displays of masculinity by which Thorpe wedded the gentleman to the alligator-man. One might expect manly posturing to be unusually exaggerated on the hunt, and Thorpe filled his stories with these little displays. What is surprising is the very extravagance of gentlemanly theatrics, so much so that the boundary line between sportsman and braggart begins to disappear. Consider the proto-safari in Thorpe's description of the "Devil's Summer Retreat in Arkansaw," a place of primeval wildness where Bob Herring, the original hired guide, introduces paying gentlemen to the twin rewards of stalking bear and sleeping on the ground. (Note that this was the 1840s; the frontier was in retreat even then.) The trip was a paid experience, Thorpe wrote with considerable irony, not open to the "effeminate citizen." Here, at the edge of the wilderness, real men paid good money to act like real men. A year later Thorpe turned the whole idea into burlesque with a parody of Sir William Stewart's expedition to the Far West, written as a series of spurious letters to the New Orleans *Intelligencer*.[16] Stewart was the gentleman-hunter's gentleman-hunter, a man with enough breeding, money, and spare time to seek renewal among the Indians and the buffalo. Stewart and his clones hauled tons of cumbersome equipment across mountain and prairie in a showy quest for the perfect kill. Like Doggett and his big bear, they are denied the transcendent moment, only this time Thorpe shows no ambivalence. In a dry voice Thorpe transformed the elaborate expedition into a slapstick version of a Louisiana bear hunt, where the buffalo intimidate the hunters, the guides stink of gin, and the only trophy anyone brings back is a pocketful of buffalo chips (another scatological reference to waste).

And in an astonishing anticipation of telescopic sights, all-terrain vehicles, and fish-finders, Thorpe focused on the gentleman-hunter's obsession with toys. The same year Thorpe published the "Big Bear" he reported on Bennet Barrow's latest foray into conspicuous waste: the custom-built, steam-powered, whiskey-fumed *Nimrod*—granddaddy of all subsequent powerboats and RVs. *Nimrod* had room for horses, a state-of-the-art armory, and—perhaps most important—an open bar with no cashbox. This was something new, and it required elaboration. "IT'S A GREAT IDEA," Thorpe explained simply, in capitals. "The thing is worthy of the large scale on which the South West is laid out!" Why? Because Barrow had contrived to carry "into the wilderness the comforts of refined life, thus mixing up the life of a perfectly wild hunter, and the associations of the drawing room." (Is this the "useful alloy" that Thorpe longed for?) "Its magnitude is sufficient to cause congestion of the brain in common men," Thorpe rejoiced with obvious sarcasm, and indeed common men such as the woodcutter who supplies the boat's fuel cannot absorb the idea. The boat is neither here nor there, the old coot puzzles. "Thar's . . . something un-natural 'bout it—*too comfortable for this world, by half*—all the crew with long-tailed coats on, and tights—no cargo, save arms, ammunition, ten horses, and a raft of hounds." Tights and tails on a ship's crew? The incongruity here, from our perspective, is that the woodcutter is the voice of civilized masculinity, not the other way around.

We can take such humor too seriously and forget that self-parody is healthy, and the fact that Thorpe's audience enjoyed his stories and rewarded him makes the Southern gentleman somehow more human. But humor is a weighty exercise in defining self. Thorpe was particularly idealistic, and his satire was an idealist's indication that the Virginia gentleman had not traveled well. Whether in Thorpe's Louisiana, or C.F.M. Noland's Arkansas, or Joseph G. Baldwin's Alabama, the patriarchal symmetry of Virginia and the Sea Islands simply did not reproduce itself. Thorpe, try as he might to graft William Elliott's patrician ethic into bear hunts and fish kills, ended up with an awareness that the gentleman of the frontier South was more an entrepreneur and a show-off (a con man and a salt-river roarer, if you will) twisted into the role of planter and patriarch.

In time, Thorpe's patience with this sort of thing began to wear thin, even while his drive to be a gentleman remained strong. As early as 1845 he began casting about, looking for other ways to distinguish himself even if the effort required him to move back home. He wrote Abraham Hart, the publisher, that he was unhappy with having to pursue business instead of writing, and he offered himself as an in-house editor/writer/traveler who could also do his own artwork. "Finally," he added, "if I should come north I would wish by industry to acquire a competency, a position in society, and whatever else pertains to a gentleman."[17] It was the same aspiration he had voiced to his college friends when he left for Louisiana years earlier, except that he now emphasized that he would rise to gentlemanly status "by industry." (Hart declined.) A year later, with a war with Mexico starting up, he hustled off to Matamoras to play war correspondent and write an account of the battles going on down there. That enterprise also failed, as did a biography of Zachary Taylor that Thorpe hoped would land him a political job. Nor was Thorpe successful in an 1852 run for state superintendent of education. Thorpe won the towns with a plea for expanded common schools; he lost the countryside.

By 1850 Thorpe's infatuation with the leisure class had largely dried up, replaced by self-pity and rage. He put his frustration on display in a eulogy he delivered that year for Seargeant S. Prentiss, the same transplanted Yankee Baldwin had memorialized. Where Baldwin's eulogy was didactic, Thorpe's was transparently autobiographical and self-pitying. Prentiss had migrated South several years earlier and established a reputation as an orator, hail fellow, and duelist. Prentiss had come upon an opportune time and place. "The era was one of extravagance," Thorpe wrote, "the virgin soil of Mississippi was pouring into the laps of her generous sons untold abundance, [and] there were thousands of her citizens, full of health and talent, who adorned the excesses of living by the tasteful procurements of wealth, and the highest accomplishments of mind. Into this world Prentiss entered, heralded by naught save his own genius." How the "excesses of living" produced high intellectual achievement was not clear here, but the image of Prentiss as a Yankee genius living among the overindulged parvenus fit Thorpe like a suit. Prentiss, Thorpe wrote, was a man "living unnoticed and unknown among the wealthiest citizens of the South" and measuring "the mighty capacity of his own soul with those whom society had placed above him. I think I see him brooding over his position, and longing to be free, as the suffocating man longs for the boundless air of heaven."[18] Suffocating himself, Thorpe finally went back North in 1854.

When he arrived there he already had in his pocket a blistering indictment of the Southern leisure class, *The Master's House*. This rambling novel labored in the shadow of *Uncle Tom's Cabin*, a thankless job given Stowe's masterful performance and Thorpe's rather pedestrian one. Still, *The Master's House* has its special merits. Unlike Stowe's book, it is not a domestic or sentimental piece but a derivation of Thorpe's considerable skills as a humorist—even though the rare bits of humor in it are bitterly ironic. It takes little interest in slaves as people, but it is the only work by a major humorist to seriously consider the effect of slavery on white behavior. It is autobiographical, certainly, but also and most poignantly it is the record of a man's disillusionment with his own ideals, for *The Master's House* brings all of what Thorpe had groped at in his humor into a long chronicle of the declension of the gentleman on the Southern frontier.

At the center of the plot is Graham Mildmay, the North Carolina aristocrat who moves west in search of fortune and ends up depressed and disgraced. It is easy enough to read parts of Thorpe's own experience into Mildmay, whose father is dead and whose mother sends him to Connecticut for an education. There Mildmay, like Thorpe, meets up with Southern boys who persuade him to pull up roots and head west. It is an agreeable prospect, since Mildmay is also in love with a refined girl and needs to "prove" himself. Leaving his old plantation in North Carolina, "he looked forward with romantic interest to the founding of . . . a home in a new and vigorous State,—where he could rise with its fortunes, and identify his name with its prosperity."

To do that, however, Mildmay must run with the same crowd that Thorpe had encountered in his own, nonfictional, journey. The novel is hard on this bunch from the start. At college, Mildmay takes offense early on at the "reckless sneers" of one Calhoun (a risky name to tag on an unsympathetic character). The fictional Calhoun, Mildmay observes, is lazy and arrogant, a victim of "his natural indolence. He will when he goes home give no useful tone to his community." Later, when Mildmay is established in Louisiana, the focus of Thorpe's satire falls on two characters, Moreton and Lee (it is also hard to imagine Thorpe not considering the weight of the name Lee). Lee is a jumped-up fraud, given to gentlemanly bombast and fake genealogies. Moreton is probably the fictional image of Barrow; he is rich, opinionated, and edgy. His estimation of slaves and common folk tends to fuse the two into a single underclass. When Mildmay suggests that slaves should be given the right to testify against whites, Moreton surprisingly endorses the idea as an effective means of social control. Slavery, Moreton orates, "is, after all, an aristocratic institution, and it is inimical to its perpetuity to give the poor white man political, or even legal, equality. The planter, to secure perfect peace, ought to have the power to arrest and punish these miserable vagrants [poor whites]; put them in the stocks, and order them out of the community, or hang them to the nearest tree." This is fairly strong stuff—a blatant contradiction of the myth of racial solidarity—and Moreton backs it up with a further denunciation of towns. "These towns, sir, if it were possible, should be abolished,—the houses razed to the ground, and their streets turned into a cotton farm, or a potato-patch." There is an echo there of Frank Meriwether's isolationism and of the kind of social displacement that Longstreet had discerned in Augusta.

Meanwhile Mildmay sets up shop as a gentleman, complete with a new house, a wife, and various slaves whom he is clearly uncomfortable presiding over as master. He also takes up the gentleman's sporting life with a vengeance. He is not the only one working toward the planter ideal, however, for Thorpe took one of Stowe's minor characters, the slave trader, and transformed him into a character every bit as provocative as Simon Legree. As a stereotype, Legree was a complete specimen; he had already perfected his own corruption when Stowe introduced him. Thorpe's slave trader, Dixon, is a work in progress. Dixon, like Mildmay, is determined to link his fortunes to a new state and share in its prosperity. Also like Mildmay, he has a Methodist mother and the semblance of a conscience. Unlike Mildmay, however, his use of violence is hard and real, with no sport to it at all. The two are bookends to a contradictory code of manhood.

In his own sick way, Dixon is an acute student of men and manliness. Next to Mildmay's dreamy visions of natural nobility and paternalistic responsibility, Dixon sees clearly the hard business sense that life in the cotton South demands and that slavery complicates. For his own part, he keeps a "Free Sile" book—newspaper clippings of runaways whom he catches and resells. "You see, Ben," he explains to a quizzical observer, "you'll never make money until you keep books." He is astonished that one of his customers would beat a slave to death, for "that is a foolish wasting of property." When a remembrance of his antislavery mother sends him into a funk of self-doubt, the words of the local preacher are like a tonic: "What," says the reverend, "is the position of the slaveholder? He is the true patriarch; the parent of a large family; his duties are sacred." Dixon listens with gratitude and, paternalistic assurances in hand, goes back to work.

Dixon's business sense marks him as the unedited voice of Thorpe's disaffection with the Louisiana gentleman. While back East making a few calls, Dixon meets a dissolute young aristocrat, Mercer, who asks him over brandy whether he could make it "down South." Dixon's reply, coming from an author who had spent years doing humor and whose work had now turned deadly serious, is worth an extended look. It is as hard an estimation of the Bennet Barrow model of Southern planter as one will find from the pen of an adopted son and country wit. "On going down the Mississippi," Dixon observes,

> every thing depends on how you start. If you can flare up, and make a figure, you'll do—but if you just go quietly to work at some honest business, selling niggers or dry goods, or teaching a school, or getting up railroads, the people will set you down as lacking spirit. The very best way is to get up a duel and kill somebody, but if you can't do that, there's other openings 'most as good; credit—if rode fast and made a short heat of, will carry a fellow through until he can marry rich, or something of that sort—but every thing depends on the way you cavort around—talk about State rights, and Southern independence—next to hard cash, splurging will set you ahead.

This is masquerade culture concisely defined: make a figure, cavort and strut, marry well, splurge, orate gustily about rights, and kill someone.

Dixon, of course, is too hard-headed for the pure showmanship he has described; Mildmay is too soft-hearted to resist it. In a sense the two men meet and merge into one unflattering portrait of the frontier planter. When Mildmay gets sucked into a pointless duel with Moreton, he does so from the peer pressure of the gentleman's code of honor. "Strange as it may seem," Thorpe wrote of Mildmay, "he cowered under the idea of having these same people, for whom he really felt so little respect, condemn him, for doing what he knew to be right." So Mildmay gives in "to a bloody Moloch," and kills, but he feels no redemption, no regeneration. At that point Dixon's estimate of a duel's social value is validated. "What a trump he is!" exclaims another planter in ironic admiration. "What a trump! he has, this morning, established himself in society; every honor and office is henceforth open to him. I wonder whether he will decide to go to Congress?" Only a trained humorist could fashion such irony.

Even more ironic is the fate of Dixon. After years of working hard in ruthless defiance of every value that Frank Meriwether would have held dear, Dixon finally buys a plantation stocked with fine furnishings and docile slaves. This charlatan-man, this Dickensian shyster who cannot read without moving his finger and mouthing the words, gets his portrait painted "sitting in a magnificent library, and holding a 'Virgil' in his hand." How many such portraits, one wonders, had Thorpe painted for how many such men?

And yet still Thorpe labored on, trying to become a sporting gentleman in absentia from his new quarters in New York. He dabbled in law, brushed up a few more canvasses, and on the very eve of civil war bought up the failing *Spirit of the Times* when Porter died, as if publishing the stories could redeem the reality that underlay them. The enterprise disappeared for good after Ft. Sumter, and it looked as if Thorpe would finally have to leave the South and gentlemanly prominence behind.

But even the Mildmays of the world have their revenge. In 1862 Thorpe went back to New Orleans, this time as a carpetbagger in the tow of Benjamin Butler—the same "Beast Butler" who had confiscated slaves as contraband and ordered rebellious Southern women to be treated as common whores. In a part of the South feeling the first hard lessons of reconstruction, Thorpe got himself elected to the legislature as a Republican, voted for the Free State constitution, looted his expense account, and left town a few days ahead of a warrant for his arrest. He went back to New York, prospered, and never returned.

5

Swamp Fevers

Henry Clay Lewis, physician and humorist, once stole a baby—a "dead nigger baby," to use his exact terms. He did it because anatomy fascinated him, and he wanted his own specimen "to while away the tedious hours with" while he waited for dinner. He also stole it simply because it was there, lying in a morgue beside the body of its mother, and it called to him with a "bond of association" which, as he explained, "held me to my place, my gaze riveted upon it." He became obsessed with the ghastly thing, so he wrapped it in a cloak, went to class, and "manfully . . . strove to be composed" until the lecture ended. Then he hurried home. This showed much daring, but his luck did not hold. Lewis divided his affections between anatomy and Lucy, a wealthy "Kentucky gal," and it was often hard for him to keep the two passions separate, even while courting her. "When holding her soft hand in mine, and gazing into the star-lit ocean of her soul, I would wonder if there was not some peculiarity of her optic nerve which gave her eyes such brilliancy." He was "daft" and he knew it, but Lucy wrote all this behavior off as "the eccentricities of genius and love" and insisted on meeting him after class, which she did on this wintry day in Louisville, despite Lewis's best efforts to avoid her. Complicating the already complicated situation was Lucy's father, who had "an aversion to Southerners" and regarded them in much the same way Lewis regarded dogs (mean and vile). As Lewis encountered Lucy on the street, the father suddenly bore down upon them, whereupon Lucy grabbed Lewis and pulled him into a doorway to hide. There a bulldog (nothing else, given Lewis's prejudices, would do) tripped them both on the ice and sent Lewis, Lucy, and the dead baby all spilling out onto the sidewalk. "My cloak flew open as I fell, and the force of the fall bursting its envelope, out, in all its hideous realities, rolled the infernal imp of darkness upon the gaze of the laughing, but now horrified spectators." Lucy's father hurried her away, and Lewis never saw her again. He went back to school and ended up in exile as a "swamp doctor."[1]

It probably never happened, but it could have; who knows? "Stealing a Baby" is one story in Lewis's collection *Odd Leaves from the Life of a Louisiana Swamp Doctor*, which is part humor, part horror, and part autobiography. The story contains most—not all—of the elements of a remarkable personal odyssey. There is the matter of Lewis's age and status: a young medical student slogging through the requisite training but loving his studies and the pure rationality of science to the point of madness. There is the concurrent promise of love and the aching loneliness for a woman, all complicated by Lewis's station as a Southerner and a penniless student. There is Lewis's attraction to and fear of deformity (he thought himself ugly) and the hidden darkness within, symbolized by the dead black child and its improbable birth, or perhaps purging, in front of a mocking crowd. There is either blind luck or Calvinistic predestination in the convergence of *that* dog and *that* ice in *that* doorway at *that* moment. There is death itself, frightfully laid out for all to see.

Lewis, who fantasized about and feared his own death in terms that would have intrigued Edgar Allan Poe, was himself dead to the literary world for over a century. The real identity of "Madison Tensas," the swamp doctor of *Odd Leaves*, was in doubt and of little concern until John Q. Anderson did the necessary research and brought Lewis out of anonymity in 1962.[2] *Odd Leaves* traveled a rocky road from the start, with its author dying at age twenty-five in a rain-swollen river only a few months after the book appeared. Dying so young, Lewis missed William Gilmore Simms's curt dismissal of his work in the *Southern Quarterly Review* (the only praise Simms voiced was for the illustrator) and the general neglect that later afflicted the book. "One of a class to which we do not seriously incline," Simms wrote.[3] A few stories have made their way into anthologies, but the volume still has not caught on, at least not the way

Longstreet's, Baldwin's, or Harris's have. A recent edition by Edwin T. Arnold acknowledges that part of the problem arises from the darkness and psychological complexity of Lewis's comic visions. The book is more torment than humor.[4]

It is torment in a vein that does not comfortably fit with most humor of the Old Southwest, even though that literature is full of pain. Lewis used a frame by telling the stories as the reminiscences of an old bachelor doctor with "haggard features and a buttonless coat," but this is not the bemused voice of the gentlemen scoffing at hicks. The book is a chronicle of a boy's coming of age, and it is starkly autobiographical and confessional. (Whether it is faithful to the truth is a matter of speculation, but the voice is realistic.) The stories are mostly in the first person, and they cover the swamp doctor's life from the act of running away from a broken home, through apprenticeship and medical school, to life as a physician on the frontier. There are sexual longings and embarrassments, hijinks and practical jokes, test taking and adventure and ambition. Some stories are excruciatingly violent and pitiless, as when Lewis and his pals set fire to a mule and send it running through a camp meeting of excitable Millerites gathered for the Second Coming. There is a good, solid frontier story about Mik-hoo-tah, "The Indefatigable Bear-Hunter," who loses a leg to one bear and beats another to death with the wooden replacement. There are also tender moments when Lewis ponders death and fate, occasionally calling out for his dead mother to come tend to him. There is poetry, one passage buried in the prose. Mostly there are grotesque stories of purging, extractions, and bodily pain. In fact the body, both male and female, is prominent and is frequently and inappropriately on display. Prevalent in all the stories is the fear of exposure and humiliation.

Edwin Arnold, one of Lewis's best modern critics, goes straight to the point in arguing that Lewis used humor to focus "on the disturbed, the deformed, and the dispossessed, the physical and psychological 'monsters' who inhabit the borderlands between solid earth and liquid swamp." This is literature that poses "those basic questions of personal identity and self-determination, of body and boundary, that engage us yet today."[5] Against a larger backdrop of fate, free will, sacrifice, and rebirth are questions that afflict any young man. Lewis has ambitions and attendant fears of failure, and he uses medicine as a metaphor to explore the corruptions and purgations he must endure to succeed. Equally complicated is Lewis's perspective on women, whom he uses to explore not only longings for love and motherhood and lost family but also more broadly his sexual desires and fears. Far from being nurturers or domestic managers, Lewis's women take charge, compete, and mock his pretensions. Similarly, Lewis used black slaves to explore his own divided personality. In his hands, blacks are the demons within that will *not* be mastered and are likely to get free, as the "dead nigger baby" does when it comes spilling out of Lewis's cloak in front of all to see. All these issues involve Lewis's sense of manhood (particularly considering his youth), and all link Lewis to Northern writers, especially Poe and Melville, who struggled with the same things. He is not bound, as Arnold wisely points out, by his region.

But Lewis was a Southerner nonetheless, and the issues he explores in *Odd Leaves* were conditioned by their Southern context and involved a Southern sense of manhood. One was the matter of Lewis's profession itself. Medicine was not his first choice of career, and it was not traditionally accorded the kind of respect and deference that he craved. As a student and especially as a country doctor, Lewis rode the borderline between patrician and mechanic, between things that are fixed in place and those that can be fixed by reason and skill. This put him in a liminal zone between settled concepts of manly status and a new professionalism whose codes were more akin to market behaviors than patrician ones. This was an uncomfortable status for upwardly mobile Southern men, as Stephen Berry has noted, who were "supposed to exemplify the *effects* of civilization," not work for it.[6] J.E.B. Stuart, just out of West Point but without an inheritance to start a plantation, found himself in the same predicament and hated it. Could he stoop, he wondered, to "the *hireling* professions . . . Law, Medicine, Engineering, and Arms." Alas, prospects weren't good. "The lawyer has his cases but *seldom* receives his fees. The physician has his patients & his sleepless nights but his patients are very patient in *waiting to pay him*."[7]

A second source of anxiety was the patriarchal decay Lewis saw around him. The solvent effect of the frontier seemed to degenerate noble qualities of manhood into laziness and/or self-serving pretensions, and in this respect Lewis's analysis was not far off Thorpe's, who lived relatively nearby. Women figure prominently here, for their capacity to challenge Lewis's manhood is all the more pronounced.

And third, there was Lewis's own preoccupation with death—a thing which drove him to dissect dead babies but which, in the swamp, threatened to dissect him. Southerners had a particular vision of how real men faced death; meeting it nobly was the final act of manly assertion, and it required courage, self-control, and mastery. Lewis's fantasies of death speak to the heavy burden Southern men may have secretly felt behind their public pronouncements of fearlessness.

Overlaying all these themes was Lewis's narrative technique, which also must be read in its Southern context. More than any other humorist before George Washington Harris, Lewis adopted the pose of the "obsessive confessor."[8] It is a pose both *un*-Southern and manipulative, and it adds to the audaciousness of Lewis's art. By and large, Southern men were averse to admitting weakness, and Lewis's frank depictions of exposure and humiliation were simply not consistent with the demands of Southern manhood. The dictates of masquerade culture required the careful maintenance of appearances—to be what one proclaimed himself to be, to avoid unmasking whatever the cost. Market behavior, by contrast, had its own masquerades in the deceits and carefully contrived personae that made up a good trader or a con artist. For either, the fear of exposure and humiliation was great, and men avoided unmasking wherever possible. Those who attempted to look behind the masks, like the humorists we have seen so far, usually did so only through surrogate personalities like Simon Suggs or Mark Littleton. Baldwin mocked himself directly, but his self-effacements—although bold for the times—were performed from a fairly stable social and economic position. Baldwin, after all, had a family, a secure and even prestigious profession, and years of experience to give him a sense of ironic detachment.[9] Lewis had only his youth and his ambition, and his sense of irony was intensely personal and hardly detached.

Odd Leaves thus becomes a rarity in Southern literature—a young man's most interior record of coming of age—and it is brilliantly destabilizing. Granted that these are stories, many still have the ring of authenticity, and their impact is disorienting, which is probably what Lewis would have wanted. His humiliations and exposures excite sympathy, ridicule, and disgust simultaneously, turning the reader into voyeur, judge, and companion all at once. David Leverenz has seen similar artistry in writers such as Whitman and Melville. "In very different ways," he writes, "American Renaissance writers try to disorient and convert their readers, especially male readers, from one style of manhood to another. In an age when possessive individualism was running wild, surrounded on every side by men striving to beat down other men, these writers fashion styles of self-dispossession."[10]

Thus there is trickery here. Lewis may act the fool and spill his guts, but his odd and erratic behaviors leave the reader unsteady. Southwestern humor had its expectations, among which was the rule that other people's humiliations were funny, not one's own. Anyone who reads *Odd Leaves*, however, is drawn intimately into the action—which is usually painful— and is forced to encounter Lewis's own dysfunctions, which were probably more typical than Southern men liked to admit. The male reader (and this was emphatically masculine literature) had to confront feelings that any manly man would rather ignore. These feelings centered on humiliation and exposure, and they were intimately bound with Lewis's vaulting ambition and insecurity.

In Lewis's case the vulnerability may have been intensified by his own outsider status: a poor boy trying to break into the carriage set, a man of science among the unlettered, literally a Jew among the Gentiles.[11] Lewis's short history was that of a man cut adrift. Like Simms he was from Charleston, although his family moved to Cincinnati when he was about four. His parents were of Italian and French Jewish descent; the mother was a Salomon and the father claimed a connection to Disraeli. In Charleston they owned a furniture store, which either did not profit or did not profit enough, so they left to undertake the same venture in Cincinnati. There Rachel Salomon died, and the father drifted off on a tour of the Southern frontier—a journey similar to that made by the father of William Gilmore Simms.[12] Simms, however, had a grandmother to help break the fall as well as a slight but adequate claim to the Carolina aristocracy. Lewis had nothing. He was left in a strange place in the care of an older brother and a sister-in-law who treated him more or less as a houseboy. This was not to his liking, so at age ten he hopped a steamboat as a cook's helper and floated south down the Ohio and the Mississippi rivers.

After a year or so of that, Lewis chanced on another brother running yet another store in Manchester, Mississippi. Here Lewis found some comfort; the brother took him in gladly and promised to help him get an education and a career. Curiously, Lewis made no attempt to contact his father, who was downstream in New Orleans at the time, where he died in 1839. Manchester (later Yazoo City) was an interesting and approachable place for a boy such as Lewis. Like Longstreet's Augusta it had newspapers, a debate club, an amateur theater troupe, schools, and politics, all centered on an economy that was pure cotton and a population that was two-thirds black. Lewis dreamed of getting an education and moving up in the world, but when the market collapsed in 1838 his dreams fell with it. His brother, beset by hard times, put him to work chopping cotton. Of all the humiliations Lewis had faced, this was the worst. He toiled in the fields alongside slaves "between whom and myself but a slight difference existed." "Was this," he asked, "the consummation of all my golden dreams?"

But his luck changed. In 1841, when Lewis was sixteen, his brother secured him an apprenticeship with a local physician, Dr. Washington Dorsey. Lewis had never given medicine a thought. "It was not the profession I would have selected had wealth given me a choice, but still it was a means of acquiring an education, a door through which I might possibly emerge to distinction." He was also flattered. "One of the first physicians in the state, taking a fancy to me, had offered to board me, clothe me, educate me in his profession, and become as a father to me," Lewis recalled. "I am not much, yet what I am he made me." Dorsey was only eleven years older than Lewis, young for a patron and a father figure, but he seems to have taken the role seriously. He made Lewis his apprentice and in 1844 sent the boy—now only nineteen—to the Louisville Medical Institute. Dorsey died unexpectedly a year later, and Lewis grieved for him. Significantly, for what follows, Dorsey and Lewis were not on good terms at the end (word of Lewis's pranks at medical school had probably trickled south). Lewis thus lost a second father.

By that point, however, he was moving ahead. In Louisville Lewis studied under some of the best in the country, certainly the best in the South.[13] Among them was Daniel Drake, whose volume *Diseases of the Interior Valley of North America* was the kind of hard spadework that was moving medicine away from folklore and toward a growing professionalization and categorization of diagnostics and treatments. Lewis flourished in this environment; he apparently worked hard and well, despite his own self-characterization of laziness. He received his degree a few months short of his twenty-first birthday and headed back to Yazoo City, where he hung out a shingle and sat around for a time waiting for patients to come in. Few did, so he decided to move. The problem was not so much public healthfulness but the tendency among town folk to treat Lewis as a boy and call him by his first name. "'Blessed J-s!'" says an old crone in one of his stories, "'Is that *thing* a doctor? why, his face's smooth as an eggshell.'" This affront to his status was too much. He boarded a riverboat and floated down to the bayou country around Richmond in northeast Louisiana (near a point called, interestingly, "Bayou Despair"), where he set up shop as a "Swamp Doctor" and started his career. He wore hunting clothes, lived in a cabin, and bartered for his fees. After a short time, he was lucky enough to become the house doctor for a planter with many slaves, and he returned a quantity discount, so to speak, for the patronage of a cotton snob. (Again, the parallel to Thorpe is provocative.) By 1848 he had moved back to town, rented a slave boy named Calvin (which is ironic given Lewis's obsession with fate) to groom him and clean up after him and run his chores, and was known for treating his chums to round after round of drinks. On one occasion he was hauled into court for defending his honor too rambunctiously, and when he died he was showing the twin results of masculine success: prosperity and debt.

All the while he was writing stories. His first, "Cupping the Sternum," is a gross piece about bleeding a slave girl from the wrong end because he had not learned that the "sternum" was the breastbone. He wrote it at age sixteen, and Porter's *Spirit of the Times* grabbed it. Others followed, the best known being "The Indefatigable Bear-Hunter"—which is very good frontier humor—and "A Tight Race Considerin'," which we will confront later on. *Odd Leaves*, however, went way beyond his meager publication record: tapping some unknown wellspring of creativity, Lewis emerged with twenty-two stories evenly proportioned among his early life and apprenticeship, his career as a medical student, and his experiences as a swamp doctor. These are mostly written in proper English, although Lewis's use of vernacular is almost as good as Harris's. Interestingly, the sketches are not arranged chronologically; time is distorted and disoriented, as again is the reader's perspective. Whether this was intentional or not is unknown, but it *is* certain that Lewis was a careful writer and reviser and left little to chance.

Chance, in fact, was the last thing Lewis wanted to leave untended. He seems to have had a passion for control—of self, of circumstance, of future—which his own hard luck and common sense denied and which feeds his humor. He had his Calvinist side, his Jewish origins notwithstanding. In his first autobiographical essay, "My Early Life," Lewis recounts how his whole career as a medical man and swamp doctor "depended when I was ten years old on a young lady wearing 'No.2' shoes when common sense and the size of her foot whispered 'fives.'" To make a complicated story short, she comes hobbling down the street and collapses in front of Lewis's porch, whereupon he gets sent for help. In the course of securing aid, he is redirected by a gentleman to run an errand to a steamboat, where he immediately forgets about the lady's sore feet, stows away, and starts anew. The rest is history, and reason or planning has nothing to do with it. "Who . . . cannot verify in his own person," he asks, "that we are the creatures of circumstances, and that there is a hidden divinity that shapes our ends, despite the endeavours of the pedagogue, man, to paddle them out of shape?"

The whole gist of *Odd Leaves*, however, works against this mindless fatalism. It is a recurring story of work, planning, and scheming, compounded with a con man's opportunism and sense of fun, all directed toward the acquisition of fame and fortune. Medicine, recall, was "not the profession I would have selected had wealth given me a choice, but still it was . . . a door through which I might possibly emerge to distinction." Distinction is the driving force, yet ambition and diligence are not enough to secure it. He plows through his studies with a vengeance, but wherever he turns (as on the ice with Lucy and the dead baby) he seems destined to slip and fall. People demean him because of his youth and beardless chin. On the brighter, more humorous side, Lewis's unsteady relationship with fate allows a certain reckless spirit to show itself. He was a vigorous man, and it shows in his stories.

Clearly Lewis's adopted profession was central not only to his fiction but to his sense of identity. His obsession with personal advancement is evident throughout these tales, and yet becoming a professional man in the South was not necessarily a direct step up. Doctoring was different than, say, the practice of law. Despite the profound changes occurring in law and lawyering, the legal profession itself had a long history of respectability and inclusion in the higher ranks. It had professional networks, and Southern lawyers, rightly or not, conceived of themselves as the best of the lot. Medicine was another matter entirely. Even in Lewis's time the profession had not fully escaped a heritage of blood-letters and barbers, and the midwives who tended the sick and birthed babies were often more skilled than the quacks who peddled elixirs made from poisonous plants or crude oil. Moreover, the Southern doctor was particularly isolated from the hubs of innovation and advancement, specifically those in Europe and Philadelphia. This sense of marginality was common among Northern doctors also, but as John Harley Warner argues, Southern medical men felt particularly outcast and unappreciated. Stuck in the woods, their "collective experience," he writes, was "properly characterized by their self-perceived marginality, isolation, low professional status and lack of community appreciation," to which he adds low pay and a "consciousness of inferiority."[14]

Their frustration was fed by the fact that doctors did not exactly fit into the social hierarchies of masquerade culture. Lawyers might change with the times, as Baldwin demonstrated, but law, changing or not, was its own theater, its own stage for performance. The same might be said of Longstreet's careers as preacher and professor or Hooper's run as a newspaper editor. These were roles acceptable to traditional notions of hierarchy and manhood. If nothing else, law provided a platform to practice oratory and impress the villagers. By contrast, as Steven Stowe's analysis reveals, the country physician lived in a shifting hierarchy of expectations and roles.[15] He was a man of science—not a manly occupation at that romantic time—and he spoke the peculiar dialect of the specialist, which was gibberish to most ears and lacked the kind of oratorical cachet of the lawyer or minister. Moreover, his own standards were changing. At the very moment Lewis was studying, the profession was moving slowly away from "heroic" all-at-once cures—a form of theater that had some appeal to the romantic—and toward more measured, if less flashy, treatments. Lewis surely learned some of this at Louisville, although as his own stories show the faculty there was riven by competing methodologies and egotistical theorizing. In the country, the physician inevitably experienced a confusion of social expectations. His role as authority figure had not fully matured, the work was hard, and it did not even pay very well. *Odd Leaves* makes it clear that Lewis felt these confusions keenly. Grateful for the chance at an education and enthusiastic about the work itself, he still displays Warner's "consciousness of inferiority" in his assessment of his profession. He exalts it as noble one moment and ridicules it the next, turns it into a game of barter and bluff, and makes himself a poet on one page and a con man the next.

Lewis's first impulse, if the placement of the stories in *Odd Leaves* is any indication, was to make the country physician into a "natural" man, to diminish his role as detached scientist and stress rather his connection to the community. "The City Physician *versus* the Swamp Doctor" opens *Odd Leaves* with a topic-by-topic recitation of the foppery of the city practitioner compared with the physical and emotional muscularity of his frontier counterpart. The city doctor is "effeminate," "fastidious," "polished," "compelled to keep up appearances," and detached, while the swamp doctor is "courageous," self-sufficient, rough-hewn, and loved. The comparison is directly couched in manly terms: "The city physician has soft hands, soft skin, and soft clothes: we have soft hearts but hard hands; we are rough in our phrases, but true in our natures; . . . we say what we mean ... for such is the character of the pioneers and pre-emptionists of the swamp." These are noble attributes, but even so Lewis opens the story with frustration and self-questioning. City physicians have resources such as "scientific and experienced coadjutors" and cultivated friends, while country doctors are "impelled by youthfulness, poverty, defective education, or the reckless spirit of adventure" (a short list of Lewis's own traits). As if that weren't enough, they hang out with semiliterates. Lewis then, early on, makes his first mention of Death. Though the city doctor may expire like Scrooge, with harpies lurking about to rob the body, the country doctor dies with "hard and manly hands [and] the tears of women" lifting him upward. The latter will still do combat with devils and get stiffed for his fees; "he, no doubt, in the battling troop of the angels above, if feasible, will continue to *charge*."

It is a pun, of course, which opens up images both of heroic struggle and market exchange. For such a young man, Lewis saw pretty clearly the fact that his place among Southern men was a matter of negotiation rather than hierarchical certainty. In "The Mississippi Patent Plan for Pulling Teeth," for example, a "huge flatsboatman" stalks into his office with a toothache and asks, "'Do you pull teeth, young one?'" Lewis, ever sensitive about his age, bristles. "'Yes, and noses too,'" replies Lewis, "fingering my slender moustache." The reference to noses could prove fatal, because one did *not* pull on another's nose and get away with it in frontier Louisiana, or any other place in the South for that matter. But the river man just lets it pass with a shrug and begins haggling over the fee. Lewis asks a dollar. "'A dollar! dollar h–ll! ... I'd see you mashed under a hogshead of pork 'fore I'd give you a dollar to pull the thing.'" They work it down to a quarter, with a dose of castor oil thrown in. At this point Lewis experiences a double-con, one on his patient and one on himself. Rather than simply extracting the tooth, Lewis straps the giant into a fixed chair surmounted with elaborate pulleys and wheels, attaches a clamp to the tooth, and begins to haul away. The ropes strain and creak, the chair begins lifting out of its moorings, the Kentuckian begins screaming, and then out comes the tooth—the wrong tooth. The Kentuckian cusses him flat, throws him a five-dollar note, gets his change, and walks out. His is the second con: the note is counterfeit.

"Pulling Teeth" is a small story, great for fun and not too deep, but it highlights Lewis's indeterminate position. He is proud of his skill; he could not have thought up the joke without a certain expertise. He is determined to be respected; hence he twiddles his thin moustache and demands respect from someone twice his size. This is manly strutting and cockfighting. The whole scene is a medical variation, however, on Longstreet's "The Horse-Swap" or any one of Simon Suggs's many schemes, and it does not flatter either the awe the medical profession might command or the real-world skills of Lewis himself. Left with the Kentuckian's worthless note and out the change he gave for it, Lewis is exposed as a bigger fool.

Lewis's pretensions are reflected in the world around him. As a young man, he wants models, yet those he is presented with almost invariably fail him. The professors in "Being Examined for My Degree" are egotists in rivalry with each other, and the humor with which he treats them is not entirely fond. "Being Examined" is Lewis's account of taking oral exams, an experience which is often a game of both skill and attitude. In going from professor to professor, Lewis essentially becomes a con artist and an unmasker, turning his superiors into suckers and letting them talk themselves into thinking highly of him, rather like Suggs had done in his various adventures. Barging in on the first one, "who, being a superannuated widower, affected youthfulness very much, and prided himself very much, like a Durham stock raiser, on the beauty of his calves, to his dismay I found him arranging a pair of elaborate false ones, which showed a great disposition to work around to the front of his spindle-shanks. I had him dead for his vote, sure." This is, again, exposure, and Lewis uses it nicely to his own advantage. He engages other examiners in cons of wordplay per Simon Suggs, including this nice exchange with a teacher who is too deaf to hear the answers to his own questions:

> "What are emetics?"
> "Medicines, that a man who has dined badly, and wants to conceal it, should never take."
> "What are the most certain?"
> "The first cigar, the first quid, or a spoiled oyster!"
> "What is their action?"
> "That of money won at gambling; going back the way it came, and taking a good deal more than it brought!"

He passed, getting a "square yard of sheepskin ... giving me free permit to kill whom I pleased without the fear of the law."

This is fun for a student, but when Lewis moved to the bayou country the absence of role models and parental figures became serious. With his own father abandoning him and his patron first disaffected and then dead, Lewis's attempt to construct a natural man out of a swamp doctor displayed a kind of desperate man-making de novo, for there was no one at hand to use as a pattern. Pretension, on the other hand, was everywhere in evidence. The very term "planter," let alone "gentleman," was absurd in this liquid world. "Every farmer in the South is a planter," Lewis wrote with some acid, "from the 'thousand baler' to the rough, unshaved, unkempt squatter, who raises just sufficient corn and cotton to furnish a cloak for stealing the year's supply." It is not surprising that Lewis hated the Virginians he encountered, who—even in the midst of swamps and bogs—insisted on contracting only "aristocratic diseases" and who choked on their "insane state pride and consequent individual importance." There is a hint of hillbilly incest in his description of one of these clans: "all of one family, or otherwise closely connected," and being "originally from Virginia, they had all the proverbial clannishness of that highly favoured race. . . . They all eat with the same tastes, and used the same pair of spectacles to view men and measures."

So it could be said of Frank Meriwether's Swallow Barn, but in the bayous this kind of self-regard degenerated into laziness and sloth, with predictable results for both masculine authority and the family. Consider this description of the patriarch of a bayou family, a self-styled "planter" named Jim Spiffle.

> He would have scorned to hoe an hour in his corn patch, and yet would not have hesitated a moment to pursue a deer or bear for days, with all the indefatigability of a German metaphysical philosopher studying an incomprehensibility. But hunting deer and bear . . . was sport; so was drinking whiskey, and between the two, Jim Spiffle had little time to extend the limits of his demesnes, or multiply the comforts of his household, wherein a wife and a dozen children attested Jim's obedience to scripture.

The striking thing about this passage is not its description of a dirt-poor swamper, but its use of a language of sport and leisure usually reserved for the idle rich. Spiffle sleeps away his time, snoring through the plug of tobacco in his mouth—which his son tries to steal, losing three fingers to a gag reflex in the process. That of course brings in the doctor (hence the story), but it is Spiffle's wife who takes command and gets the call out. Therein lies a tale itself.

This is patriarchy in decay, and its indolent men allow women to take center stage. It is very clear that the death of Lewis's mother left him desolate; such a loss would devastate any child. Running away at age ten, he sees Cincinnati disappear behind the bend of the river. "I was . . . leaving the churchyard which held my mother . . . and I thought in leaving her grave I should never see her more, for how, when she should rise again at night, would she be able to find me, rambler as I was?" This image reappears at the very end of the book, as we shall see, threading its way into the writing as a pervasive sense of loss and detachment. He has no nurturer and, in the absence of his father, "no friend to counsel me save the monitor within." The self-pitying pose extends to his role as swamp doctor, an old bachelor with a lonely bed and time on his hands to write stories, time that should have been spent raising a family. This is, to be harsh, the adolescent sentimentality of a lonely young man who might have seen better days had fate and the river given him the time and opportunity to marry and settle down.

But that did not happen, and *Odd Leaves* marks a dark take on Southern fiction's normally adoring portrait of women. Longstreet exposed the "Charming Creature" as a vain, idle thing; Simms's women showed grit and managerial force. Lewis's women, however, are participants in games of exposure and humiliation that presage the domestic anarchy of George Washington Harris's Sut Lovingood. The body bursts its bounds. Lucy, the "Kentucky gal," disrupts his scheme to steal a baby, and when all fall down on the ice they perform a sexualized dance: "our inferior extremities considerably intermingled, and her ankles not as well protected from the heat as they might have been." Similarly, Lewis describes a country boy awkwardly proposing to his belle in a grape arbor, where the lovers fidget and stutter through love's rituals, all the while stuffing themselves with grapes—and more grapes. Soon, nature literally takes hold, seizes them in its grip, and sets their hearts, or perhaps their intestines, aflutter. "What can be the matter?" Lewis marvels. "They have just read an extract from one of Cowper's bu-*colics*—but can poetry produce such an effect? They groan, and writhe their bodies about, and would press their hearts, if *they* only lay where their digestive apparatus certainly does."

One of Lewis's better-known tales, "A Tight Race Considerin'," does a nice bit of gender-bending when "granma . . . a monstrous overbearin' woman," can't resist horse-racing the local preacher to church, not knowing that the boys have put burrs under the preacher's saddle. She begins shedding bits of clothing: shoes to whip the horse and petticoats and such to lighten the load. "'Passun,' said she, 'I'll be cust if it's fair or gentlemanly for you, a preacher of the gospel, to take advantage of an old woman this way, usin' spurs when you know *she* can't wear 'em.'" It is a barely concealed play on sexual domination, but she hardly needs spurs anyway. The horse hits the churchyard at full gallop and stops short. Her own momentum pitches her buck naked through the church window, "leavin' her only garment flutterin' on a nail in the sash." Naked grandmother stories are few and risky, and this one is a gem.

These are not simple victimizations, with one person exposing another. Like Harris, who followed him brilliantly, Lewis's exposures most often involve himself, and when women are involved his fears of inadequacy are literally in plain view. "Taking Good Advice" has him bursting naked from his bunk on a steamboat when the ship runs aground. "I did look queer," he admits, and his impact on the women is not exactly flattering. "Sixteen young ladies, unmindful of nature, ran shrieking away; fourteen married ones walked leisurely to the stern of the boat . . . whilst two old maids stood and looked at me in unconscious astonishment, wonderful amazement, and inexpressible surprise." The young ladies and the old maids can be forgiven their reactions, but for experienced married women to walk "leisurely" away? That is bad.

Inevitably, it would seem, the fear of exposure turns violent. (There is, in fact, an element of violence in all the stories just mentioned.) Bertram Wyatt-Brown, Joan Cashin, and others have suggested that the pressures on young men as they moved westward to Mississippi and Louisiana were intense and disorienting. The pressure to become independent without the immediate support of an extended family, the reduction of the family itself to its nuclear core, the competing demands of honor and economic success, and the sheer isolation all made life more extreme and young men less restrained. Lewis felt all those pressures and more—he was an orphan, a professional, and a gregarious boy-man stuck in the swamps. There is absolutely no evidence that he ever hurt a woman (or a man either, for that matter, except for one single unfortunate incident of brawling), but his stories of medical school pranks, cruelty to animals and outcasts, and outright delight in inflicting pain—all are sick humor.[16] They reflect not only his own fears but also the fact that there was simply no one, father or mother, to "counsel" him. Instead, the women of his stories are reduced to comical figures, victims, and/or potential threats.

This is most evident in "The Curious Widow." Renting rooms from a widow and her three daughters, Lewis and two fellow students discover they are the objects of a snoop. "Not a pocket of any garment . . . could remain unexamined, not a letter remain on the table unopened, nor scarcely a word of conversation pass without a soft, subdued breathing at the keyhole." This is exposure of a type that Lewis and his mates will not abide, and no wonder, for all are Southerners, "possessing pretty much the same tastes and peculiarities," which in a larger sense is to say that they cannot bear to be unmasked. Hence, the mode of revenge is particularly Southern: in the dissecting room of the medical school lies the cadaver of "one of that peculiar class called Albinoes, or white negroes. Every feature was deformed and unnatural; a horrible harelip, the cleft extending halfway up his nose externally, and a pair of tushes projecting from his upper jaw." Lewis and his friends surgically remove this face, carefully wrap it in a package that would certainly excite the widow's curiosity, and place it where she is bound to find it.

Simple and sick revenge, except that Lewis distorts the story in several ways. The "white negro's" face, that of a male, is even more grotesque than the corpse of the "dead nigger baby." Nothing, literally nothing, could be more humiliating to a Southern woman than to be confronted with this device. It crosses all the boundaries at once—gender, race, and class—in a sign of sheer contempt. Had Lewis done this to a male, violence would certainly have ensued.

But the fact is that Lewis almost backed off, almost aborted the joke. As the day after the packaging begins, he descends to breakfast and feels a momentary pang of guilt. "Bless her not-despairing-of-marrying-again spirit! who could be angry with her? Such a sweet smile of ineffable goodness and spiritual innocence rested on her countenance, that I almost relented of my purpose, but my love-letters read, my duns made evident, my poetry criticized by eyes to which Love would not lend his blindness, to make perfect; and then—she is a widow!" There we have respect for maternal goodness balanced by anger at exposure—fairly normal reactions—but it is Lewis's outrage at her widowed status that tips the scale. "My heart, at this last reflection, became immediately barred to the softening influences of forgiveness, and I determined in all hostility to *face* her."

This is a very subtle contest of masculine control. The domestic symmetry of Southern identity broke down in the presence of outsiders, among them old bachelors and spinsters but especially widows. The bachelor could provide for himself, as any man was supposed to do anyway, and the spinster almost always remained dependent on fathers, brothers, or other male kin. Widows were another matter. Separated from the nuclear family by the act of marriage and thrown out into the world by the husband's death, widows were neither here nor there. They had won certain legal rights of inheritance and property dating back to the colonial period, but these protections were subject to all kinds of social pressures and legal anomalies that favored men even in Lewis's time. Still, with a little luck and a lot of work, smart, tough widows could hang on to property, run estates, and manage their own affairs, which they did to the general unease of cocksure men. Lewis's curious widow, then, operates both outside and inside male expectations of authority and control. She crosses accepted boundaries, assumes authority no male wants her to have, and must therefore be put in her place.[17]

But in typical style Lewis adds yet one more joke at his own expense. Once the bait is out, the widow grabs it. With Lewis and crew watching from the shadows, she unties the package, opens it, and confronts "the hellish countenance . . . the fiendish tushes protruding from the parted lips . . . and the eyes enclosed in their circle of red, gazing up into hers with their dull vacant stare." They wait for her to launch into hysterics, but with no luck. "Ay, but she was a firm-nerved woman," Lewis recalled in admiration. In yet another reference to the kind of gender-crossing a widow must do, Lewis gives her the most esteemed of manly qualities, battlefield courage. In another age, "her spirit must have once animated, in the chivalrous times, a steel-clad knight of the doughtiest mould." Instead of breaking down, she laughs—eerie, sustained, manic laughter, but laughter all the same. When she finally turns to the students, her cool remark is simultaneously a slap at their youth and naiveté, the generally decrepit state of men in general, and their presumption that she needs a man at all: "'I was just *smiling aloud*,'" she says of her laughter, "'to think what fools these students made of themselves when they tried to scare me with a dead nigger's face, when I had slept with a drunken husband for twenty years!'" This is social collapse: a dead and debauched patriarch, silly boys, and a fearless woman.

Dead babies, dead faces, dead husbands—images of death naturally inhabited Lewis's dark world. Death was all about him in the rotting landscape of the bayous and swamps, and it was part of his training and his calling. His mother's ghost seems to have traveled the bayous with him, reminding him that people die, and in the disease-ridden, medicine-deprived, often alcoholic and always miasmic world of the Mississippi frontier, they died in capricious and nasty ways. This could not help but color the visions of a lonely and creative man such as Lewis. Bertram

Wyatt-Brown has described a "melancholic" South alongside and a part of the honorable South.[18] Death and the social expectations attached to it compounded this melancholy, twisting it into bizarre forms and, occasionally, good art. Poe, for example, was a displaced child with a foster father who largely rejected him (a fact which gave him some kinship with most of the authors discussed here, Lewis included). If melancholy helped shape these writers' perspectives, death helped define their authorial performance: Poe's, a gloomy slide into morbid collapse; for lesser talents, a triumphal denial of anything but the manly ideal.

In a masquerade culture, where appearances were everything, one had to put on a good show even in the act of dying.[19] Lewis was steeped in the tradition, and throughout *Odd Leaves* he alludes to some of the basic assumptions that Southern men had about death. One was that a good death was, of course, public, preferably among friends and family. The "sobs of children, and the boisterous grief of the poor negroes, attest that not unregarded or unloved he hath dwelt on earth," Lewis wrote of the country doctor in the first essay of the collection. Moreover, it was best to die outside, surrounded by the soft colors of nature and illuminated by the sun, with an unobstructed path straight to heaven where, presumably, the man would carry on the good fight (recall Lewis's country doctor going off to join "the battling troop of the angels above"). This sense of continuing struggle, not quiet acceptance, was part of the man's most important engagement with death: he had to meet it fearlessly, preferably in battle. When Mik-hoo-tah, the Indefatigable Bear-Hunter with a wooden leg, got caught up in the hunt for a particularly vicious bear that was certain to eat him alive, he met the dare with joyous self-assertion. "'Oh! Doc, this was what I needed,'" he told Lewis, "'and I swore, since death were a-huggin' me, anyhow, I mite as well feel his last grip in a bar-hunt.'" The bear hunter's eagerness to meet death was not suicidal, but rather the ultimate display of mastery.

Mastery might come naturally to a fictional bear hunter, but Lewis's own sense of control was a good deal more complicated. In two starkly powerful tales, "Valerian and the Panther" and "A Struggle for Life," he confesses fear, helplessness, loneliness, and despair at the imminent threat of death. The first story casts Mik-hoo-tah's manly pose aside and sets Lewis fleeing a panther in panic (riding a horse appropriately named "Chaos") with a pocketful of the herb valerian and a stray vial of prussic acid. Fear makes him "delirious." "I imagined that I was in the midst of a well-contested battle, and in the wavering fight, and covering smoke, and turmoil of the scene, I caught the emblem emblazoned on the banner of my foe, and it was a panther *couchant*." This hallucination of cavalier steeliness flies apart when, trying to draw his "sword," he realizes that the only thing he has at hand is the vial of prussic acid. "This aroused me; and, taking it out, I determined to commit suicide, should the panther overtake me—preferring to die thus, to being devoured alive." In desperation, Lewis sacrifices the horse on the theory that, "if I kill my horse, may not the panther be satisfied with *his* blood, and allow me to escape?" So he cuts the horse's carotid artery with a penknife, rides the animal to the ground, and lets it die, "whilst I, disengaging myself, at a full run strove to make my escape. There was reason in it." The panther keeps coming nonetheless, and Lewis surrenders to the inevitable. "I uncorked the vial, and was raising it to my lips, when, as if by inspiration, came the blessed thought, that when the panther seized me, to pour the instantaneous poison down his throat." This Lewis does, and promptly faints.[20]

Lewis's power to disorient the reader and confuse the message is evident here. All things considered, using a dead horse as a decoy shows shrewdness even if the gambit does fail, and backing up against a tree with a single shot of poison takes nerve. Whether the act is suicide or a calculated defense, he is determined to meet death manfully. Reason—and doctors are trained in reason—dictates that he sacrifice the horse. Yet in other regards his reason fails him, as he does not think to rid himself of the valerian, which in calmer moments he knows full well "possesses great attraction for the cat tribe, who smell it at a great distance, and resort to it eagerly, devouring its fragrant fibres with great apparent relish." (Valerian may be thought of as potent catnip.) Moreover, he is lost in the swamp, a situation he should not be in to begin with, and he is terrified. "I strove to breathe a prayer;" he says, venting his fears for all to hear, "but my parched tongue clove to the roof of my mouth, and what I uttered served but to add to the damning chorus of hellish sounds." Of course he is alone and not surrounded by adoring family, so no one will witness his terror (which makes the later public admission all the more startling). Finally, there is the matter of fainting at the panther's last leap. Would Mik-hoo-tah, the Indefatigable Bear-Hunter, swoon? This admission of frailty and effeminate behavior is clearly not a claim to mastery, but it is probably closer to reality than the cultural mandate that men meet death with cool aplomb. It may be little wonder, then, that Simms hated the book. It violated the formulas for measuring manhood.

It is a testament to Lewis's artistic courage that he took his confession of fear a step further, driving even deeper into his own fears of anonymity and obliteration in images guaranteed to scare the wits out of a white Southern male. "A Struggle for Life," the last story in *Odd Leaves*, is as gothic as anything on offer (there is no record that Lewis read Poe, but he seems to have read everything else). Called to tend a patient deep in the swamp, Lewis is led into the trackless waste by a "negro dwarf of the most frightful appearance." It is as if the detached face in the "Curious Widow" had been reborn to punish Lewis. His "diminutive body was garnished with legs and arms of enormously disproportionate length; his face was hideous: a pair of tushes projected from either side of a double harelip; and taking him altogether, he was the nearest resemblance to the ourang outang mixed with the devil that human eyes ever dwelt upon." Critic Alan Rose has linked this misshapen figure with Lewis's own conflicted identity. It "expressed both the covert Southern fear of the demonic Negro, and Lewis's own self-destructive personality."[21] Arnold echoes this analysis, noting how Lewis used blacks at critical points to express his rage and/or undermine his dreams and hopes: the aborted dead child who ruins his romance, the disembodied instrument of revenge in the "Curious Widow," and now this hateful thing, who fights him to the death for a bottle of brandy.[22]

This time it really is Lewis's moment to die, or so it seems. He allows the dwarf to have a drink, followed by another, and the demon is unleashed. "'Give me a dram,' [the dwarf] said very abruptly, not prefacing the request by those deferential words never omitted by the slave when in his proper mind." Lewis refuses, and gets the answer every Southerner dreaded. "'D—n you, white man, I will kill you if you do not give me more brandy!'" A struggle ensues. "With a yell like a wild beast's, he precipitated himself upon me; evading my blow, he clutched with his long fingers at my throat, burying his talons in my flesh, and writhing his little body around mine, strove to bear me to the earth." Lewis is overwhelmed, choked into a death-like trance full of hallucinations and out-of-body thoughts. But he's only stunned, and he awakens next morning to find that the dwarf has stumbled drunkenly into the fire and burned to death.

The fight between the dwarf and the swamp doctor can obviously be read at many levels. The Southerner's fear of slave insurrections takes form in the story, with a lone dwarf overpowering a much larger white man. These are, the story suggests, murderous people; in the black's eyes "was the fire of brutal nature, aroused by the desire to intense malignancy." The fact that Lewis brought the brandy himself and let its consumption get out of hand reinforces Rose's assertion that the dwarf's weaknesses are Lewis's own. (Lewis was probably drinking fairly heavily at the time he wrote the story.) And the culmination of the struggle, in which Lewis "dies," goes insensate and lies there while the dwarf drinks himself into a stupor and falls into the fire, is a moment of possible redemption. Lewis awakens to the stench of burning flesh. "Great God! Can that disfigured half-consumed mass be my evil genius?" Perhaps his sins are purged.

It is, however, that time while Lewis lies there "dead" but still thinking, still aware of himself, that is most interesting. Lewis's eerie identity lives on in his "immortal mind," which refuses to die and instead begins cataloging his failures. "My body lay dead in that murderer's swamp, my mind roamed far away in thought, reviewing my carnal life." It is not a happy picture: "Again, I stood upon the steamer, a childish fugitive, giving a last look upon my fleeing home. . . . I dragged my exhausted frame through the cotton-fields of the south. My back was wearied with stooping . . . and as dreams of future distinction would break upon my soul, the strap of the cotton-sack, galling my shoulder, recalled me to myself." He calls out again to his dead mother, but nobody will weep for him or mourn his passing, not for long. He resolves to meet death manfully, but in vain. "I did not pray. I did not commend my soul to God," Lewis wrote. "I had not a fear of death. But oh! awful were my thoughts at dying in such a way—suffocated by a hellish negro in the midst of the noisome swamp." The humiliation of such an end is of course intense, as it would be to any Southern man. Lewis has simply lost the game of mastery—over himself, over his appetites, over his inferiors, and over his reputation. Most damaging to a self-made man of his vaulting ambition, no one will notice his absence. Killed off by a drunken dwarf slave, he has no audience to impress, no family to weep.

There is here a melancholy so profound it is almost comic. Southern men-on-the-make were cut loose from (to borrow once again Stephen Berry's words) the "*effects* of civilization" but expected to assume its poses, imprisoned with their slaves and their ambitions, held up to impossibly high standards of repute, esteem, éclat, or whatever word describes their code of honor, and were always surrounded by death and the even worse threat of anonymity. Yet no outlet in serious literature at the time could express that. Thus did Lewis, who felt these pressures all too keenly, insert his anguish amidst tales of whooping and bear killing and humiliated widows. A logical fit, in its own sick way.

Sadly, his inward vision proved all too accurate. By the time *Odd Leaves* appeared, he had made literally heroic efforts to avoid the trap of professional anonymity. He wanted to be more than a physician. In a certain sense the publication of the book itself was an act of gentlemanly affirmation. Beyond that, he had moved into town, run up huge bills at the tailor's and at the bar, and was learning how to brawl and boast. Yet his professional commitment stayed strong. In August of 1850 cholera broke out in the Louisiana backwaters, and Lewis wore himself out tending to the sick. On his way back to town, tired and riding an exhausted horse, he refused to heed a friend's warning and tried to cross a rain-swollen river. The horse didn't make it, and neither did Lewis, who drowned ingloriously in the murky waters. His body was recovered and buried, but, like the anonymous swamp in his last story, the exact whereabouts of Lewis's grave are unknown.

6

Notes from the Underground

THE SOUTHERN MAN OF HONOR may have been pitifully equipped for dealing with the changing marketplace, but he was a powerful ally in the coming war over who would control the expansion of slavery. The gentleman's paternalistic benevolence and his domestic values of family and home-centered responsibility were far more effective apologies for slavery than the savvy negotiations of the businessman, even though the plantation was as firmly a part of the South's market economy as a textile mill was to Massachusetts—a fact which abolitionists were particularly fond of pointing out. As the conflict worsened, even this paternalistic image began to pale beside that of its warrior twin. Manly images were all variations of a battlefield code of fearlessness and éclat, and as the crisis worsened the masculine ideal channeled itself into the Southern cavalier, the impulsive and glibly violent gallant. This was masquerade culture run amok. Probably the most rarefied masculine image of the 1850s was the filibuster, the self-selected conqueror like William Walker, who recruited his own army, set himself up for a time as president of Nicaragua, tried to appropriate Honduras, and was shot for his efforts. Filibustering and cavaliering were great fun, if one overlooked the consequences, but their sheer boisterousness oddly did not generate much humor. Attitudes had hardened, postures had become deadly serious, and when Preston Brooks caned Charles Sumner on the Senate floor in 1856 he drew the outline of what every Southern man/boy *knew* was ideal. He acted out of honor, with a flourish and without reflection—no market dithering or negotiating here. Man-making, it seemed, had settled on the most traditional, most Homeric, and—in the face of what was to come—most suicidal ideal of all.

An era was ending, in more ways than one. Joseph Baldwin's *Flush Times* was among the last really creative attempts by a humorist to satirize the gentleman gently and point out the incongruities of Southern manly ideals, and it was published in 1854—the very year Stephen Douglas introduced the Kansas-Nebraska Act and the Republican Party began to form. Humorists continued to write, of course, but even the *Spirit of the Times* began to hemorrhage subscribers and lose its punch. Local colorists like Hardin E. Taliaferro, a very gifted humorist in his own right, wrote good stories about odd characters, but his were more nostalgic than ironic.[1] Even Baldwin's masterpiece, it must be pointed out, was set in the past.

Still, there was one more attempt to push past the self-flatteries and come to grips with the incongruities of being a Southern male. In 1854, that critical year, an obscure Tennessee businessman, George Washington Harris, began recording the voice of Sut Lovingood, coward and fool, a task which took him through the war to come and which he assembled into a book in 1867.[2] Sut was the antithesis of the gentleman. In Harris's hands, Sut describes himself as a "nat'ral born durn'd fool," without "nara a soul, nuffin but a whisky proof gizzard," with "the longes' par ove laigs ever hung tu eny cackus." His sole purpose in life is to drink, romp with the girls, and get "intu more durn'd misfortnit skeery scrapes, than enybody, an' then run outen them faster, by golly, nor enybody." When challenged, he runs; when asked to explain himself, his answer is direct: "'Yu go tu *hell*, mistofer; yu bothers me.'" Anything, human or animal, is fair game, although he has a special fondness for preachers, sheriffs, and women of virtue. In one of the funniest stories in Southern humor, Sut slips two live lizards up a circuit preacher's pant leg just to watch the old windbag strip and run naked through a mostly female crowd, screaming "'Brethren, brethren.... the Hell-sarpints *hes got me!*'" In another tale, Sut breaks up Mrs. Yardley's quilting bee by tying a clothesline row of quilts to a horse's saddle horn, then splintering a fence rail over the poor animal "'bout nine inches ahead ove the root ove his tail." The horse knocks down just about everything in sight, including Mrs. Yardley, who dies either from being run over or from the shock of losing a nine-diamond quilt, depending on who tells the story. Often Harris made Sut the butt of the joke, as when he lusts a little too openly after Sicily Burns. ("Sich a buzzim! Jis' think ove two snow balls wif a strawberry stuck but-ainded intu bof on em.") Sicily, no virgin she, slips him raw baking soda as a "love potion." As the gas comes frothing out of Sut's "mouf, eyes, noes, an' years," he thinks, *Kotch agin, by the great golly! . . . same famerly dispersishun to make a durn'd fool ove myse'f . . . ef thar's half a chance. Durn dad evermore, amen!"* For a country just emerging from civil war, this was radical. Mark Twain, off in California, reviewed a collection of the Lovingood stories in 1867 and thought it very fine, except that "Eastern people will call it coarse and possibly taboo it."[3] He was of course entirely right.

How do we explain a creature such as this? Sut Lovingood exists outside respectability. His dialect, his looks, and his behavior are as unpolished as dirt. He is certainly no planter, and there is not a single cavalier in any of the stories about him, although there is the occasional dandy. He is not from the business culture; there is no evidence that he handles money at all. He is most certainly not a lawyer or journalist, although he lays claim to cracker-barrel speculations on human "nater," which is Calvinistically "onregenerit." He delights in humiliation. "Ef enything happens [to] some feller, I don't keer ef he's yure bes' frien, an' I don't keer how sorry yu is fur him, thar's a streak ove satisfackshun 'bout like a sowin thread a-runnin all thru yer sorrer. Yu may be shamed ove hit, but durn me ef hit ain't thar." Translation: everyone has a mean streak. "An' yer's a littil more; no odds how good yu is tu yung things, ur how kine yu is in treatin em, when yu sees a littil long laiged lamb a-shakin hits tail, an' a-dancin staggerinly onder hits mam a-huntin fur the tit . . . yur fingers *will* itch tu seize that ar tail, an' fling the littil ankshus son ove a mutton over the fence among the blackberry briars, not to hurt hit, but jis' to disapint hit." Translation: life is often cruel. The same impulse applies to suckling calves and babies, all of whom must be taught that "buttin won't allers fetch milk." Lovingood comes from a world of physical—not psychological—pain and deprivation, and he responds accordingly with violent and uncompromising energy. Poor people prove victims of his pranks just as surely as rich ones. There is no irony to his life, no expectations. He knows he is worthless, and so lives entirely for the moment. He was born a fool from a fool.

Fools, however, are complicated creatures.[4] From one perspective, they are agents of moral destruction, anarchists seeking revenge on those who have humiliated them or who simply appear in the wrong place at the wrong time. Sut's eloquent homage to cruelty feeds this impression. In Edmund Wilson's famous phrase, Sut is a "peasant squatting in his own filth," a purely sadistic thing "avenging his inferiority by tormenting other people."[5] In a similar vein, Kenneth Lynn used Sut's cruelty and excess to evoke a psychology of self-hate and social psychosis, one which transcended class or poverty. "Sut Lovingood's haunted imagination reflects like a cracked mirror the frantic state of mind of the secessionist South," Lynn wrote. He is "a rebel without a cause; but his guilty contempt for himself, and his paranoid hatred of the enemies whom he sees all about him tell us much" about the sickness of the Southern fire-eater, with whom Harris shared much. "More intensely than any other figure in American literature, Harris's hero embodies the worst aspects of the slavocracy, even as the name 'Sut' is an ugly contraction of 'South.'"[6]

Then again, it is possible to see Sut as weirdly conservative and proper. By attacking pomposity and pretentiousness, Sut actually reinforces the moral order of respectability and restraint. He becomes a figure of escape by which we can, in Pascal Covici's terms, "snuggle down for a titillating glimpse of raw impulses turned loose," but do so secure in the knowledge that the very impropriety of Sut's antics basically reinforces the status quo. "The effect of Harris's work was to strengthen the grip upon readers' minds and hearts of the relatively safe, relatively known world that propriety offered."[7] Sut's degradations thus fit the Russian formalist critic Mikhail Bakhtin's idea of the regenerative power of carnival, the orchestrated moment where society allows itself to be mocked. Beggars parade the streets as kings; kings momentarily abase themselves. "Degradation," Bakhtin wrote, "digs a bodily grave for a new birth; it has not only a destructive, negative aspect, but also a regenerating one."[8] Out of the dirt comes the rose, metaphorically speaking.

Fools like Sut are thus compelling precisely because they are so ambiguous and ambivalent. They sit on the dividing line between good taste and bad habits, between freedom and restraint, between moral order and durn'd foolishness. Like Henry Clay Lewis's disorienting tales, they destabilize the reader. "The effect of it," Wilson sighed, "is more disconcerting than if Sut were simply a comic monster, for it makes one feel that Sut's monstrous doings really express, like his comments on local life, George Harris's own mentality. It is embarrassing to find Caliban, at moments, thinking like a human being."⁹ Perhaps more to the point, it is embarrassing to find a human being thinking like Caliban.

Caliban's rage stemmed from his humiliation, and the connecting thread that runs through Sut's monstrous doings (and all these interpretations) is also humiliation, whether imposed on others or suffered from within. This is an integral part of masculinity. Humiliation, or rather the fear of it, drives manly codes of whatever stamp. Manly behavior in the Old South—whether based on honor, market success, or evangelical self-discipline—was fundamentally assertive and competitive, and the other humorists we have seen here had subverted or pointed out the ironies therein. Most had done so by creating fictional sociologies wherein manly ideals could be rehearsed and staged, and in so doing they had deflected a direct confrontation with their own doubts. To move directly into a confession of weakness and vulnerability was therefore hard. Henry Clay Lewis had made the step, as we have seen, and exposed his frailties and his fear of being shamed in an autobiographical confession.

Harris's Lovingood, however, took on the very essence of shame itself and projected it on a much grander stage. In any of its forms—be it public disgrace, exposure, cowardice, poverty, addiction, sexual masochism, family madness, general worthlessness—he took masculinity's nightmare monsters of humiliation and simply negated them. His satire on masquerade culture is dismissive; his attack on evangelical culture is demystifying. His weapons are the very machinery of humiliation: revelation, exposure, nakedness, weakness.

He becomes, in William Ian Miller's terms, the "obsessive confessor."¹⁰ Southern men carefully tended to appearances, yet Sut reveals himself in volleys of self-deprecation and personal exposure that took Henry Clay Lewis's own radical efforts to unplumbed depths. Where bearing and deportment were constant concerns, and no man could stand to be "unmasked" as fearful or even human, Sut readily exposes himself, literally and physically (in one sketch he tries on a starched shirt, cannot stand it, and ends up jumping buck naked from a sleeping loft). He flees confrontation. His style of "duel" involves kicking a dandified stranger in the rump and then running 119 yards between shots when the fop unexpectedly pulls a two-barrel derringer on him. Nothing in the code of Southern honor fits Sut. Consider his self-assessment:

> I'm no count, no how. Jis' look at me! Did yu ever see sich a sampil ove a human afore? I feels like I'be glad *tu be* dead, only I'se feard of the dyin. I don't

> keer for herearter, for hits onpossibil for me to hev ara soul. Who ever seed a soul in jis' sich a rack heap ove bones an' rags as this? I'se nuffin' but sum newfangil'd sort ove beas'... a sorter cross atween a crazy ole monkey an' a durn'd, wore-out hominy mill. I is one ove dad's explites at makin cussed fool invenshuns.... I blames him fur all ove hit, allers a-tryin tu be king fool.

In that one paragraph, Sut rejects both the salt-river roarer's sense of brag and the gentleman's sense of honor. He admits to being ugly, poor, afraid of dying, of dubious lineage and parenthood, indifferent to God and duty, and vengeful of his father. What's worse, he is actually proud of it.

There is a paradox here. As this obsessive confessing liberates him from masquerade culture, it simultaneously gives him the moral authority to criticize evangelical culture, which he does through ruthless and violent degradation. Fyodor Dostoevsky had done something similar with his Underground Man. "I am a sick man ... I am a spiteful man," announces Dostoevsky's nameless antihero in words very close to Sut's own.[11] He shares Sut's low estimation of human nature, an almost Calvinist extreme of original sin. "It has long been known that lack of good sense results from nothing other than depravity," the Underground Man announces. Sut's terms are simpler: everyone is a nat'ral born durned fool.

To know that—and this is a critical step in the evolution of modern satire—is to acquire moral power. This view from the bottom, as it were, liberated both Dostoevsky and Harris to attack the nostrums and petty sins of their respective societies, to set themselves up as relentlessly judgmental and contemptuous of hypocrisy. It is suggestive that both writers were religiously conservative. It takes a fool to spot a fool, so to speak, and a Christian to correct a Christian. Mrs. Burns, Sicily's exasperated mother, perceives this about Sut: she "sez ... that I ain't one half es durn'd fool" as the proper citizens around him "an' ten times more Cristshun" as well. It is also suggestive that both writers wrote in societies that were rigidly hierarchical, at least in the sense that both had systems of unfree labor. Where upward mobility was hard, there was a temptation to identify with the dispossessed. Sut may have been a Caliban, but even Caliban knew the pains of frustration, victimization, and hopelessness.

So did Harris. He was born in western Pennsylvania in 1814, and little is known of his parents, except that George was named after his father and that his mother had another son, Samuel Bell, from a previous marriage. Bell moved to the small town of Knoxville, Tennessee, a few years after

Harris was born and brought the young boy with him shortly thereafter. No one knows what happened to George's parents; they may have gone to Tennessee as well or they may have died.[12] Bell, like Benjamin Franklin's older brother or, closer to home, Henry Clay Lewis's Cincinnati kin, seems to have been more demanding than nurturing. Thus did Harris, like so many Southern humorists, grow up essentially fatherless.

Harris spent his early years learning skills and nursing his ambition. Samuel Bell was a trained metalworker who specialized in first-rate small arms, such as pistols, knives, and swords. He taught Harris the trade in a Knoxville shop, and Harris kept one hand in the profession for most of his life. But George Washington Harris seems to have been a mobile, restless youth who was not entirely happy with the limitations of his half-brother's style of life. He was a small man, reputedly quick and agile, who briefly rode jockey in local quarter-races. Like most young men he was eager to set out on his own. The opportunity came when he was only nineteen. A company took him on as captain of a steamboat making the run from the port of Knoxville along the Tennessee River to the Ohio, and Harris kept the job for five years. He was good at the work, maintained discipline, and took care of his equipment.

What would have been a dream for many young men was, for Harris, the first of many jobs in a spotted career. In 1835 he married the daughter of the inspector of the Port of Knoxville (who also owned the local race track) and began a family. It may be that he grew tired of life on the river. It may also be that his family and father-in-law pressured him to settle down. Either way, the young man's days of romantic wandering were over. In 1839 he took out a loan, bought a substantial farm near the Great Smokies, and settled into apparent respectability. The 1840 census listed his occupation as "manufacturing and trading"—which probably meant that he farmed some, traded some, and made or fixed things. He had a nice house, carpets, books, china, a bay mare, three slaves, and a family. By any measure, he had moved at a young age into what would later be called the Victorian middle class. He had also contracted that most middle-class of burdens, a large debt. He could not sustain it. By 1843 the farm and at least one of the slaves were gone, and Harris took his family back to Knoxville. There he opened a metal shop, like his half-brother, and tried again. The shop was large and could handle both delicate jobs and heavy machine work, but the venture did not last. By the end of the decade Harris had signed on as superintendent of a glass factory (more likely a large shop), while he continued to do some silversmithing on the side. He probably needed to work two jobs, for Harris still tried to maintain a large household, including two slaves and a washerwoman.

If there was any consistency to his career thus far, it seemed to be in his capacity for hard work and constant debt in the pursuit of the image of prosperity. Actual prosperity eluded him. During the 1850s Harris went through an astonishing number of jobs for someone of his age and respectability. He became a steamboat captain again in 1854 and then a mine surveyor the next year. The following year he borrowed money to start a sawmill, which failed, so he became a postmaster for a short time and then a railroad conductor. Along the way he turned fire-eater and secessionist, but he was so obscure and marginal a character that few, if any, noticed. During the Civil War he moved around, living for a while in northern Alabama and then in Georgia. After the war he went back to Tennessee to work for the railroads again. He was still in that job when he died in 1869.

Sometime in the 1840s this fairly unremarkable man, who had had only a year and a half of schooling in his life, began to write. He may have done some newspaper work for the Democratic *Knoxville Argus* in the mid-1840s, but his first attributable stories were for the *Spirit of the Times*. The *Spirit* was a natural place for Harris to start, and his first stories read pretty much like the rest of the magazine's submissions: folksy characters making fools of themselves for rich folk to snort at.

But even these stories suggest something different, something truly creative, at work. His first story of any worth, "The Knob Dance," was in most respects an ordinary tale of a hillbilly hoedown.[13] For sexual references and sheer irreverence, however, it pushed the limits for its time. Girls come to the dance "pourin out of the woods like pissants out of an old log when tother end's afire," wearing everything from homespun to calico—but not silk. Any girl who wore silk would "go home in her petticote-tale *sartin*, for the homespun would tare it off of hir quicker nor winkin, and if the sunflowers dident help the homespuns, they woudn't do the silk eny good." That is, what the dancing did not wear out, the bushes would. Everybody drinks, dances, eats, rolls on the bed, and the whole thing ends in a glorious brawl, with lust thrown in for seasoning. The narrator describes walking home with his girl, and a "rite peart *four-leged* nag she is. She was *weak* in *two* of hir legs, but 'tother two—oh, my stars and possum dogs! they make a man swaller tobacker jist to look at 'em, and feel sorter like a June bug was crawlin up his trowses and the waistband too tite for it to get out." He wants to marry her, or so he says. Porter's magazine was one of the few, perhaps the only, outlet for innuendos such as these, but on at least one occasion during these early years even Porter had to reject one of Harris's stories as too salty.

In that story we see the sort of voyeurism that characterized so much of what would evolve into the Lovingood yarns. The whole bit about petticoats and legs and trousers is exposure and titillation, the sort of thing one would expect from adolescent boys reading a dirty book and trying out new euphemisms just to see how they roll off the tongue. Coming from Harris, a grown man, such activities present complications. At heart he was a proper man. Friends called him a "blue Presbyterian," which meant simply that he took his church seriously, did not work on Sunday, and raised a strict household. For years the First Presbyterian Church of Knoxville had a Harris family pew, and one of Harris's sons was named after the pastor there.

Such habits made him part of what historian Ted Ownby has called "evangelical culture," a culture of home, church, and town that Longstreet had foreseen as early as the 1830s and which was gathering force even before the Civil War.[14] The business competitor, who had created such ambivalence in the antebellum years, merged fairly readily into this culture. In fact, he reinforced it and paid its bills. The Civil War interrupted the change and obscured it, precisely because the war mythologized the Southern cavalier and lifted him to the level of icon. After the war it was easy, even necessary, to deify the cavalier and sing his praises, but as virtually every historian from C. Vann Woodward on has argued, the key figures in the reconstructed white South were businessmen, preachers, and lawyers. These men did not come out of nowhere in 1865; they had been part of the Southern fabric for a long time, and the war cleared the way for their cultural ascension. The country gentleman/cavalier remained the textbook hero, but the workaday model for Southern manhood shifted from the republican gentleman or the cavalier to the Victorian father/provider. In the postwar South, with the plantations gone forever, it was the only really usable role a Southern man could take. Harris was such a man, if not a particularly successful one.

Harris was also a Southern fire-eater. He began and ended life a staunch Southern Democrat, but during the 1850s his politics became increasingly extreme, as if he were unraveling along with the Union itself. He supported James Buchanan in 1856, wrote a rather bad political satire about the Republican and Know-Nothing candidates, and got rewarded with a postmaster's job. That same year Harris was elected a city alderman. More importantly, Harris went to Savannah in 1856 for the Southern Commercial Convention—a loose cover for a meeting of the crazier secessionists of the time. In 1859 he went to Nashville for the Democratic state convention and was appointed to the state central committee. That was the apex of his political career. After Lincoln's election the following year, Harris wrote three vicious parodies of the new president, comparing him to a dried-out old frog nailed to a board. This sort of thing was more popular in west Tennessee, where secessionists held a majority, than in unionist east Tennessee, so Harris left Knoxville. During the war itself he pulled his family across three states, looking for sanctuary. Afterwards, Harris wrote more nasty satires—this time sniping at Grant, abolitionists, and radical Republicans. These were not his best work.

The convergence of Harris's middle-class propriety and his rabid, arrogant sectionalism is suggestive. In daily life, Harris was a fairly ordinary, proper townsman with a business to run, children to raise, and a house to maintain. His record of successes, failures, ventures, and losses was not radically different from those of his peers in towns all over the country, South and North, or even in Western Europe and England. Like it or not, Harris was a member of the urban middle class and partook of its Protestant ethics. Yet it was a weighty role, and, importantly, it gave up much of the moral and domestic authority of the traditional patriarch to the woman of the house. It also accentuated the power of the church. In critical ways evangelical culture ran counter to what Southern men had been brought up to value. "Male culture and evangelical culture were rivals," writes Ted Ownby about the postwar South.[15] Masquerade culture in the South was aggressive, crude, and often violent; it was attractive, fun, and assertive, and it did not require the moderating influence of women or religion. Male culture persisted through the poverty and humiliation of Reconstruction, and it made itself violently felt in pool rooms, in politics, and on duck hunts and fishing trips. With two divergent ethics of manhood in play simultaneously, life for someone like Harris could be fairly complicated.

The fact is that Harris fit neither model of manhood. Like his creation, Sut Lovingood, he was enigmatic and outside the tradition of Southern humor. Harris was no gentleman, even if he did own a slave or two and was a rabid secessionist, nor was he successful in the market-oriented, competitive South that existed in and alongside the planter's world. He was, rather, an example of a type of Southerner we commonly assign to the New South—the business-oriented, town-centered, Protestant family man. In Marxist terms, Harris was petit bourgeoisie. In Southern terms, he was town-folk, much like Longstreet in his moralisms, tastes, and essential propriety.

But Harris was different nonetheless, and his perspective on Southern ideals and manhoods was radically unlike that of any who had gone before him. Most of the humorists covered in this work had some claim to respectability, even if their fathers were worthless or deceased. Harris and Lewis alone were utterly stranded. Like Lewis, Harris rose up from nothingness, worked for a living at whatever came his way, and suffered the consequences of his mistakes directly, with no family safety net to cushion the blow. Unlike Lewis, he had a family of his own to provide for, which must have increased his inner tensions exponentially. All his schemes and designs for himself ultimately fizzled into mediocrity or outright failure, and the bitterness that Wilson and Lynn picked up runs through his humor like an inflamed nerve. A hint of his frustration appears in the preface to the Lovingood yarns. In that introduction Harris lets Sut explain that he will be happy if he can give a laugh to "eny poor misfortinit devil hu's heart is onder a mill-stone, hu's ragged children are hungry, an' no bread in the dresser, hu is down in the mud, an' the lucky ones a'trippin him every time he struggils tu his all fours, hu has fed the famishin an' is now hungry hisself, hu misfortins foller fas' an' foller faster, hu is so foot-sore an' weak that he wishes he were at the ferry."

The voice Harris gave to Sut is not that of a bemused gentleman laughing at the hicks or of a cultured professional mocking the snobs. It is the voice of a restless man who had changed jobs too many times and whose debts had piled too high. It is that of a man who failed at virtually everything, who could lay no claim to being a gentleman, and who knew business for what it is—a daily exercise in taking abuse and maintaining a smile, punctuated by moments of abject failure or triumphal conquest. It is the voice, in other words, of one used to humiliation but unable to do much about it. Like so many other humiliated and frustrated men he found his comfort in an edgy blend of conservative religion and radical politics, both of which he tempered with a sense of humor that tended toward the profane and which had, as its primary target, the very centers of Harris's existence: home and church.

These are carefully crafted tales, and humiliation is woven into them like fine thread. Harris's output was erratic until 1854, when he introduced

Sut Lovingood, and he spent the rest of his life revising and polishing this creation. Sut's prototype was probably Sut Miller, a local from somewhere around Ducktown, Tennessee (Harris worked there briefly as a mine inspector). Harris added "Lovingood"—sexual reference doubtlessly intentional—and put him in Pat Nash's (also a real person) saloon, talking to a respectable narrator named "George," thus creating a conversation with himself. The first tale, published in the *Spirit* and revised later for Sut Lovingood's *Yarns*, was a knockout.[16]

"Sut Lovingood's Daddy, Acting Horse" is unlike any other story of its time. Sut rides up to Pat Nash's saloon on the spindliest horse ever born and begins right away to explain that this nag is "next to the best hoss what ever shelled nubbins or toted jugs," that is, second only to his lamented Tickytail, now dead. "Yu see, he froze stiff; no, not that adzactly, but starv'd fust, an' froze arterards." From that unlikely introduction, Sut jumps cleanly into an explanation of how Tickytail's death prompted Dad to act hoss. The whole family—sixteen kids plus a "prospect"—had lazed through the winter, "hopin sum stray hoss mout cum along." It never happened, so Dad lies awake one night, "a-snortin, an' rollin, an' blowin, an' shufflin, an' scratchin' hisself, an' a-whisperin at Mam a heap—an' at breckfus' I foun' out what hit ment." Dad has decided to pull the plow himself, acting hoss.

Dad is pretty good at it, too—maybe too good. He gets Sut and Mam to fashion him a harness from pawpaw bark and a bridle from an umbrella brace and then runs around on all fours practicing snorting, kicking up his heels, and trying to bite someone. Mam "step'd back a littil an' were standin wif her arms cross'd a-restin' 'em on her stumick, an' his heel taps cum wifin a inch ove her nose. Sez she: 'Yu plays hoss better nur yu dus husban.' He jes run backards on all fours an' kick'd at her agin, an'—an' pawd the groun wif his fis." So Sut leads Dad off to the fields, and they play their parts nicely. Dad snorts and pulls, and Sut begins dreaming of the corn crop they will get in (and the whiskey it will produce).

Then come the hornets. Dad charges straight into "a ball ho'nets nes' ni ontu es big es a hoss's hed, an' the hole tribe kiver'd 'im es quick es yu culd kiver a sick pup wif a saddil blanket." Dad tears off like a scared horse through bushes and seven panels of fence. He loses the harness, his clothes, everything except the bridle and "ni ontu a yard ove plow line sailin behine, wif a tir'd-out ho'net ridin on the pint ove hit." When Dad gets to the bluff overlooking the river, he jumps in. While he bobs up and down trying to get free of the hornets, Sut begins mocking him. "'Switch 'em wif yure tail, dad.... I'll hev yer feed in the troft, redy; yu won't need eny curyin tu-nite will yu?'" Dad cusses him back so badly that Sut leaves for the mines for a few days. "Yere's luck tu the durned old fool," he toasts, "an' to the ho'nets too."

That broke the mold. Never mind that Harris's comic imagery and use of language was far ahead of anyone else's writing in the field; those are subjects in and of themselves. He had created a comic masterpiece from a most un-Southern, un-honorable, un-middle-class subject: a father's total humiliation. "Dad" is not simply made foolish; he is physically exposed and disgraced. What is more, he utterly deserves it, in a kind of weirdly Calvinist comment on human nature. As Noel Polk has observed, Sut's father is a blind bull of animal appetites, a worthless no'count who drinks too much, sires children with no thought for the future, and debases himself in public. Acting hoss is acting animal, which he is.[17] The Presbyterian assessment of "onregenirit" human nature is on display here and made even more evident in the last story, "Dad's Dog School." There, Dad dresses as a bull, trying to bait the family dog and teach it to "hold fast." Again he gets stripped, exposed, humiliated, and nearly cut to pieces. Significantly, the dog holds fast by clamping down on Dad's nose, which after the penis was a nineteenth-century man's foremost symbol of virility.[18] Sut separates the two with an axe just as the local squire rides up. "It is not a pretty picture," writes Polk, "the worthless Dad, completely degenerated, his wife cursing and beating him with her every breath, and Sut ... unleashing all his years of accumulated frustration and shame.... Dad is for Sut a sort of foolish Everyman, in whose character are crystallized all the faults of the human race."[19]

More particularly, Dad is the father and thus a patriarch, and in the antebellum South a figure of authority and manhood. Sut's response to his father's woes is complex. Dad's acting horse can be interpreted as market behavior—another worthless scheme to make something out of nothing—and Sut is fed up with it. This may be an internalization of Harris's own checkered career and numerous failed schemes, but at least he has Sut take delight in the spectacle when all goes horribly wrong. When Dad turns to training a dog for bull baiting, however, he exhibits the Southern man's obsession with sport, a passion among all classes and the special prerogative of the leisured. When this also ends in disgrace, Sut feels the humiliation keenly, especially so because the disaster happens in the presence of the local squire. All is exposure and shame. "I wer shamed ove dad, shamed ove mam's bar laigs an' open collar, shamed ove myself." This is a Presbyterian's horror in the presence of an elder who has lost control; a poor man's shame at his poverty; a Southerner's distress at being exposed.

But not just that. It is also disgust at a social order built on deceit and masquerade. The other prominent elder in the story—Squire Hanley—who comes ambling up on the horse, "were one ove the wonderfulest men in all my knowin,'" says Sut. "Wonderfulest" is an open-ended term. Hanley is evangelical culture in the flesh. "He wore a hat ten years, an' wore a nail in the church wall bright, a-hangin hit on." His horse does not kick, his firewood has no knots, and he is a perfect churchgoer. He is also a womanizer, skinflint, penny-pincher, hypocrite, and old lady. "He wer secon enjineer ove a mersheen, made outen a mess ove sturgeon-backed, sandy-heeled ole maids, devarsed wives, ur wimen what orter been wun ur tuther; an' other thin-minded pussons, fur the pupus, es they sed, ove squelchin sin in the neighborhood, among such domestic heathins es us, but really for the mindin giner'lly ove everybody else's business." A machine made of Victorian gossips, sturgeon, and sexual confusion is a powerful metaphor, if a mixed one. Hanley fuses the paternal authority of a "squire," or country gentleman, with the prudishness of a Victorian busybody and the machine-like depersonalization of an industrial spy. His sexuality is something undecided, neither virgin nor divorcee, "wun ur tuther," but hardly masculine. There is gender-bending at work here, as the paragon of patriarchal control merges with the image of clucking hens.

The gender distortions extend to Mam as well. Coming on the scene, the Squire provokes this exchange: "'Say, O ye onregenerits,'" Hanley bellows in his best Calvinistic mode, "'whar's the patriark ove this depraved famerly?'" Mam's reply is fierce and astonishing: "'Look a-yere, Squire Hanley,' sez mam, 'I'se hits patriark jis' now; mos' ove the time I'se hits tail.'" (Tail? The reference is openly sexual punning, but Mam is up to the job.) She dismisses him: "'This am a *privit soshul famerly 'musment* an' hit needs no wallin up ove eyes, nur groanin, nur secon han low-quartered pray'rs tu make hit purfeck, 'sides, we got no notes to shave, nur gals ole enuf tu convart.'" A pithy condensation of how evangelical culture was mixing up gender roles. Clearly Mam's assumption of domestic authority was morally justified: Dad is as worthless as they come; Hanley is a prig; Mam is in charge.

But was Southern society ready for assertive women and reliable father/providers? Sut thinks not. "Men," he announces, "wer made a-purpus jis' tu eat, drink, an' fur stayin awake in the yearly part ove the nites: an' wimen wer made tu cook the vittils, mix the sperits, an' help the men du the stayin awake." A woman who stepped outside that role, who wanted to take command rather than simply cater to men, was greatly to be feared. "They aint human; theyse an ekal mixtry ove stud hoss, black snake, goose, peacock britches—and d—d raskil. They wants tu be a man; an es they cant, they fixes up thar case by bein devils."[20] This comes, in proxy, from a writer who was devotedly married to one woman for thirty-two years until her death, and whose second wife was reportedly every bit as bright, intelligent, and assertive as was he. It suggests a profoundly ambivalent posture toward the reality around him and the tenacious persistence of a more independent, traditionally masculine ideal.

It became Sut's task, then, to hold evangelical culture up to its own ideals. As a confessed unregenerate, Sut can do that with impunity and creativity. William Ian Miller's interpretation of the moral authority of the Underground Man fits Sut perfectly: "He distinguishes himself from those direct and confident men, those oafs of action who feel nothing very deeply, who are untroubled by the foolishness they do, who do not even perceive their failings and pomposities."[21] The very imaginativeness of Sut's humiliating stunts is in its own way evidence of his superiority. In the tale about Parson Bullins and the lizards, for example, Sut expressly adopts the role of repentant confessor—the evangelical's very conversion experience—to lay bare hypocrisy. Parson Bullins, who gets the lizards up his pant leg, is inseparable from women, who are his primary audience and his private obsession. If he were one of the traditional Anglican clergy with a circuit to ride, an occasional dalliance would pose no threat. But he has humiliated Sut by catching him in the bushes with a girl and then tattling to the girl's mother. This calls for revenge, so Sut goes to the service, full of repentance and lizards, to hear the parson work the women into a fever with the fear of Hell-serpents. "Tole 'em how they'd quile [coil] intu thar buzzims, an' how they *wud* crawl down onder thar frock-strings . . . up thar laigs, and' travil *onder* thar garters, no odds how tight they tied 'em, an' when the two armys ove Hell-sarpents met, then—That las' remark *fotch 'em*." At this point the women are screaming, the preacher is waving his hands, and the lizards are beginning their own travels up *his* garters. It is particularly satisfying to Sut that this preacher, who has seduced half the girls in the county, gets literally exposed. He takes off running, naked as a baby, through the crowd. "Passuns ginerly hev a pow'ful strong holt on wimen;" says Sut, "but, hoss, I tell yu thar airn't meny ove em kin run start nakid over an' thru a crowd ove three hundred wimen an' not injure thar karacters *sum*."

It is Sut's genius, however, to recognize that some women will not be shocked, as Henry Clay Lewis had discovered when he jumped naked from his berth on the wrecked steamboat. Bullins's streak through the crowd gives Sut the opportunity to sort women into types:

> sum wimen screamin—they wer the skeery ones; sum larfin—they wer the wicked ones; sum cryin—they wer the fool ones, (sorter my stripe yu know;) sum tryin tu git away wif thar faces red—they wer the modest ones; sum lookin arter ole Bullins—they wer the curious ones; sum hangin clost tu thar sweethearts—they wer the sweet ones; sum on thar knees wif thar eyes shot, but facin the way the ole mud turtil wer a-runnin—they wer the 'saitful ones; sum duin nuthin—they wer the waitin ones; an' the mos' danerus ove all ove em by a durnd long site.

In Southern humor the closest approximations to this lot were Billy and Bob's harridan wives in Longstreet's "The Fight." In polite Southern literature and in the many homages to female virtue and refinement that littered Southern iconography, there was nothing even remotely close.

More explicitly, Sut rated "available" women like horses. His courtship of Sicily Burns is famously lewd, but she was certainly not Sut's only interest. Young girls were fine, and old maids could be tamed, but widows were best.

> Hits widders, by golly, what am the rale sensibil, steady-goin, never-skeerin, never-kickin, willin, sperrited, smoof pacers. They cum clost up tu the hoss-block, standin still wif thar purty silky years playin, an' the naik-veins a-throbbin, and waits fur the word, which ove course yu gives, arter yu finds yer feet well in the stirrup, an' away they moves like a cradil on cushioned rockers, ur a spring buggy runnin in damp san.' A tetch of the bridil an' they knows yu wants em to turn, an' they does hit es willin es ef the idea wer thar own.

Like Dad acting hoss or playing bull, the imagery here is purely animalistic. It denotes that "onregenerit" side of human nature that simply will not be tamed, but it also exposes Sut's yearning to be a real man, in control with a "tetch of the bridil." It's a fantasy, and it won't happen. The passage mocks its author.

Amid such lust, the home was a place of negotiation, not moral certainty or patriarchal authority. In "Rare Ripe Garden Seed" a man marries, and then leaves for Atlanta after helping his young bride put in a garden of "rare," fast-growing seeds bought off a Yankee peddler. When he comes back, four and a half months after the wedding, she presents him with a newborn baby girl. He can count at least to nine on his fingers and begins to express some doubts, but his mother-in-law quickly takes him in hand. It was eating the produce of the rare garden seed that made the baby come to term so quickly, she explains. "'This is what cums of hit, an' four months an' a half am rar ripe time fur babys, adzackly,'" she says. "'Tu be sure, hit lacks a day ur two, but Margarit Jane wer allers a pow'ful interprizin' gal, an' a yearly [early] rizer.'" The real father, incidentally, is the local sheriff, whom Sut and the husband humiliate in a later tale. Where lineage is in doubt, so is the patriarch's claim on manhood.

These stories also feminized evangelical culture and the men who were a part of it. They are *Swallow Barn* come full circle. The domesticated Frank Meriwether of Kennedy's novel had been a proud master of a small world, but master nonetheless. Longstreet's nephew George had lost some of that independence marrying his Charming Creature. Each was a variation on a patriarchal model that was never as stable as men wanted to believe, and each represented a subtle recognition of the encroachment of feminine orderliness and propriety into standards of patriarchal authority. Dad's humiliation and the interesting transformation of the "squire" into parson, penny-pincher, and old maid mark yet another drastic step away from the country republican ideal, as does the commanding voice of the woman. Who rules this new South? "'I'se hits patriark jis' now,'" hisses Mam, and the implications of her claim are profound.

And that brings us back to Dad. Dad, of course, is the fool's fool, the creation fool, the original fool. He is the antithesis of a Southern patriarch and the whole manly social order built thereon. Lineage—breeding, if you will—was so vital to the South's social order that marriages were based upon it, unlikely names came from it (for example, St. George Tucker), and whole genealogies were constructed around it. It is said that one never asks a true Southerner *who* someone is when all you want is the name. *Who* you are goes back through generations and all the way out to fifth cousins. But Sut's father is just Hoss, and when he dies, Sut and his Mam borrow a shingle cart to use as a hearse, ride the body around the field a few times, and then drop it into a convenient crack in the ground, rather like dumping waste. Later that night Mam feels what appears at first to be a tug of conscience. "'Oughtent we to a scratch'd in a littel dirt on him, say?' 'No need, mam,' sed Sall [Sut's sister], 'hits loose yeath, an' will soon cave in enuff.'" Then Mam's true motive comes out. "'But, I want to plant a 'simmon sprout at his head,' sed mam, 'on account ove the puckery taste he has left in my mouth.'"[22]

Harris wrote that particular story after the Civil War, probably for a second book of yarns. It is arguably his final comment on the collapse of the Old South, for Dad's unmarked grave is no different from many thousands dug between 1861 and 1865. In another sense, however, it looks forward—to a new South of overplowed and overworked fields, of "loose yeath" and poverty that mocked the father's ability to provide either food or direction. There was not much left that Sut, or anyone else, could do about that, and Sut marks Dad's death with neither mockery nor shame, merely acceptance. Humiliation is thus negated. This may be what William Faulkner meant when asked why he liked Sut. "He had no illusions about himself, did the best he could; at certain times he was a coward and knew it and wasn't ashamed; he never blamed his misfortunes on anyone and never cursed God for them."[23] Even an Underground Man has qualities of redemption.

But then again, Harris died before the legend of the Old South was firmly in place. In 1869 he went to Richmond with a manuscript copy of a second collection of Sut's yarns—its probable title, *High Times and Hard Times*.[24] The proposed title has an ironic quality; it pretty much describes the Southern experience up to that point. The hunt for a publisher was not successful, and on the way back, on the train for Knoxville, Harris collapsed, probably victim of an aneurism or heart attack. He lay senseless on his coach seat, ironically mistaken for a drunk, until someone took pity on him, laid him in a bed, and called for help. It was too late. His last word was "Poisoned!" The manuscript was lost.

Epilogue

WHEN WAR BROKE OUT, John Pendleton Kennedy was an elder statesman with plenty of spare time in which to reflect and opinionate. In the 1850s he had made a final attempt at obtaining national prominence, serving as secretary of the navy under Fillmore, and then had largely settled into his role as gentleman patron of Baltimore's mixed Southern and Northern elites. He dabbled in nativism, as did so many displaced Whigs, formed a fast friendship with Robert Winthrop, a peer in Boston, and generally watched the increasing sectional animosities of the 1850s in gasping frustration. The conflict, he was persuaded, was not about slavery or the extension of slavery or even about abolition, which he considered a "moral epidemic."[1] It was a war waged by and for the Southern ego, and in 1863 he placed the blame for it squarely on the people who had taken the domestic qualities he had given Frank Meriwether and turned them into a competitive, imperialistic cockiness which knew no discipline or taste.

> If I were asked to describe in a word the primal source or germ out of which this commotion has sprung, I would say it was the egotism of the Southern character. There are no people in the world who have a higher opinion of themselves and their surroundings than the inhabitants of certain districts of the South. They are accustomed to speak of themselves as possessing the very highest type of civilization; as preeminent in all the qualities of generous manhood; as hospitable, frank, brave beyond all other people; quick to resent dishonor; keen in their perception of what is great

or noble; refined and elegant in manners. They claim, besides, superior talent, more acute insight, and higher energy than their neighbors. They are prolific in statesmen, orators, and politicians. They are manly, truthful, and *chevalresque*. This is the portrait they draw of themselves.

Like many self-portraits, this one had flaws. Kennedy said, "It shows the tendency of their aspirations, which is one good step toward accomplishing them. But, on the other hand," he continued, "we may remark that this self-esteem, whilst it exalts its possessors, is apt to breed opinions derogatory of all other people outside of their boundary"—specifically the Yankee, a figure who, since colonial days,

> signified ... in the vulgar apprehension, a shrewd, cunning chapman, who invariably outwitted the credulous Southron in a bargain. [The term] has lost something of this significance in these later times, since the credulous Southron has grown more worldly, and developed some of the qualities of a chapman himself. It now rather indicates the hatred engendered by jealousy of New England growth and prosperity.

"Generous manhood," in other words, had become a posture to conceal a kind of sectional inferiority complex, but one with a noble ideal—the *chevalresque*—at its core.

In various ways Kennedy's assessment has been canonized over the years, and for good reasons. Wars and their causes are complicated things, to say the least, and the American Civil War has been particularly resistant to easy explanations. Whatever brought on the struggle, its enactment (or its "performance," if you will) can be seen as an affair of manhood, of masquerade culture taking offense at the slights and sleights-of-hand of an expansive, market-oriented, and morally assertive North. War was a forceful affirmation of manhood, and one that itself transformed and simplified the ideal. Stephen Berry terms it éclat—the Southern man's desperate effort to impart "a certain grandness to a man's vision" in a world that was rapidly becoming prosaic and pinched.[2] For that reason, the war was particularly a young man's essay into manliness, and love of country merged seamlessly with sexual performance and even a Byronesque sense of romantic doom.

These are real and compelling insights into Southern identity, but they must not be used to mask the sense of insecurity that Kennedy—thirty years after *Swallow Barn*—still perceived. No historian of Southern manhood can miss the caveat in Kennedy's short estimate of the "Southron":

alongside the bravura were the "qualities of a chapman" (a peddler) that came with cosmopolitanism and market sophistication. However powerfully the chevalier took hold of the imagination, perceptive Southerners still knew he was a construct of the mind. If Lee had not existed, it would have been necessary to invent him. In battle after senseless battle, the Virginia gentleman or the Carolina sportsman shed his domestic paternalism in favor of a warrior's stoicism and drive for self-destruction—all compounded by a tragic sense of éclat. At the other end of the manly spectrum, the salt-river roarer became transformed into the patriot soldier, his "I am the man!" brag distilled into a chilling war whoop, the rebel yell. Somewhere in between, as usual, was the unsung hero of the Confederacy, the entrepreneurial man who used his Yankee-born traits to put bacon on the fire and powder into the cannon each and every day for four years. An example was Josiah Gorgas, the quartermaster's quartermaster. Thus did chevalier, mighty hunter, and chapman ride together. Perhaps more accurately, thus did two overarching ethics of manhood, the man of honor and the man of enterprise, join for battle with the ripsnorter staffing the ranks and doing the dirty work.

During and after the war these manly images became distorted and strange. Reconstruction so fundamentally changed manly possibilities in the South that the three figures of gentleman, yeoman, and businessman evolved almost into self-parodies, devoid of irony. The New South took Longstreet's sense of self-discipline and moral energy and turned it, with Northern help, into a kind of hard capitalism that made the hoss trader look like what he was: a bit player in a small-time freak show. Business became the Southern man's business, and the New South of Henry Grady's *Atlanta Constitution* literally created a new elite—urban, sophisticated, and worldly men of industry. Longstreet's vision of the evangelical businessman took its own path and came to realization in the small towns. There, men of Longstreet's inclinations tended to small businesses and divided their pursuits into discrete blocks of time and space. They worked hard during the days and relaxed in carefully tended masculine zones around city squares, saloons, Elks clubs, and on duck hunts on weekends. The home was a woman's world, a true "separate sphere" for moral instruction, with the church forming a common ground for both sexes. This division of manly pursuits was not, however, available to the yeoman. Off in the fields, away from the towns, the alligator-wrassler found himself tamed and transformed into a sharecropper. For him the manly ideal was self-sufficiency, an elusive thing, and his roar ended up in

Epilogue 125

Populist cries for aid from, in a further stroke of irony, the very government he had once disdained.

The most distorted manly figure, however, was the postwar gentleman—or rather the postwar "conception and estimate" of the gentleman. Even before the war the gentleman had become a quaint, cartoonish thing in literature, handled and idealized much better by Harriet Beecher Stowe than by native Southern writers. Writers of real merit generally worked around him, as for example in the later work of William Gilmore Simms. Simms had made gallant attempts at creating a Southern Ivanhoe but had, by 1852's *Woodcraft*, pretty much given up the quest in favor of flawed heroes and lonely warriors. The hero of that novel, Captain Porgy, is a soft, useless thing who ends up mortgaging his slaves to a woman to stay afloat ("You have the soul of a man!" he marvels to her in an unintentional revelation).[3] Daniel Hundley's essay on Southern sociology (*Social Relations in Our Southern States*) put the gentleman at the pinnacle of Southern breeding, but like Simms softened him and made him into something rather closer to the domesticated Frank Meriwether than either he or Simms might have wanted. Porgy's feminized male reappeared after the war in the novels of James Lane Allen and Thomas Nelson Page.[4] In the run-up to the war, however, the gentleman's code of honor was, as humorists had implied, adapted and distorted by fire-eaters and hotspurs to cloak a testy defensiveness which veritably erupted into the kind of éclat only a war could provide. "Gentleman" increasingly gave way to "cavalier"—not the same thing. The war provided for the making of this ideal, as it did the making of the myth of the Lost Cause, and it is our mistake if we read the cavalier too far back into history.

None of this was particularly funny, and so humor changed accordingly. These changes were ironic, and in a way that was itself ironic. The brilliance of antebellum Southern humor depended on pricking pomposities, not reinforcing them, and while any war produces its moments of comic relief, the sheer gallantry of Lee and his type and the tragedy of what was happening was grim business. Humor survived, but after the war its subversive voice gave way to a more nostalgic one, with local colorists working the weird characters down the road for material. This strain of humor was significant in its own way, especially as it attempted to come to grips with a changed landscape of social relations. Race, which had been an infrequent visitor in Southwestern humor, became institutionalized into a nostalgia of its own, with the most prominent example of this shift being Joel Chandler Harris's Uncle Remus tales. The ironic voice fled west, with Samuel Clemens.

The war was also hard on the humorists themselves. Kennedy spent it venting his rage at his Southern counterparts, dismissing the lot as pumped-up martinets. The rest were thrown into motion and restlessness. Harris wandered around Tennessee and Alabama before he collapsed on that train; pure genius that he was, he kept writing until he died. Baldwin, off in California, arranged a cross-country trip to take care of his affairs and see what was going on back east. He dropped by the White House, where Lincoln told him that he kept a copy of *Flush Times* near at hand when the nighttime hours got bleak. Baldwin was no doubt flattered, but his sympathies were Southern—yet not to the point that he joined up. Ever the lawyer, he went back to California to continue work on its legal code and later died there of tetanus, probably contracted from a rusty scalpel used during a routine operation. Hooper was sickly and too frail to carry a weapon, despite his sportsman's knowledge of dogs and guns. He died, probably from consumption, while pushing paper at Confederate headquarters in Richmond, a lost and wandering soul. Thorpe bought the *Spirit of the Times* when Porter became too old and sick to manage it. The paper folded and Thorpe, ever questing for status, tried practicing a little law in New York. When New Orleans fell, he returned to Louisiana and practiced a little fraud instead. Perhaps the saddest fate (other than Lewis's untimely death in 1850) belonged to Longstreet. The war drove him from South Carolina, and he settled in Mississippi on the plantation of his son-in-law, L.Q.C. Lamar. In November 1862, long before the catastrophes at Vicksburg and Gettysburg, he wrote Lamar a simple and prescient warning: "Your plantation will soon be a battlefield. We shall be whipped on it, and the Yankees will make a desert of it. . . . The prospect before us is awful."[5]

It always had been. Southern men had never reconciled their opposing ideologies of manhood and needed a war, in a cruel sense, to do the job for them. The competitive, exploitative, and nervously masculine image of the entrepreneur and social climber was a good fit for these men, for they shared modernity with the North. Yet that image was constantly sapped and sidetracked by the demands of honor and masquerade culture, compounded exponentially by the requirements of mastering slaves. The ambivalences tore Southern men apart. The ideal of the country republican was ultimately a feminized, domestic thing unfit (at least as men would define unfit) for a competitive world, and Southern men knew it. Still, it *was* the ideal, made necessary by the internal logic of mastering slaves, where domesticity and a sense of the father's care could be worked into an ideal despite the hard realities of slave driving and making a crop. The tension between these ideals was real enough, and what the South would have looked like without the war's intervention is anybody's guess. The war did intervene, however, removing all the grey areas and fashioning the Old South into a legend and a myth that has—of all such myths—the most sticking power in our national memory. If there is any humor in that, I have not seen it.

Notes

INTRODUCTION: *Negotiating Manhood in the Old South*

1. This was accomplished most recently and superbly by Justus in *Fetching the Old Southwest*, a really good book that deserves attention from historians, folklorists, and humor critics alike. The literature on antebellum Southern humor is dauntingly large, most of it appearing at the hands of literary critics and folklorists. Rather than run this footnote to absurd lengths, I refer the reader to specialized studies that appear below and in the succeeding chapters, to Justus's bibliography, and especially to the bibliographic section in a collection of essays edited by Inge and Piacentino, *Humor of the Old South*.

2. Again we confront a dauntingly large literature. For the precapitalist, premodern view, see any of the influential works by Eugene Genovese and Elizabeth Fox-Genovese, esp. *Fruits of Merchant Capital*; the classic *Political Economy of Slavery*; and the recent *Mind of the Master Class*. For the "progressive" perspective, see any of several works by O'Brien, esp. *Conjectures of Order*; his essays in *Placing the South*; and the essays in *Rethinking the South*. See also Oakes, *The Ruling Race*; Shore, *Southern Capitalists*; plus specialized studies cited below.

3. Jones, "The Work of Gender," in Morris and Reinhardt, eds., *Southern Writers and Their Worlds*, 41–56.

4. Leverenz, *Manhood and the American Renaissance*, 4 and passim.

5. Jones, "The Work of Gender," 51.

6. Hundley, *Social Relations in Our Southern States*.

7. See O'Brien, *Conjectures*, ch. 9, for a fine discussion of Hundley.

8. On Simms's world view, see esp. Ridgely, *William Gilmore Simms*, 22–23 and passim.

9. Greenberg, *Honor and Slavery*, quoted on 25; Wyatt-Brown, *Southern*

Honor; also see Wyatt-Brown's *Shaping of Southern Culture*; Stowe, *Intimacy and Power in the Old South*; plus specialized studies noted below.

10. In addition to the "modernists" listed in note 2 above, see Ownby, *Subduing Satan*; Quist, *Restless Visionaries*; Wells, *The Origins of the Southern Middle Class, 1800–1861*; Bode, "Formation of Evangelical Communities in Middle Georgia."

11. Leverenz, *Manhood*, 72–73.

12. Taylor, *Cavalier and Yankee*, 152.

13. On Porter, see Yates, *Porter*. Again, Justus's *Fetching the Southwest* is the best of the recent studies of Southwestern humor. See also Justus's introduction to Inge and Piacentino, eds., *Humor of the Old South*, and the introduction to Cohen and Dillingham, eds., *Humor of the Old Southwest*, xiii–xxviii, a fine anthology of stories and tales.

14. Parks, "Three Streams of Southern Humor," 147–59.

15. Bier, *Rise and Fall of American Humor*, 63.

16. Bergson, *Laughter*.

17. Lynn, *Mark Twain and Southwestern Humor*; see also his introduction to an anthology, *Comic Tradition in America*. Cohen and Dillingham echo this assessment, although not as stridently; see *Humor of the Old Southwest*, xv–xvi. For variations, see also Fellman, "Alligator Men and Cardsharpers," and Bruce, *Violence and Culture in the Antebellum South*, esp. ch. 10. Justus, however, utterly rejects Lynn's analysis as "clabbered up in its inapt hygienic metaphor" (in Inge and Piacentino, *Humor of the Old South*, 7).

18. Oring, *Israeli Humor*, 129. See also Oring's other works, esp. *Jokes and Their Relations*, a superb book on humor theory that stresses appropriate incongruity, and Oring, ed., *Folk Groups and Folklore Genres*. See also Walker and Dresner, eds., *Redressing the Balance*, xix–xxxiv, reprinted as "Women's Humor in America," in Walker, ed., *What's So Funny*, 171–84. Alternate approaches to humor are nicely collected in Corrigan, ed., *Comedy*, esp. Corrigan's introduction, 1–13. Anyone studying humor must also read Bakhtin, *Rabelais and His World*.

19. The analysis that follows is taken from a collective profile of the humorists used in Cohen and Dillingham's anthology, *Humor of the Old Southwest*, supplemented by biographical information gleaned from various sources. A spreadsheet divided into categories of birth, parentage, occupation, residence, education, political affiliation, and ownership of slaves was constructed; the results are summarized in the text.

20. Bier, *Rise and Fall*, 75.

21. Turner, *Ritual Process*.

CHAPTER 1. *The Conception and Estimate of a Gentleman*

1. The literature on the gentleman is large, and more specialized references will follow in the text as appropriate. For a varied and often contradictory sam-

pling, see Gray, *Writing the South*, esp. ch. 2; Taylor, *Cavalier and Yankee*; Isaac, *The Transformation of Virginia, 1740–1790*; Lynn, *Mark Twain and Southwestern Humor*, esp. ch. 1; Rozbicki, *The Complete Colonial Gentleman*; Sydnor, *American Revolutionaries in the Making*; and Kilbride, *An American Aristocracy*.

2. See Breen, *Tobacco Culture*.

3. See J. D. Miller, *South by Southwest*.

4. Unidentified source in Wirt, *Sketches of the Life and Character of Patrick Henry*, 32–33. Taylor's discussion of Wirt and his book is expert; see *Cavalier and Yankee*, 85ff.

5. There are two editions of the book. The original, *Swallow Barn, or A Sojourn in the Old Dominion*, was in two volumes and published in Philadelphia by Carey & Lea, 1832. The later, 1852 edition has been edited and includes an introduction by Lucinda H. MacKeithan. All citations in the text are from MacKeithan's edition, which as she notes is a slightly less gloomy, more nostalgic variant of the original, and which drops a key chapter on Captain John Smith. These differences have not changed my interpretation except where noted, and MacKeithan's edition is superbly executed as well as being readily available.

6. As quoted in Bohner, *Kennedy*, 86. Bohner's is the best, indeed only, thorough modern study of Kennedy's life.

7. *New England Magazine* 3 (1832), 79, quoted in Bohner, *Kennedy*, 87.

8. *John Pendleton Kennedy*, 46, still an excellent study despite its brevity and age.

9. *Main Currents in American Thought*, vol. 2, 46. Parrington has held up well on basic points of interpretation.

10. Most of this biographical discussion is taken from Bohner, *Kennedy*. The Kennedy Papers (hereafter JPKP) at the Enoch Pratt Free Library in Baltimore are extensive.

11. Quoted in Bohner, *Kennedy*, 40.

12. Ibid., 135. See also Brown, "John Pendleton Kennedy's *Quodlibet* and the Culture of Jacksonian Democracy," 625–44.

13. To Philip Pendleton, n.d. (1853?), quoted in Hubbell, *The South in American Literature*, 487.

14. To Elizabeth G. Kennedy, August 19, 1828, JPKP.

15. To Philip Clayton Pendleton, October 17, 1844, JPKP.

16. To Philip Clayton Pendleton, June 5, 1841, JPKP.

17. The cordon sanitaire is Lynn's term (see *Mark Twain and Southwestern Humor*), although the framing device is a well-established literary trope. See Blair, *Native American Humor*.

18. See two pieces by Lorri Glover, *All Our Relations*, and "An Education in Southern Masculinity," 39–70. See also Jones and Donaldson, *Haunted Bodies*, esp. ch. 1.

19. *The Education of Henry Adams*, 57.

20. See Grammer, *Pastoral and Politics in the Old South*, chs. 1 and 2; O'Brien,

Conjectures of Order, vol. 2, 882ff. O'Brien also has an excellent discussion of Kennedy in the same book, vol. 1, 318ff.

21. Romine, *Narrative Forms of Southern Community*, 78. Ridgely, *Kennedy*, makes fundamentally the same point.

22. See Ferguson, *Law and Letters in American Culture*; also the essays in Bodenhamer and Ely, eds., *Ambivalent Legacy*.

23. Bohner, *Kennedy*, 27.

24. See Horwitz, *Transformation of American Law, 1790–1860*; also Ferguson, *Law and Letters*.

25. Wyatt-Brown, *Southern Honor*, 177; see also Leverenz, *Manhood and the American Renaissance*, esp. ch. 3.

26. Almost alone in his opinion, Michael O'Brien sees the falconry scene as farce, not realism. See "The Lineaments of Antebellum Southern Romanticism," in *Rethinking the South*, 54.

27. *A Family Venture*, 26.

28. Ibid., 35.

29. John Lyde Wilson, *The Code of Honor*.

30. *Violence and Culture*, 17. See also Stowe, *Intimacy and Power in the Old South*, esp. ch. 1.

31. Simpson, *Dispossessed Garden*, esp. 43–51; Bakker, *Pastoral in Antebellum Southern Romance*. See also the comparison with Harriet Beecher Stowe in MacKeithan, "Domesticity in Dixie," in Jones and Donaldson, *Haunted Bodies*, 223–42.

32. Taylor makes much of the cavalier/scout dichotomy in *Cavalier and Yankee*, esp. 31ff.

CHAPTER 2. *Georgia Theatrics, Georgia Yankees*

1. To T. H. White, April 10th, 1836, in Scafidel, "The Letters of Augustus Baldwin Longstreet," 100.

2. All citations are from Kibler's 1992 reprint of Longstreet's 1840 edition of *Georgia Scenes*. The reprint includes Kibler's excellent introduction.

3. See Kibler's introduction to Longstreet's *Georgia Scenes*, vii–xxii, and Rachels, "A Biographical Reading of A. B. Longstreet's *Georgia Scenes*," in Inge and Piacentino, eds., *Humor of the Old South*, 113–28.

4. Fitzgerald, *Judge Longstreet*, 15.

5. Ibid., 14.

6. Martin, "The Prison House of Gender," in Inge and Piacentino, eds., *Humor of the Old South*, 87–100. The citation is found on 88.

7. Bier, *Rise and Fall of American Humor*, 61.

8. Bergson, *Laughter*. Kenneth Lynn's approach is essentially the same; see *Mark Twain and Southwestern Humor*, 72ff and passim. For a sampling of other views, see the essays in Corrigan, ed., *Comedy*.

9. Romine, *Narrative Forms of Southern Community*, 34.

10. The key work here is Wells, *Origins of the Southern Middle Class, 1800–1861*, but the groundwork for his superb analysis has been laid by others. See notes below.

11. Ownby, *Subduing Satan*. Ownby's book, while post war, contains directions for antebellum historians. A similar point is stressed in James David Miller's excellent *South by Southwest*, esp. ch. 1.

12. See a fine piece by Christopher Morris, "What's So Funny?" in Morris and Reinhardt, eds., *Southern Writers and Their Worlds*, 9–26.

13. General treatments of Longstreet begin with King, *Augustus Baldwin Longstreet*; Scafidel's introduction to the letters (see above); the introduction by Kibler in the reprint of *Georgia Scenes* used here; Meriwether, "Augustus Baldwin Longstreet," 351–64; Wade, *Augustus Baldwin Longstreet*; as well as Fitzgerald's piece, cited above. Both Parrington, *Main Currents in American Thought*, vol. 2, 166–72, and Hubbell, *The South in American Literature*, 666ff, are still worthy treatments. See also specialized studies below.

14. See Wade, *Longstreet*, 14ff.

15. See O'Brien, *Conjectures of Order*, vol. 1, 153ff.

16. Of the many good studies of South Carolina, see esp. Burton, *In My Father's House Are Many Mansions*; Ford, *Origins of Southern Radicalism*; McCurry, *Masters of Small Worlds*; also McCurry, "The Politics of Yeoman Households in South Carolina," 22–38.

17. See Lepore, *Name of War*, 203–4.

18. *In My Father's House Are Many Mansions*, 92.

19. Ford, *Origins of South Carolina Radicalism*, 32. On Georgia evangelism, see also Bode, "Formation of Evangelical Communities in Middle Georgia." See also Boles, *The Great Revival, 1787–1805*.

20. Samuel A. Townes to George F. Townes, June 6, 1833, quoted in Ford, *Origins of Southern Radicalism*, 68. On McDuffie, see Edwin Green, *George McDuffie*.

21. Quoted in Wade, *Longstreet*, 22.

22. To William B. Sprague, May 1, 1849, in Scafidel, "Letters," 434–42.

23. To Louisa(?), March 6, 1870, in Scafidel, "Letters," 655–62. This long letter on the death of his wife is autobiographical.

24. To Board of Trustees, South Carolina College, May 5, 1858, in Scafidel, "Letters," 560.

25. *Main Currents*, vol. 2, 168.

26. *A Voice from the South: Comprising Letters from Georgia to Massachusetts, and to the Southern States*, in Scafidel, "Letters," 324.

27. For a fairly typical Longstreet affirmation of states' rights, see among others his letter to "Seneca" in *State Rights' Sentinel*, September 11, 1834, in Scafidel, "Letters," 67–73.

28. See also two letters to James K. Polk, November 3, 1844, and November

28, 1844, Scafidel, "Letters," 229ff. These are long letters in which he urges retrenchment and term limits in order to reduce the size of government and keep the "Federal" party from reestablishing its exploitative policies.

29. To "Seneca," in *Augusta Chronicle*, November 3, 1832, in Scafidel, "Letters," 30.

30. To Mirabeau B. Lamar, n.d. (prob. 1838), in Scafidel, "Letters," 105.

31. To "Seneca," in *State Rights' Sentinel*, November 3, 1832, in Scafidel, "Letters," 30–32.

32. See for comparison Ryan, *Cradle of the Middle Class*, who argues that by the 1850s women had forged at home the cult of domesticity, and men, the myth of the self-made man. Both were "built on the assumption that the household was no longer the place of production, the locus of breadwinning." This was a "privatizing trend" that kept the women at home and made them domestic managers, but gave rise, for men, to "the domain of the self, the individual, of 'manly independence'" (147).

33. Greenberg, in *Honor and Slavery*, makes much of the concept of "unmasking," as in different ways does Morris in "What's So Funny?"

34. This is a much-studied sketch. The most influential interpretation of the sketch is Lynn's *Mark Twain*, 70–72, although he chooses to emphasize Longstreet's class biases and tends to overemphasize the role of Ransy Sniffle. Less political, and equally good, is Newlin, "*Georgia Scenes*." See also Meriwether, "Augustus Baldwin Longstreet." My own work, "The Theater of Public Esteem," is the source from which much of this material is adapted.

35. On the dynamics of sociability and gambling, see especially Greenberg, *Honor and Slavery*, esp. ch. 3, and Wyatt-Brown, *Southern Honor*, 327–61.

36. See Dale, "William Gilmore Simms's Porgy as Domestic Hero"; Ridgely, *Kennedy*, 65–91; Wimsatt, *Major Fiction of William Gilmore Simms*, 156–72; and Mayfield, "'The Soul of a Man!'"

37. Kimball King takes this essay very seriously (*Longstreet*, 74–77), although most critics do not. He sees it primarily as a sermon on domestic economy and false beauty and a companion piece to Longstreet's novel, *William Mitten*, written possibly for the instruction of his famous nephew, James Longstreet. He is, in my opinion, exactly right.

38. The following analysis adapts some of the material from Mayfield, "Being Shifty in a New Country," in Friend and Glover, eds., *Southern Manhood*, 113–35. Scott Romine also assigns a weighty role to the piece, although with somewhat different conclusions. He sees it as redemption of the redneck from the moral emptiness of "Georgia Theatrics." See *Narrative Forms of Southern Community*, 60ff.

39. See also Thompson, *Major Jones's Chronicles of Pineville*.

40. Wade, *Longstreet*, 341.

CHAPTER 3. *Counterfeit Presentments*

1. To D. B. Hooper, December 30, 1833, quoted in Hooper, *Simon Suggs*, edited by Shields, xix. All pertinent quotations in the text are from this edition.

2. Parts of the following are adapted from Mayfield, "Being Shifty in a New Country," in Friend and Glover, eds., *Southern Manhood*, 113–35.

3. Baldwin, *Flush Times*, edited by Justus, 83. All pertinent quotations in the text are from this edition.

4. Baldwin, *Party Leaders*, 338.

5. See Noland, *Cavorting on the Devil's Fork*. See also Feinberg, "Colonel Noland of the *Spirit*," and Christopher Morris, "What's So Funny?" in Morris and Reinhardt, eds., *Southern Writers and Their Worlds*, 9–26.

6. I have found the anthropologist Victor Turner's work on liminal cultures and their interpreters to be provocative, although the connections between them and con men should not be overstressed. See Turner, *The Ritual Process*.

7. The literature on con men and gamblers is large. For a sampling, see Lenz, *Fast Talk and Flush Times*; Kuhlmann, *Knave, Fool, and Genius*, esp. ch. 1; Halttunen, *Confidence Men and Painted Women*; Fabian, *Card Sharks, Dream Books, and Bucket Shops*; Fellman, "Alligator Men and Cardsharpers"; and Hauck, *A Cheerful Nihilism*. Carolyn Karcher's examination of Melville's *Confidence Man* is worth reading for context; see *Shadow over the Promised Land*.

8. See the fascinating treatment of this idea in Agnew, *Worlds Apart*. "Counterfeit presentment" is taken from *Hamlet*, Act IV.

9. Johanna Nicol Shields's introduction to *Adventures* is the best biographical profile; see also her superb psychological analysis in "A Sadder Simon Suggs." See also Somers, *Johnson J. Hooper*, and Hoole, *Alias Simon Suggs*.

10. See Shields's introduction to *Adventures*, xviii.

11. To D. B. Hooper, August 23, 1836, quoted in Shields's introduction to *Adventures*, xxi.

12. "Sadder Simon Suggs," 137.

13. *A Family Venture*, 99. For a different view, one that stresses continuity, see Jane Turner Censer, "Southwestern Migration among North Carolina Planter Families."

14. *Sporting with the Gods*, 90.

15. *Honor and Slavery*, 25.

16. Rosengarten, *Tombee*.

17. Philip Beidler's fine preface to the edition of *Dog and Gun* cited here discusses Hooper's crisis of identity.

18. Ibid., 7.

19. The only full-length biography of Baldwin is Samuel Stewart's dissertation, "Joseph Glover Baldwin," which contains correspondence hard to find otherwise. A more modern but shorter analysis is James Justus's very fine introduction to the edition used here of *Flush Times*.

20. Cornelius Clarke Baldwin, "Memoir of Joseph G. Baldwin," quoted in S. Stewart, "Baldwin," 14.
21. Speech before Alabama House, quoted S. Stewart, 148.
22. Cornelius Clarke Baldwin to Hugh B. Grigsby, August 1, 1875, in Grigsby Family Papers, Virginia Historical Society. Recently, Adam L. Tate has examined Baldwin's (and Hooper's) conservatism very carefully in *Conservatism and Southern Intellectuals, 1789–1861*, 246–354. See also Tate's article, "From Humor to History."
23. *Party Leaders*, 227.
24. See Mary Ann Wimsatt, "Bench and Bar," in Inge and Piacentino, eds., *Humor of the Old South*, 187–98.
25. *The Transformation of American Law, 1780–1860*, 253. More particularly, see the essays in Bodenhamer and Ely, eds., *Ambivalent Legacy*.
26. *Law and Letters in American Culture*, 202. See also the essay by Michael Grossberg, "Institutionalizing Masculinity," in Carnes and Griffin, eds., *Meanings for Manhood*.
27. *Party Leaders*, 20.
28. Ibid., 278.
29. Ibid., 284.
30. February 22, 1855, quoted in S. Stewart, "Baldwin," 308.

CHAPTER 4. *Useful Alloys*

1. Thorpe, *Master's House*, 350. See also Hayne, "Yankee in the Patriarchy."
2. For the best biographies of Thorpe see Rickels, *Thorpe*, and David C. Estes, ed., his introduction to *A New Collection of Thomas Bangs Thorpe's Sketches of the Old Southwest*, 3–79. A thorough bibliography of articles and other studies may be found in Inge and Piacentino, eds., *Humor of the Old South*, 304–5; also in Griffith, *Humor of the Old Southwest*, 191–208. Pertinent specialized studies are cited in the notes below. Thorpe's personal correspondence is scanty and scattered, and I have relied on Rickels's extensive use of quotations.
3. Cited in Rickels, *Thorpe*, 28.
4. See Edwin Adams Davis, ed., *Plantation Life in the Florida Parishes of Louisiana, 1836–1846, as Reflected in the Diary of Bennet H. Barrow*; also Edwin A. Davis, "Bennet H. Barrow, Ante-Bellum Planter of the Felicianas."
5. See Wyatt-Brown, *House of Percy*.
6. See Padgett, "The West Florida Revolution of 1810," 11.
7. Thorpe actually bought part interest in the *Spirit* in 1859, long after he had left the South. For a full discussion of the paper and its genre and contributors, see Yates, *Porter*. See also Estes, "The Rival Sporting Weeklies of William T. Porter and Thomas Bangs Thorpe."
8. Proctor, *Bathed in Blood*, which also contains a thorough bibliography on the subject. See also Higgs, "The Sublime and the Beautiful"; Bruce, *Violence*

and Culture; and Theodore Rosengarten's introduction to Elliott, *Carolina Sports*.

9. Elliot, *Carolina Sports*, 15, 251, 24.

10. Slotkin, *Regeneration Through Violence*, and his companion volume, *The Fatal Environment*. Also see Oriard's very interesting *Sporting with the Gods*; Martin, "The Prison House of Gender," in Inge and Piacentino, eds., *Humor of the Old South*, 87–100; and Ownby, *Subduing Satan*.

11. "Pictures of Buffalo-Hunting," (originally included in Thomas Bangs Thorpe, *The Mysteries of the Backwoods* [1846]) and reprinted in Estes, ed., *New Collection*, 283–99. Thorpe published at least three collections of his stories, including *Mysteries* and the more popular *The Hive of the "Bee-Hunter," A Repository of Sketches, including Peculiar American Character, Scenery, and Rural Sports*. Estes's collection is superb, with full textual notes, and is readily available. All subsequent citations to Thorpe's stories are taken from this anthology.

12. For a similar view, see Estes, "Thomas Bangs Thorpe's Backwoods Hunters."

13. The story has been extensively studied, with the best piece being Lemay's "The Text, Tradition, and Themes of 'The Big Bear of Arkansas,'" which calls it "elegiac and tragic." Lynn made much of it in *Mark Twain and Southwestern Humor*, 88–99. See also Littlefield, "Thomas Bangs Thorpe and the Passing of the Southwestern Wilderness"; Perry, "The Common Doom"; and Rickels, *Thorpe*, 49–61.

14. "My First Dinner in New Orleans," in Estes, ed., *New Collection*, 203–6.

15. Again see Proctor's excellent analysis, *Bathed in Blood*, esp. ch. 2.

16. See McDermott, "T. B. Thorpe's Burlesque of Far West Sporting Travel."

17. December 5, 1845, quoted in Rickels, *Thorpe*, 113.

18. *Spirit of the Times*, August 3, 1850; quoted in Rickels, *Thorpe*, 162.

CHAPTER 5. *Swamp Fevers*

1. Lewis, *Odd Leaves* (Arnold, ed.). All quotations from Lewis's stories are taken from this edition.

2. Anderson, *Louisiana Swamp Doctor*, "Introduction," 1–71.

3. *Southern Quarterly Review* 17 (July 1850): 537.

4. See Arnold's article, "Facing the Monster," 179–91, and his introduction to *Odd Leaves*, xi–xliv.

5. Arnold, introduction to *Odd Leaves*, xiv. See also Israel, "Henry Clay Lewis's *Odd Leaves*"; Keller, "'Aesculapius in Buckskin.'"

6. Berry, *All That Makes a Man*, 34.

7. Stuart to Bettie Hairston, October 28, 1853, quoted in Berry, 36.

8. The term is used, profitably, in William Ian Miller's excellent study on humiliation and honor, *Humiliation*, quotation on 170 and passim. See also the following chapter in this work on George Washington Harris.

9. I have made a similar point in "Being Shifty in a New Country," in Friend and Glover, eds., *Southern Manhood*, 113–35.

10. *Manhood and the American Renaissance*, 6.

11. I have taken most of this biographical information from Anderson's study (see note 2, above). Much, however, is contained in Lewis's own stories.

12. See Arnold, "Facing the Monster," and Mayfield, "'The Soul of a Man!'"

13. See Anderson, "Henry Clay Lewis, Louisville Medical Institute Student, 1844–1846."

14. Warner, "The Idea of Southern Medical Distinctiveness," 205.

15. See Stowe, *Doctoring the South*, and "Seeing Themselves at Work."

16. The whole of Southern humor is, according to Jesse Bier, sick humor. See *Rise and Fall of American Humor*, esp. 62.

17. See Wyatt-Brown, *Southern Honor*, esp. 240ff; also Lebsock, *The Free Women of Petersburg*.

18. *Hearts of Darkness*. See also Michael O'Brien, "The Lineaments of Antebellum Southern Romanticism," in O'Brien, *Rethinking the South*, ch. 2.

19. See Greenberg, *Honor and Slavery*, esp. ch. 4.

20. See Watts, "In the Midst of a Noisome Swamp."

21. Rose, "The Image of the Negro in the Writings of Henry Clay Lewis." See also Rose, *Demonic Vision*, esp. 25–38.

22. See Arnold's introduction to *Odd Leaves*, xliii and passim.

CHAPTER 6. *Notes from the Underground*

1. Taliaferro (pronounced "Tolliver") is worth study. See the collection of his tales and the introduction by Craig, *The Humor of H. E. Taliaferro*.

2. Harris, *Sut Lovingood*. All pertinent quotations are from this edition.

3. Quoted in Rickels, *Harris*, 121. The literature on Harris and *Sut* is so large that the selected bibliography of works on him in Inge and Piacentino's collection of essays (*Humor of the Old South*) runs over five pages, more than that of any other humorist in the work. Historians, to their discredit, are largely absent from this list. See also the very fine collection of essays, *Sut Lovingood's Nat'ral Born Yarnspinner*, Caron and Inge, eds.

4. See esp. ch. 7 in Rickels, *Harris*. Much of this chapter is a revised version of my own "George Washington Harris," in Morrison, ed., *The Human Tradition in Antebellum America*, 229–43, although my interpretive stance has evolved.

5. E. Wilson, *Patriotic Gore*, 509–10.

6. Lynn, *Mark Twain and Southwestern Humor*, 136–37.

7. Covici, "Propriety, Society, and Sut Lovingood," in Caron and Inge, eds., 246–60. The citation is found on 255.

8. Bakhtin, *Rabelais and His World*, 21. For amplification of this theory, see Lachmann, "Bakhtin and Carnival"; Kelly, "Revealing Bakhtin"; and the essays in Hirschkop and Sheperd, eds., *Bakhtin and Cultural Theory*.

9. E. Wilson, *Patriotic Gore*, 516.

10. See W. I. Miller, *Humiliation*, 170 and passim.

11. Dostoevsky, *Notes from Underground*, translated by Mirra Ginsburg, 1, 3. I am taking my cue here from W. I. Miller, *Humiliation*, esp. 170ff. See also Kelly, "Revealing Bakhtin," esp. 44.

12. The best biography is found in Rickels's fine book, *Harris* (which also explores the notion of Sut as fool, though from a different perspective). See also the various essays in Caron and Inge, eds., esp. Donald Day, "The Life of George Washington Harris," 33–68.

13. "The Knob Dance—A Tennessee Frolic," in Inge, ed., *High Times and Hard Times*, 44–53.

14. Ownby, *Subduing Satan*. See also Olsen, *Political Culture and Secession in Mississippi*, esp. ch. 1.

15. Ownby, *Subduing Satan*, 14.

16. See Rickels's careful study, *Harris*, 44–48 and passim.

17. Polk, "Blind Bull," in Caron and Inge, eds., 148–75.

18. Greenberg, *Honor and Slavery*, 16ff.

19. Polk, "Blind Bull," 163.

20. "Sut Lovingood's Chest Story," in Inge, ed., *High Times and Hard Times*, 120.

21. W. I. Miller, *Humiliation*, 171. See also Walker, "Sut and His Sisters: Vernacular Humor and Genteel Culture," in Caron and Inge, eds., 261–71, on Sut's protest against hypocrisy.

22. "Well, Dad's Dead," in Inge, ed., *High Times and Hard Times*, 211.

23. Quoted in Rickels, *Harris*, 95.

24. M. Thomas Inge's collection of yarns not found in the 1867 edition (*High Times and Hard Times*) probably encompasses most of the material in the lost manuscript, but we will never know with certainty.

Epilogue

1. Paul Ambrose (John Pendleton Kennedy's pseudonym), *The Slave Question*. The lengthy quotations in the text following this notation are from this piece.

2. Berry, *All That Makes a Man*, 21 and passim. See also Wyatt-Brown, *Shaping of Southern Culture*, and Olsen, *Political Culture and Secession in Mississippi*.

3. See Mayfield, "'The Soul of a Man!'"

4. See the fine article by Caroline Gebhard, "Reconstructing Southern Manhood," in Jones and Donaldson, *Haunted Bodies*, 132–55.

5. To L.Q.C. Lamar, November 13, 1862, in Scafidel, "Letters," 643–44.

Bibliography

Primary Texts and Editions

JOSEPH GLOVER BALDWIN

Baldwin, Joseph G. *The Flush Times of Alabama and Mississippi, A Series of Sketches.* New York: D. Appleton, 1853. Edited with an introduction by James H. Justus. Baton Rouge: Louisiana State University Press, 1987.

———. *Party Leaders; Sketches of Thomas Jefferson, Alex'r Hamilton, Andrew Jackson, Henry Clay, John Randolph, of Roanoke, Including Notices of Many Other Distinguished American Statesmen.* New York: D. Appleton, 1855.

GEORGE WASHINGTON HARRIS

Harris, George Washington. *Sut Lovingood: Yarns Spun by a "Nat'ral Born Durn'd Fool" Warped and Wove for Public Wear.* New York: Dick & Fitzgerald, 1867.

Inge, M. Thomas, ed. *High Times and Hard Times: Sketches and Tales by George Washington Harris.* Kingsport, Tenn.: Vanderbilt University Press, 1967.

JOHNSON JONES HOOPER

Hooper, Johnson Jones. *Adventures of Captain Simon Suggs, Late of the Tallapoosa Volunteers; together with "Taking the Census" and Other Alabama Sketches.* N.p.: 1845, 1858. Reprinted and edited with an introduction by Johanna Nicol Shields. Tuscaloosa: University of Alabama Press, 1993.

———. *Dog and Gun: A Few Loose Chapters on Shooting, Among Which Will Be Found Some Anecdotes and Incidents.* New York: Orange Judd, 1856. Reprinted with an introduction by Philip D. Beidler. Tuscaloosa: University of Alabama Press, 1992.

JOHN PENDLETON KENNEDY

Kennedy, John Pendleton [Paul Ambrose, pseudonym]. *The Slave Question: A Pretext to Lead the Masses On to Revolution*. Washington, D.C.: 1863. Reprinted from *National Intelligencer*, March 1863.

———. *Swallow Barn, or A Sojourn in the Old Dominion*. 2 vols. Philadelphia: Carey and Lea, 1832.

———. *Swallow Barn, or A Sojourn in the Old Dominion*. 2nd ed. 1852. Edited with an introduction by Lucinda H. MacKeithan. Baton Rouge: Louisiana State University Press, 1986.

HENRY CLAY LEWIS

Anderson, John Q., ed. *Louisiana Swamp Doctor: The Writings of Henry Clay Lewis, Alias "Madison Tensas, M.D."* Baton Rouge: Louisiana State University Press, 1962.

Lewis, Henry Clay. *Odd Leaves from the Life of a Louisiana Swamp Doctor*. Edited with a new introduction by Edwin T. Arnold. Baton Rouge: Louisiana State University Press, 1997.

AUGUSTUS BALDWIN LONGSTREET

Longstreet, Augustus B. *Georgia Scenes, Characters, Incidents, andc., in the First Half Century of the Republic*. 2nd ed. New York: Harper and Brothers, 1840. Reprinted with an introduction by James E. Kibler Jr. Nashville: J. S. Sanders, 1992.

———. *Master William Mitten: or, a Youth of Brilliant Talents, Who Was Ruined by Bad Luck*. Macon, Ga.: Burke, Boykin, 1864.

THOMAS BANGS THORPE

Estes, David C., ed. *A New Collection of Thomas Bangs Thorpe's Sketches of the Old Southwest*. Baton Rouge: Louisiana State University Press, 1989.

Thorpe, T[homas] B[angs]. *The Hive of the "Bee-Hunter," A Repository of Sketches, including Peculiar American Character, Scenery, and Rural Sports*. New York: D. Appleton, 1854.

———. *The Master's House: A Tale of Southern Life*. N.p.: 1854.

Secondary Works and Other Editions

Adams, Henry. *The Education of Henry Adams*. New York: Book League of America, 1928.

Agnew, Jean-Christophe. *Worlds Apart: The Market and the Theater in Anglo-American Thought, 1550–1750*. New York: Cambridge University Press, 1986.

Allen, Michael. *Western Rivermen, 1763–1861: Ohio and Mississippi Boatmen and the Myth of the Alligator Horse*. Baton Rouge: Louisiana State University Press, 1990.
Anderson, John Q. "Henry Clay Lewis, Louisville Medical Institute Student, 1844–1846." *Filson Club Historical Quarterly* 32 (1958): 30–37.
———, ed. *With the Bark On: Popular Humor of the Old South*. Kingsport, Tenn.: Vanderbilt University Press, 1967.
Arnold, Edwin T. "Facing the Monster: William Gilmore Simms and Henry Clay Lewis." In *William Gilmore Simms and the American Frontier*, edited by John C. Guilds and Caroline Collins, 179–91. Athens: University of Georgia Press, 1997.
Bakhtin, Mikhail. *Rabelais and His World*. Translated by Helene Iswolsky. Cambridge, Mass.: M.I.T. Press, 1968.
Bakker, Jan. *Pastoral in Antebellum Southern Romance*. Baton Rouge: Louisiana State University Press, 1989.
Beidler, Philip D. *First Books: The Printed Word and Cultural Formation in Early Alabama*. Tuscaloosa: University of Alabama Press, 1999.
Bergson, Henri. *Laughter: An Essay on the Meaning of the Comic*. New York: Macmillan, 1911. Reprint, New York: Cosimo Inc., 2005.
Berry, Stephen W., II. *All That Makes a Man: Love and Ambition in the Civil War South*. New York: Oxford University Press, 2003.
Bier, Jesse. *The Rise and Fall of American Humor*. New York: Holt, Rinehart, and Winston, 1968.
Blair, Walter. *Native American Humor*. 1937. San Francisco: Chandler Publishing, 1960.
Bode, Frederick A. "The Formation of Evangelical Communities in Middle Georgia: Twiggs County, 1820–1860." *Journal of Southern History* 60 (November 1994): 711–48.
Bodenhamer, David J., and James W. Ely Jr., eds. *Ambivalent Legacy: A Legal History of the South*. Jackson: University Press of Mississippi, 1984.
Bohner, Charles H. *John Pendleton Kennedy: Gentleman from Baltimore*. Baltimore: Johns Hopkins University Press, 1961.
Boles, John B. *The Great Revival, 1787–1805: The Origins of the Southern Evangelical Mind*. Lexington: University Press of Kentucky, 1972.
Bolton, Charles C. *Poor Whites of the Antebellum South: Tenants and Laborers in Central North Carolina and Northeast Mississippi*. Durham, N.C.: Duke University Press, 1994.
Bond, Bradley G. *Political Culture in the Nineteenth-Century South: Mississippi, 1830–1900*. Baton Rouge: Louisiana State University Press, 1995.
Booth, Wayne C. *A Rhetoric of Irony*. Chicago: University of Chicago Press, 1974.
———. *The Rhetoric of Fiction*. Chicago: University of Chicago Press, 1961.
Breen, Timothy H. *Tobacco Culture: The Mentality of the Great Tidewater Planters on the Eve of Revolution*. Princeton: Princeton University Press, 1985, 1987.

Brod, Harry, ed. *The Making of Masculinities: The New Men's Studies.* Boston: Allen and Unwin, 1987.

Brown, Thomas. "John Pendleton Kennedy's *Quodlibet* and the Culture of Jacksonian Democracy." *Journal of the Early Republic* 16 (Winter 1996): 625–44.

Bruce, Dickson D., Jr. *Violence and Culture in the Antebellum South.* Austin: University of Texas Press, 1979.

Budd, Louis J. "Gentlemanly Humorists of the Old South." *Southern Folklore Quarterly* 17 (December 1953): 222–40.

Burgett, Bruce. *Sentimental Bodies: Sex, Gender and Citizenship in the Early Republic.* Princeton: Princeton University Press, 1999.

Burton, Orville Vernon. *In My Father's House Are Many Mansions: Family and Community in Edgefield, South Carolina.* Chapel Hill: University of North Carolina Press, 1985.

Carnes, Mark C., and Clyde Griffin, eds. *Meanings for Manhood: Constructions of Masculinity in Victorian America.* Chicago: University of Chicago Press, 1990.

Caron, James E. "Backwoods Civility, or How the Ring-Tailed Roarer Became a Gentle Man for David Crockett, Charles F. M. Noland, and William Tappan Thompson." In *Humor of the Old South*, edited by Inge and Piacentino, 161–86.

———. "Playin' Hell: Sut Lovingood as Durn'd Fool Preacher." In *Sut Lovingood's Nat'ral Born Yarnspinner*, edited by Caron and Inge, 272–98.

Caron, James E., and M. Thomas Inge, eds. *Sut Lovingood's Nat'ral Born Yarnspinner: Essays on George Washington Harris.* Tuscaloosa: University of Alabama Press, 1996.

Cash, W. J. *The Mind of the South.* New York: Vintage Books, 1941.

Cashin, Joan E. *A Family Venture: Men and Women on the Southern Frontier.* New York: Oxford University Press, 1991.

———. "The Structure of Antebellum Planter Families: 'The Ties that Bound Us Was Strong.'" *Journal of Southern History* 56 (February 1990): 55–70.

Cecil-Fronsman, Bill. *Common Whites: Class and Culture in Antebellum North Carolina.* Lexington: University Press of Kentucky, 1992.

Censer, Jane Turner. *North Carolina Planters and Their Children, 1800–1860.* Baton Rouge: Louisiana State University Press, 1984.

———. "Southwestern Migration among North Carolina Planter Families: 'The Disposition to Emigrate.'" *Journal of Southern History* 57 (August 1991): 407–26.

Clinton, Catherine. *The Plantation Mistress: Woman's World in the Old South.* New York: Pantheon Books, 1982.

Cobb, James C. "Does Mind No Longer Matter? The South, the Nation, and *The Mind of the South*, 1941–1991." *Journal of Southern History* 57 (November 1991): 681–718.

Cohen, Hennig, and William B. Dillingham, eds. *Humor of the Old Southwest.* 2nd ed. Athens: University of Georgia Press, 1975.

Corrigan, Robert W., ed. *Comedy: Meaning and Form.* Scranton, Penn.: Chandler Publishing, 1965.

Covici, Pascal, Jr. *Mark Twain's Humor: The Image of a World.* Dallas: Southern Methodist University Press, 1962.

———. "Propriety, Society, and Sut Lovingood: Vernacular Gentility in Action." In *Sut Lovingood's Nat'ral Born Yarnspinner*, edited by Caron and Inge, 246–60.

Cox, James M. "Humor of the Old Southwest." In *The Comic Imagination in American Literature*, edited by Louis D. Rubin Jr., 101–12. New Brunswick, N.J.: Rutgers University Press, 1973.

Craig, Raymond C., ed. *The Humor of Hardin E. Taliaferro.* Knoxville: University of Tennessee Press, 1987.

Dale, Corinne. "William Gilmore Simms's Porgy as Domestic Hero." *Southern Literary Journal* 13 (1980): 55–71.

Davis, Edwin Adams. "Bennet H. Barrow, Ante-Bellum Planter of the Felicianas." *Journal of Southern History* 5 (November 1939): 431–46.

———, ed. *Plantation Life in the Florida Parishes of Louisiana, 1836–1846, as Reflected in the Diary of Bennet H. Barrow.* New York: Columbia University Press, 1943. Reprint, New York: AMS Press, 1967.

Day, Donald. "The Life of George Washington Harris." In *Sut Lovingood's Nat'ral Born Yarnspinner*, edited by Caron and Inge, 33–68.

Dostoevsky, Fyodor. *Notes from Underground.* Translated by Mirra Ginsburg. New York: Bantam, 1992.

Douglas, Mary. "The Social Control of Cognition: Some Factors in Joke Perception." *Man* 3 (1968): 361–76.

Eaton, Clement. *The Mind of the Old South.* Revised edition. Baton Rouge: Louisiana State University Press, 1969.

Elliott, William. *William Elliott's Carolina Sports by Land and Water: Including Incidents of Devil-Fishing, Wild-Cat, Deer, and Bear Hunting, etc.* 1846. Reprinted with an introduction by Theodore Rosengarten. Columbia: University of South Carolina Press, 1994.

Escott, Paul D. *Many Excellent People: Power and Privilege in North Carolina, 1850–1900.* Chapel Hill: University of North Carolina Press, 1985.

Estes, David C. "Folk Humor in Thomas Bangs Thorpe's 'Letters from the Far West.'" *Louisiana Folklore Miscellany* 7 (1992): 50–58.

———. "The Rival Sporting Weeklies of William T. Porter and Thomas Bangs Thorpe." *American Journalism* 2 (1985): 135–43.

———. "Thomas Bangs Thorpe's Backwoods Hunters: Culture Heroes and Humorous Failures." *University of Mississippi Studies in English* 5 (1984–87): 158–71.

Etcheson, Nicole. "Manliness and the Political Culture of the Old Northwest, 1790–1860." *Journal of the Early Republic* 15 (Spring 1995): 60–77.

Fabian, Ann. *Card Sharks, Dream Books, and Bucket Shops: Gambling in 19th-Century America.* Ithaca, N.Y.: Cornell University Press, 1990.

Faust, Drew Gilpin. "The Peculiar South Revisited: White Society, Culture, and Politics in the Antebellum Period, 1800–1860." In *Interpreting Southern History: Historiographical Essays in Honor of Sanford W. Higginbotham*, edited by John B. Boles and Evelyn Thomas Nolen, 78–119. Baton Rouge: Louisiana State University Press, 1987.

———, ed. *The Ideology of Slavery: Proslavery Thought in the Antebellum South, 1830–1860*. Baton Rouge: Louisiana State University Press, 1981.

Feinberg, Lorne. "Colonel Noland of the *Spirit*: The Voices of a Gentleman in Southwest Humor." *American Literature* 53 (May, 1981): 232–45.

Fellman, Michael. "Alligator Men and Cardsharpers: Deadly Southwestern Humor." *Huntington Library Quarterly* 49 (Autumn 1986): 307–23.

Ferguson, Robert A. *Law and Letters in American Culture*. Cambridge, Mass.: Harvard University Press, 1984.

Filene, Peter G. *Him/Her/Self: Gender Identities in Modern America*. 3rd ed. Baltimore: Johns Hopkins University Press, 1974, 1998.

Fitzgerald, Oscar Penn. *Judge Longstreet: A Life Sketch*. Nashville: Barber and Smith, 1891.

Flynt, J. Wayne. *Dixie's Forgotten People: The South's Poor Whites*. Bloomington: Indiana University Press, 1979.

Ford, Lacy K., Jr. *Origins of Southern Radicalism: The South Carolina Upcountry, 1800–1860*. New York: Oxford University Press, 1988.

Fox-Genovese, Elizabeth, and Eugene D. Genovese. *Fruits of Merchant Capital: Slavery and Bourgeois Property in the Rise and Expansion of Capitalism*. New York: Oxford University Press, 1983.

Fox-Genovese, Elizabeth, and Eugene D. Genovese. *The Mind of the Master Class: History and Faith in the Southern Slaveholders' Worldview*. New York: Cambridge University Press, 2005.

Friedman, Jean E. *The Enclosed Garden: Women and Community in the Evangelical South, 1830–1900*. Chapel Hill: University of North Carolina Press, 1985.

Friend, Craig Thompson, and Lorri Glover, eds. *Southern Manhood: Perspectives on Masculinity in the Old South*. Athens: University of Georgia Press, 2004.

Garner, Stanton. "Thomas Bangs Thorpe in the Gilded Age: Shifty in a New Country." *Mississippi Quarterly* 36 (Winter 1982–83): 35–52.

Gebhard, Caroline. "Reconstructing Southern Manhood: Race, Sentimentality, and Camp in the Plantation Myth." In *Haunted Bodies*, edited by Jones and Donaldson, 132–55. Charlottesville: University Press of Virginia, 1997.

Genovese, Eugene. *The Political Economy of Slavery*. New York: Pantheon Books, 1961.

———. *The Slaveholders' Dilemma: Freedom and Progress in Southern Conservative Thought, 1820–1860*. Columbia, S.C.: University of South Carolina Press, 1992.

———. "Yeoman Farmers in a Slaveholding Democracy." *Agricultural History* 49 (1975): 331–42.

Glover, Lorri. *All Our Relations: Blood Ties and Emotional Bonds among the Early South Carolina Gentry.* Baltimore: Johns Hopkins University Press, 2000.

———. "An Education in Southern Masculinity: The Ball Family of South Carolina in the New Republic." *Journal of Southern History* 69 (February 2003): 39–70.

Gorn, Elliott J. "'Gouge and Bite, Pull Hair and Scratch': The Social Significance of Fighting in the Southern Backcountry." *American Historical Review* 90 (February 1985): 18–43.

Grammer, John M. *Pastoral and Politics in the Old South.* Baton Rouge: Louisiana State University Press, 1996.

Gray, Richard. *Writing the South: Ideas of an American Region.* New York: Cambridge University Press, 1986.

Green, Edwin L. *George McDuffie.* Columbia, S.C.: The State Company, 1936.

Green, Fletcher M. *The Role of the Yankee in the Old South.* Athens: University of Georgia Press, 1972.

Greenberg, Kenneth S. *Honor and Slavery: Lies, Duels, Noses, Masks, Dressing as a Woman, Gifts, Strangers, Humanitarianism, Death, Slave Rebellions, The Pro-Slavery Argument, Baseball, Hunting, and Gambling in the Old South.* Princeton: Princeton University Press, 1996.

Griffith, Nancy S. *Humor of the Old Southwest: An Annotated Bibliography of Primary and Secondary Sources.* New York: Greenwood Press, 1989.

Gross, Theodore L. *The Heroic Ideal in American Literature.* New York: Free Press, 1971.

Grossberg, Michael. "Institutionalizing Masculinity: The Law as a Masculine Profession." In *Meanings for Manhood: Constructions of Masculinity in Victorian America*, edited by Mark C. Carnes and Clyde Griffin. Chicago: University of Chicago Press, 1990.

Hahn, Steven. *The Roots of Southern Populism: Yeoman Farmers and the Transformation of the Georgia Upcountry, 1850–1890.* New York: Oxford University Press, 1983.

Halttunen, Karen. *Confidence Men and Painted Women: A Study of Middle-class Culture in America, 1830–1870.* New Haven: Yale University Press, 1982.

Harris, J. William. *Plain Folk and Gentry in a Slave Society: White Liberty and Black Slavery in Augusta's Hinterlands.* Middletown, Conn.: Wesleyan University Press, 1985.

Hauck, Richard B. *A Cheerful Nihilism: Confidence and 'The Absurd' in American Humorous Fiction.* Bloomington: Indiana University Press, 1971.

Hayne, Barrie. "Yankee in the Patriarchy: T.B. Thorpe's Reply to *Uncle Tom's Cabin.*" *American Quarterly* 20 (Summer 1968): 180–95.

Higgs, Robert J. "The Sublime and the Beautiful: The Meaning of Sport in Collected Sketches of Thomas B. Thorpe." *Southern Studies* 25 (Fall 1986): 235–56.

Hirschkop, Ken, and David Sheperd, eds. *Bakhtin and Cultural Theory.* Manchester, England: Manchester University Press, 1989.

Hoole, William Stanley. *Alias Simon Suggs: The Life and Times of Johnson Jones Hooper*. Tuscaloosa: University of Alabama Press, 1952.
Horwitz, Morton. *The Transformation of American Law, 1790–1860*. Cambridge, Mass.: Harvard University Press, 1977.
Hubbell, Jay B. *The South in American Literature: 1607–1900*. Raleigh, N.C.: Duke University Press, 1954.
Hudson, Arthur Palmer, ed. *Humor of the Old Deep South*. New York: Macmillan, 1936.
Hundley, D[aniel] R., Esq. *Social Relations in Our Southern States*. New York: Henry B. Price, 1860.
Inge, M. Thomas, ed. *The Frontier Humorists: Critical Views*. Hampden, Conn.: Archon Books, 1975.
Inge, M. Thomas, and Edward J. Piacentino, eds. *The Humor of the Old South*. Lexington: University Press of Kentucky, 2001.
Inscoe, John C. *Mountain Masters: Slavery and the Sectional Crisis in Western North Carolina*. Knoxville: University of Tennessee Press, 1989.
Isaac, Rhys. *The Transformation of Virginia, 1740–1790*. Chapel Hill: Published for Omohundro Institute of Early American History and Culture by University of North Carolina Press, 1999.
Israel, Charles. "Henry Clay Lewis's *Odd Leaves*: Studies in the Surreal and Grotesque." *Mississippi Quarterly* 28 (1975): 61–69.
Jones, Anne Goodwyn. "The Work of Gender in the Southern Renaissance." In *Southern Writers and Their Worlds*, edited by Christopher Morris and Stephen G. Reinhardt, 41–56. College Station: Texas A&M University Press, 1996.
Jones, Anne Goodwyn, and Susan V. Donaldson. *Haunted Bodies: Gender and Southern Texts*. Charlottesville: University Press of Virginia, 1997.
Justus, James H. *Fetching the Old Southwest: Humorous Writing from Longstreet to Twain*. Columbia: University of Missouri Press, 2004.
Karcher, Carolyn L. *Shadow over the Promised Land: Slavery, Race, and Violence in Melville's America*. Baton Rouge: Louisiana State University Press, 1980.
Keller, Mark A. "'Aesculapius in Buckskin': The Swamp Doctor as Satirist in Henry Clay Lewis's *Odd Leaves*." *Southern Studies* 18 (1979): 425–48.
Kelly, Aileen. "Revealing Bakhtin." *The New York Review of Books*, September 24, 1992: 44–48.
Kilbride, Daniel. *An American Aristocracy: Southern Planters in Antebellum Philadelphia*. Columbia: University of South Carolina Press, 2006.
Kimmel, Michael. *Manhood in America: A Cultural History*. New York: Free Press, 1996.
King, Kimball. *Augustus Baldwin Longstreet*. Boston: Twayne, 1984.
Kreyling, Michael. "The Hero in Antebellum Southern Narrative." *Southern Literary Journal* 16 (1984): 3–20.
Kuhlmann, Susan. *Knave, Fool, and Genius: The Confidence Man as He Appears in Nineteenth-Century American Fiction*. Chapel Hill: University of North Carolina Press, 1973.

Lachmann, Renate. "Bakhtin and Carnival: Culture as Counter-Culture." *Cultural Critique* (Winter 1988): 115–52.
Lebsock, Suzanne. *The Free Women of Petersburg: Status and Culture in a Southern Town, 1784–1860*. New York: W. W. Norton, 1984.
Lemay, J. A. Leo. "The Text, Tradition, and Themes of 'The Big Bear of Arkansas.'" *American Literature* 47 (1975): 321–42.
Lenz, William E. *Fast Talk and Flush Times: The Confidence Man as a Literary Convention*. Columbia: University of Missouri Press, 1985.
———. "The Function of Women in Old Southwestern Humor: Rereading Porter's *Big Bear* and *Quarter Race* Collections." In *Humor of the Old South*, edited by Inge and Piacentino, 36–51.
Lepore, Jill. *The Name of War: King Philip's War and the Origins of American Identity*. New York: Knopf, 1998.
Leverenz, David. *Manhood and the American Renaissance*. Ithaca, N.Y.: Cornell University Press, 1989.
———. "Poe and Gentry Virginia: Provincial Gentleman, Textual Aristocrat, Man of the Crowd." In *Haunted Bodies*, edited by Jones and Donaldson, 79–108.
Littlefield, Daniel F., Jr. "Thomas Bangs Thorpe and the Passing of the Southwestern Wilderness." *Southern Literary Journal* 11 (1979): 56–65.
Luckenbill, David F., and Daniel P. Doyle. "Structural Position and Violence: Developing a Cultural Explanation." *Criminology* 27 (1989): 419–36.
Lynn, Kenneth S. *The Comic Tradition in America: An Anthology of American Humor*. Garden City, N.Y.: Doubleday Anchor, 1958, 1959.
———. *Mark Twain and Southwestern Humor*. Boston: Little, Brown, 1959.
MacKeithan, Lucinda H. "Domesticity in Dixie: The Plantation Novel and *Uncle Tom's Cabin*." In *Haunted Bodies*, edited by Jones and Donaldson, 223–42.
Mangan, J. A., and James Walvin, eds. *Manliness and Morality: Middle-class Masculinity in Britain and America, 1800–1940*. New York: St. Martin's, 1987.
Martin, Gretchen. "The Prison House of Gender: Masculine Confinement and Escape in Southwestern Humor." In *Humor of the Old South*, edited by Inge and Piacentino, 87–100.
Mayer, Kurt Albert. "Augustan Nostalgia and Patrician Disdain in A. B. Longstreet's *Georgia Scenes*." In *Humor of the Old South*, edited by Inge and Piacentino, 101–12.
Mayfield, John. "Being Shifty in a New Country: Southern Humor and the Masculine Ideal." In *Southern Manhood: Perspectives on Masculinity in the Old South*, edited by Friend and Glover, 113–35.
———. "George Washington Harris: The Fool from the Hills." In *The Human Tradition in Antebellum America*, edited by Michael A. Morrison, 229–43. Wilmington, Del.: Scholarly Resources Inc., 2000.
———. "'The Soul of a Man!': William Gilmore Simms and the Myths of Southern Manhood." *Journal of the Early Republic* 15 (Fall 1995): 477–500.

———. "The Theater of Public Esteem: Ethics and Values in Longstreet's *Georgia Scenes*." *Georgia Historical Quarterly* 75 (Fall 1991): 566–86.
McCardell, John. "Biography and the Southern Mind: William Gilmore Simms." In *"Long Years of Neglect": The Work and Reputation of William Gilmore Simms*, edited by John C. Guilds, 202–16. Fayetteville: University of Arkansas Press, 1988.
———. "Poetry and the Practical: William Gilmore Simms." In *Intellectual Life in Antebellum Charleston*, edited by Michael O'Brien and David Moltke-Hansen, 186–210. Knoxville: University of Tennessee Press, 1986.
McCurry, Stephanie. *Masters of Small Worlds: Yeoman Households, Gender Relations and the Political Culture of the Antebellum South Carolina Low Country*. New York: Oxford University Press, 1995.
———. "The Politics of Yeoman Households in South Carolina." In *Divided Houses: Gender and the Civil War*, edited by Catherine Clinton and Nina Silber, 22–38. New York: Oxford University Press, 1992.
McDermott, John Francis. "T. B. Thorpe's Burlesque of Far West Sporting Travel." *American Quarterly* 10 (Summer 1958): 175–80.
Meriwether, James B. "Augustus Baldwin Longstreet: Realist and Artist." *Mississippi Quarterly* 35 (Fall 1982): 351–64.
Miller, James David. *South by Southwest: Planter Emigration and Identity in the Slave South*. Charlottesville: University of Virginia Press, 2002.
Miller, William Ian. *Humiliation: and Other Essays on Honor, Social Discomfort, and Violence*. Ithaca, N.Y.: Cornell University Press, 1993.
Morris, Christopher. "What's So Funny?: Southern Humorists and the Market Revolution." In *Southern Writers and Their Worlds*, edited by Christopher Morris and Stephen G. Reinhardt, 9–26. College Station: Texas A&M University Press, 1996.
Newlin, Keith. "*Georgia Scenes*: The Satiric Artistry of Augustus Baldwin Longstreet." *Mississippi Quarterly* 41 (Winter 1987–88): 21–37.
Noland, Charles Fenton Mercer. *Cavorting on the Devil's Fork: The Pete Whetstone Letters of C.F.M. Noland*. Edited with an introduction by Leonard Williams. Fayetteville: University of Arkansas Press, 2006.
Oakes, James. *The Ruling Race: A History of American Slaveholders*. New York: Alfred A. Knopf, 1982, 1983.
O'Brien, Michael. *Conjectures of Order: Intellectual Life and the American South, 1810–1860*. 2 vols. Chapel Hill: University of North Carolina Press, 2004.
———. *Placing the South*. Jackson: University Press of Mississippi, 2007.
———. *Rethinking the South: Essays in Intellectual History*. Baltimore: Johns Hopkins University Press, 1988.
Olsen, Christopher J. *Political Culture and Secession in Mississippi: Masculinity, Honor, and the Antiparty Tradition, 1830–1860*. New York: Oxford University Press, 2000.
Oriard, Michael. "Shifty in a New Country: Games in Southwestern Humor." *Southern Literary Journal* 12 (1980): 14.

———. *Sporting with the Gods: The Rhetoric of Play and Game in American Culture*. New York: Cambridge University Press, 1991.
Oring, Elliott. *Israeli Humor: The Content and Structure of the Chizbat of the Palmah*. Albany: State University of New York Press, 1981.
———. *Jokes and Their Relations*. Lexington: University Press of Kentucky, 1992.
———, ed. *Folk Groups and Folklore Genres*. Logan: Utah State University Press, 1986.
Ownby, Ted. *Subduing Satan: Religion, Recreation, and Manhood in the Rural South, 1865–1920*. Chapel Hill: University of North Carolina Press, 1990.
Padgett, James A. "The West Florida Revolution of 1810, as Told in the Letters of John Rhea, Fulwar Skipwith, Reuben Kemper, and Others." *Louisiana Historical Quarterly* 21 (January 1938):3–41.
Parks, Edd Winfield. "The Three Streams of Southern Humor." *Georgia Review* 9 (Summer 1955): 147–59.
Parrington, Vernon Louis. *Main Currents in American Thought: An Interpretation of American Literature from the Beginnings to 1920*. 3 vols. New York: Harcourt, Brace, 1927, 1930.
Perry, Alice Hall. "The Common Doom: Thorpe's 'The Big Bear of Arkansas.'" *Southern Quarterly* 10 (1958): 24–31.
Piacentino, Edward J. "Contesting the Boundaries of Race and Gender in Old Southwestern Humor." In *Humor of the Old South*, edited by Inge and Piacentino, 52–71.
Pitt-Rivers, Julian. "Honor and Social Status." In *Honour and Shame*, edited by J. Péristiany. Chicago: University of Chicago Press, 1966: 19–77.
Polk, Noel. "The Blind Bull, Human Nature: Sut Lovingood and the Damned Human Race." In *Sut Lovingood's Nat'ral Born Yarnspinner*, edited by Caron and Inge, 148–75.
Porter, William T., ed. *The Big Bear of Arkansas, and Other Sketches, Illustrative of Characters and Incidents in the South and South-West*. Philadelphia: T. B. Peterson, 1843. Reprint, New York: AMS Press, 1973.
———, ed. *A Quarter Race in Kentucky, and Other Sketches, Illustrative of Scenes, Characters, and Incidents, Throughout "The Universal Yankee Nation."* Philadelphia: Carey and Hart, 1847. Reprint, New York: AMS Press, 1973.
Proctor, Nicholas W. *Bathed in Blood: Hunting and Mastery in the Old South*. Charlottesville: University Press of Virginia, 2002.
Pugh, David G. *Sons of Liberty: The Masculine Mind in Nineteenth-Century America*. Westport, Conn.: Greenwood Press, 1983.
Quist, John W. *Restless Visionaries: The Social Roots of Antebellum Reform in Alabama and Michigan*. Baton Rouge: Louisiana State University Press, 1998.
Rachels, David. "A Biographical Reading of A. B. Longstreet's *Georgia Scenes*." In *Humor of the Old South*, edited by Inge and Piacentino, 113–28.
Rickels, Milton. *George Washington Harris*. New York: Twayne, 1965.
———. "George Washington Harris." In *American Humorists, 1800–1950*, edited by Stanley Trachtenberg, 180–88. Detroit: Gale Research, 1982.

———. "The Grotesque Body of Southwestern Humor." In *Critical Essays on American Humor*, edited by William Bedford Clark and W. Craig Turner, 155–66. Boston: G. K. Hall, 1984.

———. *Thomas Bangs Thorpe, Humorist of the Old Southwest*. Baton Rouge: Louisiana State University Press, 1962.

Ridgely, Joseph V. *John Pendleton Kennedy*. New York: Twayne, 1966.

———. *William Gilmore Simms*. New York: Twayne Publishers, 1962.

Romine, Scott. "Darkness Visible: Race and Pollution in Southwestern Humor." In *Humor of the Old South*, edited by Inge and Piacentino, 72–83.

———. *The Narrative Forms of Southern Community*. Baton Rouge: Louisiana State University Press, 1999.

Rose, Alan. *Demonic Vision: Racial Fantasy and Southern Fiction*. Hampden, Conn.: Archon, 1976.

———. "The Image of the Negro in the Writings of Henry Clay Lewis." *American Literature* 41 (May 1969): 255–63.

Rosengarten, Theodore. *Tombee: Portrait of a Cotton Planter, with the Journal of Thomas B. Chaplin*. New York: Quill/William Morrow, 1992.

Rotundo, Anthony. *American Manhood: Transformations in Masculinity from the Revolution to the Modern Era*. New York: Basic Books, 1993.

Rourke, Constance M. *American Humor: A Study of the National Character*. New York: Harcourt Brace Jovanovich, 1931, 1959.

Rozbicki, Michal J. *The Complete Colonial Gentleman: Cultural Legitimacy in Plantation America*. Charlottesville: University Press of Virginia, 1998.

Rubin, Louis D., Jr. *The Edge of the Swamp: A Study in the Literature and Society of the Old South*. Baton Rouge: Louisiana State University Press, 1989.

———. *The Teller in the Tale*. Seattle: University of Washington Press, 1967.

———. *William Elliott Shoots a Bear: Essays on the Southern Literary Imagination*. Baton Rouge: Louisiana State University Press, 1975.

Ryan, Mary P. *Cradle of the Middle Class: The Family in Oneida County, New York, 1790–1865*. New York: Cambridge University Press, 1981.

Scafidel, James R., ed. "The Letters of Augustus Baldwin Longstreet." Ph.D. diss., University of South Carolina, 1977.

Shields, Johanna Nicol. "A Sadder Simon Suggs: Freedom and Slavery in the Humor of Johnson Hooper." *Journal of Southern History* 56 (November 1990): 641–64.

Shore, Laurence. *Southern Capitalists: The Ideological Leadership of an Elite, 1832–1885*. Chapel Hill: University of North Carolina Press, 1986.

Simms, William Gilmore. "The Humourous in American and British Literature." In *Views and Reviews in American Literature, History and Fiction*, edited by William Gilmore Simms, 142–84. 2nd series. New York: Wiley and Putnam, 1845.

Simpson, Lewis P. *The Dispossessed Garden: Pastoral and History in Southern Literature*. Athens: University of Georgia Press, 1975.

Skaggs, Merrill Maguire. *The Folk of Southern Fiction*. Athens: University of Georgia Press, 1972.

Slotkin, Richard. *The Fatal Environment: The Myth of the Frontier in the Age of Industrialization, 1800–1860*. New York: Atheneum, 1985. Reprint, New York: Harper-Perennial, 1994.

———. *Regeneration Through Violence: The Mythology of the American Frontier, 1600–1860*. Norman: University of Oklahoma Press, 1973.

Smith-Rosenberg, Carroll. *Disorderly Conduct: Visions of Gender in Victorian America*. New York: Oxford University Press, 1985.

Somers, Paul, Jr. *Johnson J. Hooper*. Boston: Twayne, 1984.

Stewart, Randall. "Tidewater and Frontier." In *The Frontier Humorists: Critical Views*, edited by M. Thomas Inge, 281–91. Hampden, Conn.: Archon, 1975.

Stewart, Samuel B. "Joseph Glover Baldwin." Ph.D. diss., Vanderbilt University, 1941.

Stowe, Steven M. *Doctoring the South: Southern Physicians and Everyday Medicine in the Mid-Nineteenth Century*. Chapel Hill: University of North Carolina Press, 2004.

———. *Intimacy and Power in the Old South: Ritual in the Lives of the Planters*. Baltimore: Johns Hopkins University Press, 1987.

———. "Seeing Themselves at Work: Physicians and the Case Narrative in the Mid-Nineteenth-Century South." *American Historical Review* 101 (February 1996): 41–79.

Sydnor, Charles S. *American Revolutionaries in the Making: Political Practices in Washington's Virginia*. 1952. New York: Free Press, 1965.

Sypher, Wylie. "The Meanings of Comedy." In *Comedy: Meaning and Form*, edited by Robert W. Corrigan, 18–60. Scranton, Pa.: Chandler Publishing, 1965.

Taliaferro, Hardin, E. *The Humor of H. E. Taliaferro*. Edited with an introduction by Raymond C. Craig. Knoxville: University of Tennessee Press, 1987.

Tandy, Jennette. *Crackerbox Philosophers in American Humor and Satire*. New York: Columbia University Press, 1925. Reprint, Port Wasthington, N.Y.: Kennikat Press, 1964.

Tate, Adam L. *Conservatism and Southern Intellectuals, 1789–1861: Liberty, Tradition, and the Good Society*. Columbia: University of Missouri Press, 2005.

———. "From Humor to History: Joseph Glover Baldwin and *Party Leaders*." *Alabama Review* 60.2 (2007): 83–110.

Taylor, William R. *Cavalier and Yankee: The Old South and American National Character*. New York: Harper Torchbooks, 1961, 1969.

Thompson, William Tappan. *Major Jones's Chronicles of Pineville*. Facsimile of 1843 edition. Upper Saddle River, N.J.: Gregg Publishers, 1969.

———. *Major Jones's Courtship. Detailed, with Humorous Scenes, Incidents and Adventures*. Philadelphia: T. B. Peterson and Brothers, 1844, 1879.

Thornton, J. Mills, III. *Politics and Power in a Slave Society: Alabama 1800–1860*. Baton Rouge: Louisiana State University Press, 1978.

Thorp, Willard. "Suggs and Sut in Modern Dress: The Latest Chapter in Southern Humor." *Mississippi Quarterly* 13 (1960): 169–75.
Toews, John E. "Intellectual History after the Linguistic Turn: The Autonomy of Meaning and the Irreducibility of Experience." *American Historical Review* 92 (October 1987): 879–907.
Tompkins, Jane. *Sensational Designs: The Cultural Work of American Fiction, 1790–1860.* New York: Oxford University Press, 1985.
———. "The Reader in History: The Changing Shape of Literary Response." In *Reader-Response Criticism: From Formalism to Post-Structuralism*, edited by Jane Tompkins, 201–26. Baltimore: Johns Hopkins University Press, 1980.
Turner, Victor W. *The Ritual Process: Structure and Anti-structure.* Chicago: Aldine Publishing, 1969.
Wade, John Donald. *Augustus Baldwin Longstreet: A Study of the Development of Culture in the South.* New York: Macmillan, 1924.
Walker, Nancy. "Sut and His Sisters: Vernacular Humor and Genteel Culture." In *Sut Lovingood's Nat'ral Born Yarnspinner*, edited by Caron and Inge, 261–71.
———. *A Very Serious Thing: Women's Humor and American Culture.* Minneapolis: University of Minnesota Press, 1988.
Walker, Nancy A., and Zita Dresner. "Women's Humor in America." In *What's So Funny: Humor in American Culture*, edited by Nancy A. Walker, 171–84. Wilmington, Del.: Scholarly Resources, 1998.
Warner, John Harley. "The Idea of Southern Medical Distinctiveness: Medical Knowledge and Practice in the Old South." In *Science and Medicine in the Old South*, edited by Ronald L. Numbers and Todd L. Savitt. Baton Rouge: Louisiana State University Press, 1989.
Watson, Ritchie Devon, Jr. *Yeoman Versus Cavalier: The Old Southwest's Fictional Road to Rebellion.* Baton Rouge: Louisiana State University Press, 1993.
Watts, Edward. "In the Midst of a Noisome Swamp: The Landscape of Henry Clay Lewis." *Southern Literary Journal* 22 (1990): 119–28.
Watts, Steven. "Masks, Morals, and the Market: American Literature and Early Capitalist Culture, 1790–1820." *Journal of the Early Republic* 6 (Summer 1986): 126–48.
Wells, Jonathan Daniel. *The Origins of the Southern Middle Class, 1800–1861.* Chapel Hill: University of North Carolina Press, 2004.
Williams, Benjamin Buford. *A Literary History of Alabama: The Nineteenth Century.* Cranbury, N.J.: Associated University Presses, 1979.
Wilson, Edmund. *Patriotic Gore: Studies in the Literature of the American Civil War.* New York: Oxford University Press, 1966.
Wilson, John Lyde. *Code of Honor, or Rules for the Government of Principals and Seconds in Duelling.* Charleston, S.C.: Printed by T. J. Eccles, 1838.
Wimsatt, Mary Ann. "Bench and Bar: Baldwin's Lawyerly Humor." In *Humor of the Old South*, edited by Inge and Piacentino, 187–98.

———. *The Major Fiction of William Gilmore Simms: Cultural Traditions and Literary Form.* Baton Rouge: Louisiana State University Press, 1989.
Wirt, William. *Sketches of the Life and Character of Patrick Henry.* Revised ed. Ithaca, N.Y.: Mack, Andrus, 1818, 1845.
Woodward, C. Vann. *American Counterpoint: Slavery and Racism in the North-South Dialogue.* Boston: Little, Brown, 1971.
Wright, Gavin. *The Political Economy of the Cotton South: Households, Markets, and Wealth in the Nineteenth Century.* New York: W. W. Norton, 1978.
Wyatt-Brown, Bertram. *Hearts of Darkness: Wellsprings of a Southern Literary Tradition.* Baton Rouge: Louisiana State University Press, 2002.
———. *The House of Percy: Honor, Melancholy, and Imagination in a Southern Family.* New York: Oxford University Press, 1994.
———. *The Shaping of Southern Culture: Honor, Grace, and War, 1760s–1880s.* Chapel Hill: University of North Carolina Press, 2001.
———. *Southern Honor: Ethics and Behavior in the Old South.* New York: Oxford University Press, 1982.
Yates, Norris W. *William T. Porter and the Spirit of the Times: A Study of the Big Bear School of Humor.* Baton Rouge: Louisiana State University Press, 1957.
Young, Jeffrey Robert. *Domesticating Slavery: The Master Class in Georgia and South Carolina, 1670–1837.* Chapel Hill: University of North Carolina Press, 1999.

Index

Abbeville, S.C., 31
Abolition and abolitionists, 35, 61, 81, 105, 114, 123
Adams, Henry, 13
Addison, Richard, xx
Adventures of Captain Simon Suggs (Hooper), 52, 55–60, 135n9
Agriculture. *See* Cotton; Tobacco
Ahab (fictional character), 71
Alabama: civil code of, 66; cotton in, 54, 60; David Hundley in, xvi; as frontier, 48–49, 52; gentlemen in, 78; George Washington Harris in, 112, 127; Johnson Jones Hooper in, xxi, 48, 54; Joseph Glover Baldwin in, xxi, 16, 48, 60, 66, 78; literary depictions of, 58, 78; and migration, 2; planters in, 60; politics in, 56, 59, 60–61; southwest, 61; state bank of, 64; Virginians in, 61
Albany, N.Y., 69
Alias Simon Suggs... (Hoole), 135n9
Allen, James Lane, 126
Alligator-men and alligator-wrasslers: Augustus Baldwin Longstreet and, 47; John Pendleton Kennedy and, 20; Johnson Jones Hooper and, xxv; Joseph Glover Baldwin and, xxv, 50;

mentioned, xiii, 70; during Reconstruction, 125; Thomas Bangs Thorpe and, 68, 73, 76–77
"Alligator Men and Cardsharpers..." (Fellman), 135n7
Ambrose, Paul (pseudonym for John Pendleton Kennedy), 139n1
American Renaissance, 87
Anderson, John Q., 84, 138n11
Anglicans, 30, 119
Animals: alligators, 53; bears, 68, 71, 73, 74, 77, 78, 85, 100, 104; birds, 73, 75, 76; buffalo, 68, 72, 75, 77; cattle, 107, 117; deer, 67, 68, 71, 75; devilfish, 75; dogs, 17, 59, 68, 73, 76, 84, 117, 127; falcons, 20, 21; fish, 71, 78; foxes, 29, 39, 71; game, 73; geese, 25, 26, 29, 39; hogs, 34; mastery over, 71; mules, 85; panthers, 100, 101; pigs, 63; quail, 59; woodcocks, 76. *See also* Horses
Appomattox, Va., 4
Arator (Taylor), 14
Arkansas, 51, 74, 78
Arnold, Edwin T., 85, 86, 102
Art of Courtly Love (Capellanus), 20
Athens, Ga., 36
Atlanta Constitution, 125

157

Augusta, Ga.: Augustus Baldwin Longstreet in, 25, 33, 34, 36, 80, 88; businesses in, 30, 33; and class, 32; debt in, 36; description of, 30–32; and Great Revival, 32; masquerade culture in, 31; mentioned, 27, 37; theater in, 30, 31; and violence, 31
Augusta, Maine, 37
Augusta Chronicle, 35
Augustus Baldwin Longstreet (King), 133n13
"Augustus Baldwin Longstreet" (Meriwether), 133n13
Austen, Jane, 43–44

Bakhtin, Mikhail, 108, 138n8
"Bakhtin and Carnival ..." (Lachmann), 138n9
Bakhtin and Cultural Theory (Hirschkop and Sheperd), 138n8
Bakker, Jan, 22
Baldwin, Joseph Glover: biography/personal life of, 16, 48, 50, 60–62, 65–66, 87, 127; and frontier, 49, 52, 55; and language, xxvi, 65; and law, 62, 92; and leadership, 60–61; as leading Southern humorist, xx–xxi; literary techniques of, 87; on manhood, 65; and market/evangelical culture, 51, 60; mentioned, 70, 78; and politics, 60–61; scholarship on, 135n19, 136n22; and Seargeant S. Prentiss, 78; in Virginia, xxi, 62; works by, xx, xxv–xxvi, xxvii, 65, 85
Baltimore, Md., 7, 8, 10, 123
Baptists, 30, 32, 53, 58
Barrow, Bennet, 69–70, 71, 77, 80, 81
Bathed in Blood ... (Proctor), 136n8
Baton Rouge, La., 69, 70
Bayou Despair, La., 89
Bear-eaters and bear-wrasslers, xiii, xxvi, 39, 68
"Being Shifty in a New Country ..." (Mayfield), 134n38, 138n9
Bell, Samuel, 110–11
Bergson, Henri, xxi, 26

Berry, Stephen, 86, 103, 124
Biedler, Philip, 135n17
Bier, Jesse, xx, xxii, xxiii, 26, 138n16
"Big Bear of Arkansas, The" (Thorpe), 1, 68, 73–74, 75, 77, 137n13
Blacks, xiv, xxiv, 58, 98, 102–3. *See also* Slavery; Slaves
Blackstone, William, 16
Bohner, Charles H., 131n6
Boston, Mass., 123
Boyhood, 19, 24, 55. *See also* Manhood
Brace, Ned (fictional character), 37, 52, 53. *See also Georgia Scenes* (Longstreet)
Bracebridge Hall (Irving), 5
Brooks, Preston, xxviii, 30, 106
Bruce, Dickson David, 21
Buchanan, James, 113
Burruss, John William, 69
Burton, Vernon, 31
Butler, Benjamin, 82

Caldwell, Erskine, 40
Calhoun, John C., 30–31, 33, 34, 35
Caliban, 108–9, 110
California, 66, 107, 127
Calvin (slave), 90
Calvin, John, 64
Calvinists, 53
Cane Ridge, Ky., 58
Card Sharks, Dream Books, and Bucket Shops (Fabian), 135n7
Carolina cavaliers. *See* Cavaliers
Carolinas, 49, 50, 76, 88
Carolina Sports (Elliott), 71, 75
Carolina sportsmen, 52, 54, 125
Caron, James E., 138n3, 139n12, 139n21
Caruthers, William Alexander, 3, 6
Cashin, Joan, 20, 55, 97
Catholics, 60
Cavalier and Yankee ... (Taylor), 131n4, 132n32
Cavaliers: characteristics of, 59; and display, 32; evolution of, 126; literary foils for, 43; as literary type, xvi, xix, 1, 105–6, 107; and migration, 72; in *Odd*

Leaves, 100; as post-war icon, 113; in *Swallow Barn*, 20, 23. *See also* Virginia gentleman
Censer, Jane Turner, 135n13
Cervantes, Miguel de, 3
Chaplin, Thomas B., 57
Charles River Bridge (legal case), 18
Charleston, S.C., 48, 88
Cheerful Nihilism, A, . . . (Hauck), 135n7
Cherokees, xiv, 18, 31, 49. *See also* Indians
Chevaliers and chivalry, 19, 20, 23, 125
Chevalresque, 124
Chicago, Ill., xvi
Choctaws, 49. *See also* Cherokees; Indians
Cincinnati, Ohio, 88, 96, 111
Civil War: Augustus Baldwin Longstreet and, 47; causes of, 124; and cavalier myth, 113; and evangelical culture, 113; George Washington Harris and, 112, 114; John Pendleton Kennedy and, 123–24, 127; literature before and after, xix, 7, 107, 122; and manhood, xv, xxiv, 124–25, 127; and masquerade culture, 124; mentioned, 82; middle class and, xxiii; and New South, 29; perspectives after, 21; and slavery, 123
Class: as boundary, 98; and cotton cultivation, 31, 34, 42, 76; and debt, 35, 42; elites, 5, 12–14, 21, 24, 27, 31, 32, 35, 42, 46, 49, 72, 73, 88, 123, 125; and evangelical culture, 29, 44; fluidity of, 31, 42; on frontier, 5, 50; in *Georgia Scenes*, 25, 26, 27, 28, 29, 40–41, 42; and honor, 31; and humor, xxii; and hunting, 31, 71–73, 75–78; and language, 29, 50–52; lawyers and, 91; lower/common, 13, 27, 29, 32, 39–40, 45–46, 49, 50, 71, 73, 75, 80, 125–26; and manhood, xv, 6, 7, 12–14; and marketplace and market/evangelical culture, 29, 44, 45, 86; and masquerade culture, 28, 31, 44; middle/bourgeoisie, xxiii, 27, 28, 29, 31, 32, 47, 58, 60, 62, 111, 114, 133n10; and migration, 5, 50; and occupation, 50,

86, 91–92; and patriarchy, 6, 13, 27; and Reconstruction, 125; and religion, 32; salt-river roarers and, 50; scholarship on, xiii–xiv, xvi–xvii, 29, 86, 133n10; and slavery, 3, 4, 22, 32, 49; and social rituals, 31, 42; Southern humorists and, xxiii; and sports, 117; in *Swallow Barn*, 40; and tobacco cultivation, 31; and upward mobility, 30, 44, 50, 55, 69, 75, 86; and violence, 31, 40, 75–76; and virtue, 42; William Wirt on, 3–4; women and, 43. *See also* Elites; Planters; Virginia gentleman
Clay, Henry, 10, 52, 65
Clemens, Samuel. *See* Twain, Mark
Cohen, Hennig, 130n13, 130n17, 130n19
College of South Carolina, 35, 47
Comedy: Meaning and Form (Corrigan), 130n18, 132n8
Competition: Augustus Baldwin Longstreet and, 34; on frontier, 57, 72; and gender, 43; and law, 62; and manhood, xv, xviii, xxi, 19, 46, 65, 109; and partisanship, 65; and sports, 39; and violence, 39
Confederacy, 60, 125
Confidence Man (Melville), 135n7
Confidence Men and Painted Women . . . (Halttunen), 135n7
Congress, U.S., 9. *See also* Senate, U.S.
Conjectures of Order . . . (O'Brien), 129n2, 131n20
Con men: characteristics and definitions of, 37, 38, 52, 65, 91; gentlemen as, 78; and language, xxvi, 51–52, 56, 94; lawyers as, 63; and mastery, 51, 56, 57, 58; mentioned, xxv; and modernity, 51; prominence of, 47; scholarship on, 135n7; and tradition, 51. *See also* Suggs, Simon (fictional character)
Conservatism and Southern Intellectuals, 1789–1861 . . . (Tate), 136n22
Cooper, 59, 72
Cordon sanitaire, xxii, 11, 26, 29, 131n17
Corrigan, Robert W., 130n18, 132n8

Index 159

Cotton: in Alabama, 54; Andrew Jackson and, 14; in Black Belt, 54; and class, xvi, 31, 32, 34, 42, 49, 51, 57, 61, 67, 73, 90; gentlemen and, 76; in Georgia, 30, 31, 36; Henry Clay Lewis and, 89; mentioned, 80, 81; mills for, 36, 60; in Mississippi, 88; prices of, 31, 36; production of, xiv, 76, 89, 95, 103; short-staple, 30, 31; and tobacco, 2, 5

Cotton gin, 31, 34
Covici, Pascal, 108
Cowper, William, 96
Cradle of the Middle Class . . . (Ryan), 134n32
Craig, Raymond C., 138n1
Crawford, William, 33
Cruse, Peter Hoffman, 8
Cruthers, William Alexander, 3
"Cupping the Sternum" (Lewis), 90

"Dad's Dog School" (Harris), 117
Day, Donald, 139n12
Death, xvii, 86–87, 99, 100, 101
DeBerniere, Charlotte, 54
Debt: Augustus Baldwin Longstreet and, 34, 35, 36; and class, 35, 42; and cotton, 31; court cases over, 60; George Washington Harris and, 111, 112, 115; growth of, 32; Henry Clay Lewis and, 90, 104; literary depictions of, 12, 45; and masquerade culture, 81; and violence, 31
Declaration of Independence, 54
Deliverance (Dickey), 68
Democrats, xxiii, 9, 26, 35, 58, 113, 114
"Devil's Summer Retreat in Arkansaw" (Thorpe), 76–77
Dickey, James, 40, 68
Dillingham, William B., 130n13, 130n17, 130n19
Diseases of the Interior Valley of North America (Drake), 89
Disraeli, Benjamin, 88
Dog and Gun (Hooper), 59, 135n7
Domesticity: and authority, 118; on frontier, 55; gentlemen and, 7, 49, 105; in *Georgia Scenes*, 43, 46; literary depictions of, 59; and manhood, 20; patriarchy/paternalism and, 12–13, 45, 59, 114; planters and, 19; in *Swallow Barn*, 7, 13, 15, 22, 46, 54–55, 59, 69, 123; and westward expansion, 47

Dorsey, Washington, 89
Dostoevsky, Fyodor, xxvii, 110
Douglas, Stephen, 106
Drake, Daniel, 89
Ducktown, Tenn., 116
Dueling. *See under* Violence

East Alabamian, 54
Edgefield County, S.C., 30, 31, 32, 33
Ellicott, Thomas, 16
Elliott, William, 71–72, 75, 76, 78
Emancipation, 22
England, 114
English sporting gentleman, 59
Episcopalians, 48, 54, 58
Estes, David C., 136n2, 136n7, 137n11
Europe, 30, 60, 69, 91, 114
Evangelical culture. *See* Marketplace and market/evangelical culture

Fabian, Ann, 135n7
Fast Talk and Flush Times . . . (Lenz), 135n7
Faulkner, William, 40, 122
Federalists, 8
Fellman, Michael, 135n7
Ferguson, Robert A., 16, 62
Fetching the Old Southwest . . . (Justus), 129n1, 130n13
Fielding, Henry, 10
Fighting: in *Georgia Scenes*, 25, 29, 39–42, 120; in "The Knob Dance," 112; in *Odd Leaves*, 102–3; in *Swallow Barn*, 5, 20–21; in U.S. Senate, xxviii, 30, 106
Filibuster, 105–6
Fillmore, Millard, 123
Fire-eaters, 108, 112, 113, 126
First Presbyterian Church of Knoxville, 113

Fitzgerald, Oscar Penn, 133n13
Florida, 70. *See also* Louisiana
Flush Times in Alabama and Mississippi (Baldwin), xxvii, 18, 62–65, 106, 127, 135n19
Fools. *See* Lovingood, Sut (fictional character)
Ford, Lacy, 32
Forrest, Edwin, 31
Fox-Genovese, Elizabeth, 129n2
Franklin, Benjamin, 44, 52, 111
Freud, Sigmund, xxi
Friend, Craig Thompson, 134n38, 138n9
Friendly Grove Factory (Va.), 60
"From Humor to History..." (Tate), 136n22
Frontier: Alabama as, 48–49, 52; characteristics of, 49, 50; and class, 5, 50; competition on, 57, 72; cotton culture on, 51; death on, 99; domestic sphere on, 55; gentlemen and, 52, 78, 95; Georgia and, 48; Henry Clay and, 65; identity on, 51; land on, 49; law and lawyers on, 49, 50; literary depictions of, 79, 85; Louisiana as, 70, 93; and manhood, 49–50, 55, 86; and masquerade culture, 50; Mississippi as, 99; and patriarchy/paternalism, 86; planters and, 49, 82, 95; pressures on, 97; profanity and, 49; religion on, 49; retreat of, 77; salt-river roarers on, 78; scholarship on, 55; slavery on, 50, 51; Southern writers and, xix, xx, xxi, xxv, 6–7, 69; and violence, xxvi
Fruits of Merchant Capital... (Fox-Genovese), 129n2
Ft. Sumter, 82

Gamblers and gambling: and class, 42; faro, 57, 58; literary depictions of, 53, 57, 58; scholarship on, 134n35, 135n7
Gardner, Brother Dave, xix
Gender: as boundary, 98; and church, 125; and competition, 43; and display, 43; and evangelical culture, 118; and humor, xxi, xxii–xxiii; and identity, xiv; in North, 15; and postwar South, 125; roles and spheres of, 37, 43; scholarship on, xiv, xvi, 134n32; and sports, 68; in Sut Lovingood stories, 118–19. *See also* Manhood; Women
Genovese, Eugene, 27, 129n2
Gentlemen: characteristics of, 53, 55; as depicted in *The Master's House*, 79–82; and domestic sphere, 105, 127–28; in *Flush Times,* 61–62; and frontier, 52, 78, 95; in *Georgia Scenes,* 26–27; Harriet Beecher Stowe and, 126; and honor, 56, 126; humorists as, 26; and hunting, 71–73; and manhood, xxv; and market economy, 61–62, 64, 105; and masquerade culture, 81; in North Carolina, 79; and paternalism, 105; and Reconstruction, 125–26; scholarship on, 9, 126, 130n1; and slavery, 105; social mores of, 46; and social rituals, 56–57; and violence, 68; William Gilmore Simms and, 126. *See also* Class: elites; Meriwether, Frank (fictional character); Planters; Virginia gentleman
"George Washington Harris" (Mayfield), 138n4
George Washington Harris (Rickels), 139n12
Georgia: agriculture in, 30; Augustus Baldwin Longstreet in, xxi; and Cherokee lands, 31; class in, 28, 58; eastern, 49; and frontier, 48; George Washington Harris in, 112; masquerade culture in, 38; middle, 30; and New South, 30; slavery in, 28; and social ethics, 30; topography of, 30
Georgia Scenes (Longstreet): "The Ball," in, 44; "The Character of a Native Georgian," in, 37; characters in, 29, 32; charateristics of, 25, 26; "The Charming Creature," in, 44–45; and class, xxv, 25, 26, 27, 28, 29, 40–41, 42; "The Dance," in, 43; domesticity in, 43, 46;

Index 161

Georgia Scenes (Longstreet), *continued*
evangelical culture in, 28–29; "Fight, The," in, 39–42, 44, 120; "Fox Hunt, The," in, 39; "Gander Pulling, The," in, 39; "Georgia Theatrics" in, 27–28, 29–30; "Horse-Swap, The," in, 37–38; language in, 28, 29, 38, 45, 63; law and lawyers in, 28; leadership in, 42, 45; literary impact of, 25–26, 45; Longstreet on, 25; marketplace and market culture in, 29, 37–39, 45; masquerade culture in, 28, 29, 32; narrators in, 26–27, 28, 29–30, 36–37, 41, 45–46; place in, 30; profanity in, 26; publication of, 33; purposes of, 25; race in, 42; scholarship on, 26–27, 132n2, 133n13, 134n34, 134n37; "The Shooting Match," in, 45; as Southwestern humor, xxv; towns and town culture in, 29, 37–38, 46–47; "The Turf," in, 42–43, 44; violence in, 25, 26, 27–28, 29, 44; women in, 25, 26, 37, 40, 41, 42, 43–45; writing of, 45

"*Georgia Scenes*: The Satiric Artistry of Augustus Baldwin Longstreet" (Newlin), 134n34

Gettysburg, Pa., 127
Glover, Lorri, 13, 134n38, 138n9
Gone with the Wind (Mitchell), 5–6
Good ole boys, 25, 27
Gorgas, Josiah, 125
Grady, Henry, 125
Graniteville textile works, 30
Grant, Ulysses S., 114
Gray, Dorian (fictional character), 53
Gray, Edward, 8, 10
Great Chain of Being, xvii
Great Revival, 32
Great Smokies, 111
Greenberg, Kenneth, xvii, 56, 134n33, 134n35
Gregg, William, 30
Griffith, Nancy, 136n2
Guy Rivers (Simms), 52

Halttunen, Karen, 135n7
Hamilton, Alexander, 65

Hamlet (Shakespeare), xv, 7
Hammond, James Henry, 30
Harris, George Washington: as author, 117; biography/personal life of, xxiv, 110–12, 113–15, 116, 119, 122, 127; and evangelical culture, xxvii; and humiliation, 97; in Knoxville, xxi; and language, 90; as leading Southern humorist, xx–xxi; literary techniques of, 87; and masquerade culture, xxvii; and New South, xxvi, xxvii; and Old South, xxvi; and religion, 110; scholarship on, 115, 138n3, 139n12; and social ethics, 30; and women, 96; works by, xx, xxvii, 85, 112–13, 114, 115. *See also* Lovingood, Sut (fictional character)
Harris, Joel Chandler, 127
Hart, Abraham, 78
Harvard, xv
Hauck, Richard B., 135n7
Hazard, Ned (fictional character), 11, 19–21, 23, 40, 41, 55
Hegel, Georg Wilhelm Friedrich, 52, 61
Henry, Patrick, 3
High Times and Hard Times (Harris), 122, 139n24
Hirschkop, Ken, 138n8
Hive of the "Bee-Hunter," The . . . (Thorpe), 137n11
Honduras, 105
Honor: adaption of, 126; challenges to, 55; and Civil War, 47, 123, 125; and class, 31; and debt, 31; and dueling, 33, 82; fool's rejection of, 110; on frontier, 49–50, 61; gentlemen and, 46, 53, 55, 56, 58, 61, 63, 82, 126; George McDuffie and, 33; in *Georgia Scenes*, 39, 46; Henry Clay Lewis and, 90; and law, 16; as liability, 24; and manhood, 24, 50, 109; and marketplace, xviii, 97, 103, 105, 106, 125, 127–28; and masquerade culture, xxviii; scholarship on, xiii, xvii, 55, 56, 100, 137n8; and social order, 55; in Sut Lovingood stories, 109, 110, 117; Virginia gentleman and, xxv, 2, 4, 63

Honor and Slavery . . . (Greenberg), 134n33, 135n35
Hoole, William Stanley, 135n9
Hooper, Archibald, 54
Hooper, George, 54
Hooper, Johnson Jones: in Alabama, xxi; biography/personal life of, xxiv, 48, 50, 52, 54, 57, 59–60, 92, 127, 135n17; and class, 58; and frontier, 52, 55; and gentleman, 52; and language, xxvi; as leading Southern humorist, xx–xxi; literary alter ego of, 62; and market/evangelical culture, 51; mentioned, 70; in North Carolina, xxi; physical characteristics of, 53; on planters, 61; on political biographies, 52; and politics, 54, 58, 59–60, 61; and religion, 58; scholarship on, 135n17, 136n22; works by, xv, xx, xxv–xxvi, 54
Horses: and death of Henry Clay Lewis, 104; frontier planters and, 71; in *Georgia Scenes*, 25, 37–38, 42–43, 96; as objects of paternalism, 13; in *Odd Leaves*, 96–97, 100, 101; ship accommodations for, 77; in Simon Suggs stories, 53; in Sut Lovingood stories, 106–7, 116, 117, 118, 120; in *Swallow Barn*, 5, 13, 21, 22–23
Horse-shoe Robinson (Kennedy), 24, 43
"Horse-Swap, The" (Longstreet), 37–38, 94
Horwitz, Morton, 18, 62
House of Burgesses (Va.), 14
Hubbell, Jay B., 133n13
Huckleberry Finn (Twain), 56
Human Tradition in Antebellum America, The (Morrison), 138n4
Humiliation: fear of, 85; George Washington Harris and, 115; Henry Clay Lewis and, 89; and humor, 26; Joseph Glover Baldwin and, 87; and manhood, xviii–xix, 87, 109; and mastery, 103; in *Odd Leaves*, 87, 88, 91, 94, 96–97, 103, 109; and poverty, 118; scholarship on, 108, 137n8; in Simon Suggs stories, 87; Southern men's fears of, xviii–xix; and Southwestern humor, 88; in Sut Lovingood stories, 107, 109, 110, 115, 117, 119, 121; in *Swallow Barn*, 87; and violence, 41
Humiliation: and Other Essays on Honor, Social Discomfort, and Violence (Miller), 137n8, 139n11
Humor: characteristics of, xix; and class, xxii; English, xix; frontier, 27, 39, 70; and identity, xxii; and irony, xix; and manhood, xiii; purposes of, 26; scholarship on, xiii, xxi, 130n18; Southern, xix–xx, xxi–xxiii, xxiv, xxvi, xxvii, 51, 74, 126–27, 129n1, 130n17, 138n16; Southwestern, 87–88, 126, 130n13
Humorists, Southern, xx–xxi, xxiii–xxiv
Humor of H. E. Taliaferro, The (Craig), 138n1
Humor of the Old South, The (Inge and Piacentino), 129n1, 130n13, 135n9, 136n2, 138n3
Humor of the Old Southwest (Cohen and Dillingham), 130n13, 130n17, 130n19
Humor of the Old Southwest . . . (Griffith), 136n2
Hundley, Daniel, xv–xvi, xix, 126
Hunting: and class, 31, 71–73, 75–78; and mastery, 71, 75; and postwar male culture, 114; in *Spirit of the Times*, 51, 68–69, 71; in works by Henry Clay Lewis, 104; in works by Johnson Jones Hooper, 59; in works by Thomas Bangs Thorpe, 67, 68–69, 71, 72–74, 75–78

Identity: and class, xv, xvii, xxiv; and competition, 29; and deception, 37, 52, 53; and English country gentleman, 6; in *Flush Times*, 64; on frontier, 51–52; and gender, xiv; in *Georgia Scenes*, 37, 39, 45; Henry Clay Lewis and, 91; and humor, xxii, xxvii; John Pendleton Kennedy and, 124; Johnson Jones Hooper and, 135n17; and market-evangelical culture, xxvii, 29, 37, 64; and masquerade culture, 28, 37; and

Index *163*

Identity, *continued*
   modernity, 51; in *Odd Leaves,* 98–99, 102, 103; and outsiders, 98–99; in Simon Suggs stories, 53, 56, 57, 59; and slavery, xxiv
"Indefatigable Bear-Hunter, The" (Lewis), 90
Independence, 20, 125–26
Indians, 68, 72, 74, 77. *See also* Cherokees
Inge, M. Thomas: as coeditor of *Humor of the Old South,* 129n1, 130n13, 135n9, 136n2, 138n3; as coeditor of *Sut Lovingood's Nat'ral Born Yarnspinner,* 139n12, 139n21; as editor of *High Times and Hard Times,* 139n24
Intelligencer, 77
Ireland, 7
Irving, Washington, xx, 5, 8

Jackson, Andrew, 14, 16, 49, 52, 65
Jefferson, Thomas, 3, 65
Jews, xxii, 88, 90
John Pendleton Kennedy (Ridgely), 132n21
John Pendleton Kennedy: Gentleman from Baltimore (Bohner), 131n6, 131n8
Johnson J. Hooper (Somers), 135n9
Jokes and Their Relations (Oring), 130n18
Jones, Anne Goodwyn, xiv, xv, xvii, xxi
Jones, Tom (fictional character), 20
"Joseph Glover Baldwin" (Stewart), 135n19
Judge Longstreet: A Life Sketch (Fitzgerald), 133n13
Justus, James H., 129n1, 130n13, 135n19

Kansas-Nebraska Act, xxvii, 106
Karcher, Carolyn, 135n7
Katharine Walton (Simms), 43
Kelly, Aileen, 138n8, 139n11
Kemper, Reuben, 70
Kennedy, John Pendleton: and abolition, xxiv, 123; biography/personal life of, xxiv, 7–10, 14, 16, 19, 60, 123; and Civil War, 123–24, 127; depictions of women by, 43, 44; on Henry Clay, 65; as leading Southern humorist, xx–xxi; on planters' authority, 37; and politics, 123; pseudonym for, 139n1; as publisher, 8; and race, xxiv; scholarship on, xxv, 9, 16, 131n6, 131n20; on Southern insecurity, 124–25; in Virginia, xxi; writing process of, 5; writings of, xx, xxv, 6, 9, 24. *See also Swallow Barn* (Kennedy)
Kentucky, 57, 65
Kibler, James, 26, 132n2, 133n13
King, Kimball, 133n13, 134n37
King Philip (Indian leader), 31
Knave, Fool, and Genius . . . (Kuhlmann), 135n7
Knights of the Golden Horseshoe (Caruthers), 3
"Knob Dance, The" (Harris), 112–13
Know-Nothing party, 113
Knoxville, Tenn., xxi, 110, 111, 113, 114, 122
Knoxville Argus, 112
Kuhlmann, Susan, 135n7

Lachmann, Renate, 138n8
Lafayette, Ala., 54
Lamar, L. Q. C., 127
Land and land speculation, 2, 60, 62
Language: Augustus Baldwin Longstreet and, 63; characteristics of, 50–51; and class, 29, 50–52; con men and, xxvi, 51–52, 56, 94; George Washington Harris and, 90; in *Georgia Scenes,* 28, 29, 38, 45, 63; Henry Clay Lewis and, 90; Johnson Jones Hooper and, xxvi; Joseph Glover Baldwin and, xxvi, 65; and law and lawyers, 51–52, 63–64; and manhood, 50–52, 56; and mastery, xxvi, 50–51, 56, 63, 65; purposes of, 50–52; and social control, 50–51, 56; in *Swallow Barn,* 12, 14, 50–51, 63
Law and lawyers: Augustus Baldwin Longstreet and, 25, 33, 34; and boundary disputes, 60; and class, 86, 90; and commerce; and competition, 62; and cotton culture, 31; and

debt, 60; evolution of, 16, 62, 92; in *Flush Times,* 62–64; on frontier, 49, 50; in *Georgia Scenes,* 28; and honor, 16; John Pendleton Kennedy and, 16, 24; Johnson Jones Hooper and, 48, 54; Joseph Glover Baldwin and, 48, 60, 62, 127; and land speculation, 62; and language, 51–52, 63–64; and mastery, 51, 63; and migration, 50; and modernity, 51; and New South, 113; and politics, 61; scholarship on, 62; in *Swallow Barn,* 5, 11, 16–19, 24; Thomas Bangs Thorpe and, 82, 127; and towns, 29; and tradition, 51; women and, 99

Leadership: in *Georgia Scenes,* 39, 41–42, 45, 65; Joseph Glover Baldwin and, 60–61, 65, 66; in *Swallow Barn,* 6; and violence, 41; Virginia gentlemen and, 49

Lee, Robert E., xvii, xviii, 1, 4, 125, 126

Legare, Hugh, 33

Legree, Simon (fictional character), 71, 80

Lemay, J. A. Leo, 137n13

Lenz, William E., 135n7

Lester, Jeeter (fictional character), 25

"Letters of Augustus Baldwin Longstreet, The" (Scafidel), 133n13

Leverenz, David, xv, xviii, 87

Lewis, Henry Clay: and brawling, 97, 104; childhood and education of, xxiv, xxvi, 84, 88–89, 92, 95–96, 111, 115, 138n11; compared to Edgar Allan Poe, xxvi, 86, 100; compared to Thomas Bangs Thorpe, 86, 90; death of, 84, 104, 127; disorienting effects of works by, 108; and humiliation, 109; as leading Southern humorist, xx; literary techniques of, 87, 90; personal characteristics of, xxvi, 84, 86–87, 89, 90, 91, 99, 102, 103, 104; as physician, 83, 84, 86, 89–90, 91, 104; works by, xx, xxvi, 90; writing habits of, 90. *See also Odd Leaves from the Life of a Louisiana Swamp Doctor* (Lewis)

Lexington, Va., 60

"Life of George Washington Harris, The" (Day), 139n12

Lincoln, Abraham, 114, 127

"Lineaments of Antebellum Southern Romanticism" (O'Brien), 132n26

Litchfield, Conn., 33, 34

Littleton, Mark (fictional character), 87. *See also Swallow Barn* (Kennedy): "Mark Littleton" (narrator) in

Longstreet, Augustus Baldwin, 51; biography/personal life of, xxiii–xxiv, 26, 30, 33–35, 41, 43, 47, 92, 127; characters created by, 70; and Civil War, 127; and class, 50, 58; compared to George Washington Harris, 115; and con men, 52; and evangelical culture, 113, 125; frontier humorists and, 51; in Georgia, xxi, 35, 36, 58; and language, 63; as leading Southern humorist, xx–xxi; letters written by, 133n23, 133n27, 133n28; literary alter egos of, 62; and market/evangelical culture, xxv, xxvi–xxvii, 49, 62; and masquerade culture, 36; as Methodist, 37; and politics and government, xx, 35, 36, 37, 47, 133n27, 133n28; scholarship on, 133n13, 134n34; and social displacement, 80; and women, 43–44, 96; works by, xx, xxv, 47, 65, 85, 94, 120, 134n37; as writer, 35, 36. *See also Georgia Scenes* (Longstreet)

Longstreet, James, 134n37

Longstreet, William, 33–34

Lost Cause, 126

Louisiana: cholera epidemic in, 104; cotton plantations in, 76; as frontier, 70, 93; gentlemen in, 78, 81; Henry Clay Lewis in, xxi, xxvi, 89–90, 104; history of, 70; hunting in, 77; literary depictions of, 67–68, 76, 77, 80; and migration, 97; planters in, 90; residents of, 70–71; Thomas Bangs Thorpe in, xxi, 68, 69, 70, 71, 78, 127

Louisiana Swamp Doctor . . . (Anderson), 138n11

Index 165

Louisville, Ky., 83, 89, 92
Louisville Medical Institute, 89
Lovingood, Sut (fictional character): analysis and descriptions of, 106–10, 114, 115, 116–20, 121–22; and analysis and descriptions of, 113; and anarchy, xxvii, 96; and evangelical culture, 119–21; as fool, 106, 107–8, 139n12; mentioned, xxvii, 1; scholarship on, 117, 139n12, 139n21; as Tennessee character, xxi; William Faulkner on, 122
Lynn, Kenneth: on Augustus Baldwin Longstreet, 26; on cordon sanitaire, 131n17; on gentlemen, 9; on *Georgia Scenes*, 134n34; on Henry Clay Lewis, 115; on humor and humiliation, 132n8; on humorists, xxii, xxiii; on Sut Lovingood, 108; on Thorpe's "The Big Bear of Arkansas," 137n13

MacKeithan, Lucinda H., 131n5
Madison, James, 70
Main Currents in American Thought . . . (Parrington), 131n9, 133n13
Maine, 64
Major Jones's Courtship (Thompson), 46–47
Manchester, Miss., 88
Manhood: and boyhood, 19, 24; as capital venture, 64–65; characteristics of, xvii, xviii, 55, 109; and *chevalresque*, 124; and chivalry, 19; and Civil War, xv, xxiv, 124–25, 127; and class, xv, 6, 7, 12–14; and codes of behavior, xvii, 19, 105; and competition, xv, xviii, xxi, 19, 46, 65, 109; and death, 86–87, 100; definitions of, xiv–xv, xvii; and domesticity, 20; and exploitation, 57–58; fluidity of, 46; and frontier, 49–50, 55, 86; gentlemen and, xxv; and honor, 24, 50, 109; and humiliation, xviii–xix, 87, 109; and humor, xiii; and independence, 20, 125–26; and inferiority, 124; and insecurity, 124–25; Joseph Glover Baldwin on, 65; and language, 50–52, 56; literary explorations of, 6–7; and market/evangelical culture, xviii, xxvii, 109, 127–28; and masquerade culture, xvii–xviii, xxvii–xxviii; and occupation, 92; and partisanship, 65; and patriarchy, 7; postwar spheres of, 125; and race, xv, xxiv; and Reconstruction, 125–26; and religion, xviii; scholarship on, xv, xviii; and slaves, 7, 23–24; and Southern humor, xxi; and values, xiii, xiv; and violence, xv; William Gilmore Simms on, xvii, 6; and women, 7, 85–86. *See also* Virginia gentleman
Marketplace and market/evangelical culture: Augustus Baldwin Longstreet and, xxv, xxvi–xxvii, 49, 62, 113, 125; characteristics of, xviii, 29, 38–39, 74; and Civil War, 125; and class, 29, 44, 45, 86; and competition, 46; fools and, 110; and gender, 37, 118, 121; gentlemen and, 61–62, 64, 105; George Washington Harris and, 113, 114; and honor, xviii, 97, 103, 105, 106, 125, 127–28; and humiliation, 87; and identity, xxvii, 29, 37, 64; Johnson Jones Hooper and, 51; Joseph Glover Baldwin and, 51, 60; literary depictions of, 28–29, 37–39, 45, 58, 81, 118, 119–21; and manhood, xviii, xxvii, 109, 127–28; and masquerade culture, xviii, xxiv–xxv, 37, 127; and mastery, 8; New South and, xviii, 29; North and, 124; and patriarchy/paternalism, 24, 43, 64; plantations and, 105; relationships in, 51; scholarship on, xviii, 29, 113, 114, 133n11; and slavery, 81; Southern humorists and, xxv, xxvi–xxvii; and towns, 29
Mark Twain and Southwestern Humor (Lynn), 131n17, 132n8, 134n34, 137n13
Martinsburg, Va. (now W. Va.), 8
Maryland, 8, 9
Masquerade culture: Augustus Baldwin Longstreet and, 36, 37; characteristics of, xvii, xxviii, 29, 31, 114; and Civil War, 124; and class, 28, 31, 44; and cotton culture, 31; and death, 100; and debt, 81; doctors and, 92; dominance

166 Index

of, xxvii–xxviii; expectations of, 57; fools and, 110; and frontier, 50; gentlemen and, 81; George Washington Harris and, xxvii; in Georgia, 31, 38; and honor, xxviii, 50; and humiliation, 87; and identity, 28, 37; literary depictions of, 28, 29, 32, 37, 81; and manhood, xvii–xviii, xxvii–xxviii; and marketplace and market/evangelical culture, xviii, xxiv–xxv, 37, 127; and slavery, 127; and Southern cavalier, 105; Southern humorists on, xxvii; and violence, xxvi; women and, 114

Massachusetts, 31, 69, 105

Master's House, The (Thorpe), 65, 67, 68, 79–82

Mastery: con men and, 51, 56, 57, 58; and death, 86, 100, 101; and exploitation, 57–58; and facade, 57; Henry Clay Lewis and, 103; and humiliation, 103; and hunting, 71, 75; Joseph Glover Baldwin and, 61; and language, xxvi, 50–51, 56, 63, 65; lawyers and, 51, 63; literary depictions of, 100–101; and marketplace, 8; and masculinity, 58; and patriarchy, xiv; and slavery, 58, 127, 128; and violence, xxvi; Virginia gentlemen and, 2, 3, 4, 24, 121

Matamoras, Mex., 78

Mayfield, John, 134n38

McCullough v. Maryland, 35

McDuffie, George, 30, 32–33, 34

Medicine, 31, 89, 91–92. *See also* Occupations: doctors

Melville, Herman, 86, 87, 135n7

Meriwether, Frank (fictional character): and domestic sphere, 54–55, 59, 69, 123; as gentleman, 52, 126; as isolationist, 80; and language, 51, 63; as master, 121; mentioned, 29, 30, 95; and paternalism, 34; values of, 82; and violence, 41–42. *See also Swallow Barn* (Kennedy): "Frank Meriwether" (main character) in

Meriwether, James B., 133n13

Methodists: and abolition, 32; Augustus Baldwin Longstreet as, 34, 37, 41, 43; and class, 30; literary depictions of, 80; in New England, 69

Mexico, 78

Migration: and class, 5, 50; and domesticity, 47; Joseph Glover Baldwin and, 60; Kennedy family and, 7; planters and, 2, 55; slaves and, 2; to West Florida (now Louisiana), 70; westward, 2, 10, 97; Yankees and, 50, 72, 78

Miller, James David, 133n11

Miller, Sut, 116

Miller, William Ian, 109, 119, 137n8, 139n11

Millerites, 85

Mind of the Master Class, The, . . . (Fox-Genovese and Genovese), 129n2

Mississippi: Augustus Baldwin Longstreet in, 127; cotton culture in, 88; as frontier, 99; Henry Clay Lewis in, 88; Joseph Glover Baldwin in, 60; and migration, xxv, 97; population of, 88; Seargeant S. Prentiss in, 79; as setting for *Uncle Tom's Cabin*, 71

Mississippi River, 71, 81, 88

Monroe, James, 2, 14

Montgomery, Ala., 56

Morris, Christopher, 134n33

Morrison, Michael A., 138n4

Morse, Samuel, 9

"My Early Life" (Lewis), 90–91

Mysteries of the Backwoods, The (Thorpe), 137n11

Narrative Forms of Southern Community, The (Romine), 134n38

Nash, Pat, 116

Nashville, Tenn., 114

Nativism, 123

New Collection of Thomas Bangs Thorpe's Sketches of the Old Southwest, A (Estes), 136n2

New England, 67, 68, 69, 124

New England Magazine, 6

Newlin, Keith, 134n34

New Orleans, La., 68, 71, 77, 82, 88, 127

Index   167

Newport, R. I., 7
New South: and capitalism, 125; culture of, xxv; George Washington Harris and, xxvi, xxviii, 114, 122; and market/evangelical culture, xviii, 29, 30, 125; men in, 115; middle class and, xxiii, 29; roots of, xviii, xxvii; scholarship on, 113; women and, 121
New York, N.Y., 7, 44, 69, 82, 127
Nimrod (ship), 77
Noble savage. *See* Indians
No'counts, 20, 25, 40, 117
Noland, C.F.M., xx–xxi, 51, 78
North (U.S.), xxiii, 15, 32, 79
North Carolina, xxi, 54, 79
Northerners. *See* Yankees
Nullification, xx, 35

O'Brien, Michael, 129n2, 131n20, 132n26
Occupations: bankers, 50, 56; barbers, 91; bartenders, 50; blood-letters, 91; bookbinders, 69; businessmen, 113, 125–26; doctors, 50, 83, 86, 89, 91–93; editors, xx, 50, 78, 92; engineering, 86; factory superintendents, 111; farmers, 12, 31, 38, 45, 73; flatsboatmen, 93; horse traders, 29, 38; journalists, 29, 54, 60, 71, 78, 92; and manhood, 92; manufacturing, 111; metalworkers, 111; middle-class, 50; midwives, 91; military service, 86; mine surveyors, 112, 116; overseers, 70; peddlers, 38; postmasters, 112; preachers, 28, 29, 92, 113; publishers, 78; railroad conductors, 112; railroading, 81; scholarship on, 86; sharecroppers, 125–26; silversmiths, 111; slave traders, 80–82; steamboat captains, 111, 112; storekeeping, 81; teaching, 29, 81; trading, 111; washerwomen, 112; woodcutters, 77. *See also* Law and lawyers; Planters; Professionals
Odd Leaves from the Life of a Louisiana Swamp Doctor (Lewis): analysis and descriptions of, xxvi, 84, 85–88, 90, 91, 92–94, 100–104; popularity of, 84–85; scholarship on, 84, 85, 86, 102, 103; stories from, 50–51, 84; William Gilmore Simms on, 84
Ohio River, 88, 111
Old Dominion. *See* Virginia
Old South: Cherokee removal from, xiv; and class, 27; cotton production in, xiv; and dealth, 99–100; evangelism in, 29; geographical size of, xiv; intellectual history of, xx; as legend, 122; and market/evangelical culture, xxvii; mythology of, 128; and patriarchy, 6; public life in, 27; regions of, xxiii; scholarship on, xiii–xiv, xvi–xvii; towns in, 29. *See also* New South
Oriard, Michael, 55
Origins of the Southern Middle Class, 1800–1861, The (Wells), 133n10
Oring, Eliot, xxii, xxvii, 130n18
Ownby, Ted, xviii, 29, 113, 114, 133n11

Page, Thomas Nelson, 126
Palmah, xxii, xxiii, xxvii
Panic of 1819, 32, 50
Panic of 1837, 50
Parrington, Vernon, 7, 35, 131n9, 133n13
Party Leaders (Baldwin), 65, 66
Patriarchy and paternalism: Augustus Baldwin Longstreet and, 34; and civic duty, 13–14; and class, 6, 13, 27; during colonial era, 20; and domestic sphere, 12–13, 45, 59, 114; fathers' roles in, xxiv; and female challenges to, 95; feminization of, 19, 24; and frontier, 86; and humiliation, 121; and lineage, 121; literary depictions of, 7, 12–13, 27; and localism, 13; and manhood, 7; and marketplace, 24, 43, 64; masculine ideals in, 6; and mastery, xiv; Northern, 24; and prewar conflict, 105; and race, 13; scholarship on, xiv, xv; and self-control, 21; and slavery, 22, 81; and social rituals, 46; in Sut Lovingood stories, 117, 118; and towns and town culture, 43
Pendleton, Nancy, 8, 9

Pendleton, Philip, 8
Pendleton family, 11, 14
Percy, Walker, 70
Perry, Oliver Hazard, 9
Petigru, James, 33
Philadelphia, Pa., 7, 91, 131n5
Piacentino, Edward J., 129n1, 130n13, 135n9, 136n2, 138n3
Placing the South (O'Brien), 129n2
Planters: Anglo, 70; Augustus Baldwin Longstreet and, 35; and authority, 51; in Black Belt, 61; characteristics of, 2; and class, 27, 31, 32, 35; and competition, 19; and cotton, 31, 54; and debt, 35; and domestic sphere, 19; and drinking, 71; and French, 70; and frontier, 49, 82, 95; in *Georgia Scenes*, 29; Henry Clay Lewis on, 95; Joseph Glover Baldwin and, 60; literary depictions of, 6, 37, 67–68, 71; in Louisiana, 70, 71, 90; and migration, 2, 50, 55; mores of, 19; and politics, 61; popular perceptions of, 10; as rulers, 14; scholarship on, xvi, 55; and slaves, 31; in Southwest, 70; and Spanish, 70; and tobacco, 2, 37, 71; and violence, 35; in Virginia, 71; and Virginia social structure, 49; and voting rights, 60. *See also* Virginia gentleman
Poe, Edgar Allan: as author, 100; biography/personal life of, 100; Henry Clay Lewis and, 84, 86, 102; John Pendleton Kennedy and, 8; and Southern humor, xix, xx; and Southern sensibilities, xxvi
Political Economy of Slavery, The (Genovese), 129n2
Polk, Noel, 117
Pope, Alexander, xvi
Populism, 126
Porter, William T.: collections published by, 68, 74; death of, 82; *Spirit of the Times* published by, xix, 41, 51, 52, 71, 82, 90, 113, 127
Port of Knoxville, 111
Prentiss, Seargeant S., 64, 78–79

Presbyterians and Presbyterianism, 113, 117, 118
Princeton (college), 11, 19, 33
Princeton, N.J., 33
Proctor, Nicholas, 71, 136n8
Profanity, 20, 26, 29, 49
Professionals: Augustus Baldwin Longstreet as, xxiii, 47, 50; and class, 50, 86, 89; George Washington Harris as, xxiii; Henry Clay Lewis as, xxiii, 86, 89, 97, 104; John Pendleton Kennedy as, xxiii; Johnson Jones Hooper as, xxiii, 50; Joseph Glover Baldwin as, xxiii, 50; and language, 50–51; and market culture, 86; mentioned, 115; occupations of, 50, 89; and patriarchy, 50; and race, 50; Simon Suggs as, 52; in Southwest, 50–51; Thomas Bangs Thorpe as, xxiii, 50; Yankees as, 19, 50
Protestantism, xviii, 32, 65, 114, 115

Quidor, John, 69
Quodlibet (Kennedy), 9

Race: as boundary, 98; in *Georgia Scenes*, 42; and humor, xxi, 126–27; and manhood, xv, xxiv; scholarship on, xiii–xiv, xvi–xvii; and social distinctions, 42
Rachels, David, 26
Randolph, John, 2, 65
Reconstruction, 82, 114, 125–26
Red Book, 8
Religion: and antebellum culture, 114; Augustus Baldwin Longstreet and, xxv, 35, 41, 58; Dostoevsky and, 110; on frontier, 49; and gender, 125; George Washington Harris and, 110, 115; and Great Revival, 32; Johnson Jones Hooper and, 58; literary depictions of, 58–59; and manhood, xviii; scholarship on, 32; Sut Lovingood and, 115; William Tappan Thompson and, 58. *See also* specific denominations
Republicans and Republican Party, xxvii, 82, 106, 113, 114
Rethinking the South . . . (O'Brien), 129n2

"Revealing Bakhtin" (Kelly), 138n8, 139n11
Richmond, La., 89
Richmond, Va., 60, 122, 127
Rickels, Milton, 136n2, 139n12
Ridgely, Joseph, 6, 132n21
Ripsnorters, 39, 40, 68, 73, 125
"Rival Sporting Weeklies of William T. Porter and Thomas Bangs Thorpe, The" (Estes), 136n7
Roarers, 50. *See also* Salt-river roarers
Rogers, Will, xvi, xix
Romine, Scott, 26–27, 134n38
Rose, Alan, 102, 103
Ryan, Mary P., 134n32

"Sadder Simon Suggs, A" (Shields), 135n9
Salamagundi Papers (Irving), 8
Salomon, Rachel, 88, 95, 99
Salt-river roarers: characteristics of, 110; and Civil War, 125; and class, 70; on frontier, 78; as literary type, xiii, 50, 70, 74
Saratoga, N.Y., 7
Savannah, Ga., 114
Savannah River, 30, 33
Scafidel, James R., 133n13
Scott, Walter, 7, 19
Scrooge (fictional character), 93
Sea Islands, 78
Secessionists, 112, 114
Senate, U.S., xxviii, 30, 106
Shadow over the Promised Land (Karcher), 135n7
Shakespeare, William, xvi, 7, 10, 53, 64
Shenandoah Valley, 9, 11, 48, 49
Sheperd, David, 138n8
Shields, Johanna Nicol, 54, 55, 135n9
Simms, William Gilmore: in Charleston, S.C., 88; and con men, 52; and gentlemen, 126; on identity and manhood, xvii, 6; and Indians, 72; on manhood, xvii, 6; mentioned, 59; and *Odd Leaves from the Life of a Louisiana Swamp Doctor,* 84, 101; as Southern humorist, xx; and women, 43, 44, 96
Simpson, Lewis, 22
Slavery: apologists for, 23; and capitalism, xiii–xiv, xxiv; and Civil War, 123; and democracy, xiii–xiv; expansion of, 105; on frontier, 50, 51; gentlemen and, 80, 105; as issue, 3, 4; literary depictions of, 13, 79, 80; and market/evangelical culture, 81; and masquerade culture, 127; and mastery, 58, 127, 128; New England attitudes toward, 67; and paternalism, 81, 128; Southern focus on, 3, 4; in *Swallow Barn* (Kennedy), 5, 21–22
Slaves: activities of, 31; antebellum depictions of, xvi; Augustus Baldwin Longstreet and, 34; and class, 4, 22, 32; confiscation of, 82; and cotton, 31, 76; and dependency, 20; George Washington Harris and, 111, 112, 114; Henry Clay Lewis and, 89; Hooper family and, 54; and hunting, 76; Joseph Glover Baldwin and, 60; in Louisiana, 70, 71; and manhood, 7, 23–24; in *Master's House, The,* 80, 81; mentioned, xviii; and migration, 2; in *Odd Leaves,* 86, 102–3; and patriarchy, xv; and poor whites, 32; rebellions by, 10; scholarship on, xiv; Southern fears of, 102; Southern humorists and, xxiii, xxiv; and Southern identity, 4; in *Swallow Barn,* 5, 6, 11, 12, 13, 15, 21–24; U.S. census counts of, 60–61; Virginia gentlemen and, 1, 3; and Virginia social structure, 49; and whiskey, 32
Slotkin, Richard, 72
Smith, John, 5, 23, 131n5
Sniffle, Ransy (fictional character), 1, 25–26, 39–40, 42, 70, 134n34. *See also Georgia Scenes* (Longstreet)
Snopeses (fictional characters), 25
Social Relations in Our Southern States (Hundley), xvi, 126
Somers, Paul, Jr., 135n9

170 Index

South. *See* New South; Old South
South by Southwest . . . (Miller), 133n11
South Carolina, 2, 30, 33, 57, 71, 72, 127
South Carolinians, 76
Southern Commerce Convention, 114
Southern Honor: Ethics and Behavior in the Old South (Wyatt-Brown), 134n35
Southern Manhood . . . (Friend and Glover), 134n38, 138n9
Southern Quarterly Review, 84
South in American Literature, The . . . (Hubbell), 133n13
Southwest, 70, 85. *See also* Frontier
"Southwestern Migration among North Carolina Planter Families . . ." (Censer), 135n13
Spirit of the Times: circulation of, 106; con men in, 52; fight stories in, 41; George Washington Harris and, 112–13, 116; hunting tales in, 51, 68–69, 71; Johnson Jones Hooper and, 52; Southern humorists and, xix; Thomas Bangs Thorpe and, 41, 68–69, 71, 76, 82, 127, 136n2
Sports: and class, 71, 117; and gender, 68; in *Georgia Scenes,* 39; literary depictions of, 59, 67; and mastery, 71; racing, 42–43, 96–97; scholarship on, 71, 72; shooting, 46. *See also* Horses; Hunting; Violence
Sportsmen, 47, 51, 73
Spotswood, Alexander, 3
States' rights, xxiii, 13, 34, 35, 60, 81, 133n27
States Rights' Sentinel, 35
Staunton, Va., 60
Steamboats: Frank Meriwether on, 13; George Washington Harris and, 111, 112; Henry Clay Lewis and, 88, 90, 97, 120; in Thorpe's "Big Bear of Arkansas," 68, 73; William Longstreet and, 34
Stephens, Alexander H., 30
Sterne, Laurence, 3, 10
Stewart, Samuel, 135n19

Stewart, William, 77
Stoicism, 14
Stowe, Harriet Beecher, 71, 79, 126
Stowe, Steven, 92
Strother, Francis, 64
Stuart, J.E.B., 86
Subduing Satan . . . (Ownby), 133n11
Suggs, Simon (fictional character), xv, 1, 52–54, 55–59, 87, 94
Sumner, Charles, xxviii, 30, 106
Sumter County, Ala., 60
"Sut and His Sisters . . ." (Walker), 139n21
Sut Lovingood . . . (Harris), 138n3
"Sut Lovingood's Daddy, Acting Horse" (Harris), 116–17
Sut Lovingood's Nat'ral Born Yarnspinner (Caron and Inge), 138n3, 139n12
Swallow Barn (Kennedy): characters in, 8, 10–11, 12–13, 15–16, 18, 19, 23; and class, 40; as comedy of manners, 6, 11; compared to Sut Lovingood stories, 121; contemporary reactions to, 5–6; debt in, 12; domesticity in, 7, 13, 15, 22, 46; editions of, 131n5; falcons and falconry in, 5, 20, 21, 132n26; feminization in, 15; fighting in, 5, 20–21, 40, 41; "Frank Meriwether" (main character) in, 10–11, 12, 13, 14–15, 18, 19, 22–23; geographical setting for, 5, 7, 11–12; horses in, 5, 13, 22–23; irony and satire in, 6, 11, 12, 15, 18–19, 20; Kennedy on, 5, 7; language in, 12, 14, 50–51, 63; law and lawyers in, 5, 11, 14, 16–19, 62; as literary turning point, 45; "Mark Littleton" (narrator) in, 5, 10, 11, 12, 13, 14, 15, 17, 18, 20–21, 22; mentioned, 25, 26, 124; "Ned Hazard" (secondary character) in, 11, 19–21, 23, 40, 41; planters in, 6; plot and focus of, 10, 21; purposes of, 5, 10, 21; scholarship on, xxv, 6, 22, 132n26; significance of, xxv, 6, 7; slaves and slavery in, 5, 7, 11, 12, 13, 21–22, 23–24; temporal setting for, 7; women in, 7, 11, 13, 17, 20, 21, 44

Index 171

Swearing. *See* Profanity
Swift, Jonathan, xvi

Taliaferro, Hardin E., 106, 138n1
Tate, Adam L., 136n22
Taylor, John, 2, 14, 17, 19, 35
Taylor, William R., xix, 131n4, 132n32
Taylor, Zachary, 78
Tennessee, xxi, 106, 111, 112, 114, 127
Tennessee River, 111
Tensas, Madison (fictional character). *See* Lewis, Henry Clay
Texas, 54, 63
"Text, Tradition, and Themes of 'The Big Bear of Arkansas,' The" (Lemay), 137n13
Thomas Bangs Thorpe, Humorist of the Old Southwest (Rickels), 136n2
Thompson, William Tappan, xx, 46–47
Thoreau, Henry David, 75
Thorpe, Thomas Bangs: as abolutionist, xxiv; biography/personal life of, xxiv, xxvii, 68–69, 71, 74–75, 78–79, 80, 82, 127; compared to Henry Clay Lewis, 86, 90; fight stories by, 41; as leading Southern humorist, xx–xxi; and migration, 50; perspective of, xxvi; and race, xxiv; and salt-river roarers, 70; scholarship on, 69, 136n1; and *Spirit of the Times*, 136n7; success of, 78; topics addressed by, 51; and violence, 69; works by, xxvi, 65, 68, 71, 72, 73, 74–75, 137n11; as Yankee, 50. *See also Master's House, The* (Thorpe)
"Tight Race Considerin', A" (Lewis), 90
Tobacco: and cotton, 2, 5; decline of, 14, 20; and plantation life, 1; planters and, 2, 37; prices of, 10, 20; in Virginia, 1, 2, 31
Toombs, Robert, 30
Towns and town culture, 29, 37–38, 46–47
Tucker, George, 3
Tucker, St. George, 121
Turner, Victor, xxvi, 135n7
Tuscaloosa, Ala., 54, 57

Twain, Mark, xix, 107, 127

Uncle Tom's Cabin (Stowe), 79
Underground Man (fictional character), 110
Union Bank of Baltimore, 16
University of Georgia, 36
Upper Hogthief, Georgia, 45, 46

Valley of Shenandoah (Tucker), 3
Van Buren, Martin, 52
Vick, Newett, 69
Vicksburg, Miss., 69, 127
Violence: Augustus Baldwin Longstreet and, 35; beatings, 70; and class, 31, 40, 75–76; and competition, 39; and debt, 31; dueling, 21, 29, 33, 35, 64, 67, 81, 82; on frontier, 55; and frontier humor, 27; in *Georgia Scenes*, 25, 26, 27, 29; and humiliation, 41; and male aggression, 39; and manhood, xv; and masquerade culture, xxvi; and mastery, xxvi; and moral leadership, 41; in *Odd Leaves*, 97; planters and, 35; and postwar male culture, 114; purposes of, 26, 40–41; and sports, 39; women and, 44; in works by Thomas Bangs Thorpe, 67, 68, 69, 80–81, 85. *See also* Fighting; Hunting
Virginia: agriculture in, 10, 14; class in, 3–4, 8, 11, 31, 49; and frontier, 48; gentlemen in, 61, 78; and industrialization, 22; John Pendleton Kennedy and, xxi, 7, 10; John Randolph of Roanoke and, 65; Joseph Glover Baldwin and, xxi, 62, 66; Kennedy family in, 8, 10; and migration, 2, 50; migration from, 2, 10; planters in, 1, 2, 10, 49, 71; popular perceptions of, 9; slaves in, 4, 10, 49; in *Swallow Barn*, 3–4, 5, 6, 7, 11–12, 13, 16, 22; Tidewater region in, 7
Virginia gentleman: authority of, 2–3; characteristics of, 1–2, 3, 4, 13–14, 63; and Civil War, 125; and class, 3, 49; and dependency, 24; as divisive image,

172   Index

5; domestication/feminization of, 7; and domesticity, 49; evolution of, 1–5; feminization of, 15, 19, 24; in *Georgia Scenes*, 42; as humorous figure, 42; and Jacksonian era, 14; John Randolph of Roanoke as, 65; and leadership, 49; literary depictions of, 3–5, 10–11, 12–16; and mastery, 2, 3, 4, 24; other terms for, 1; and slaves, 3; and sports, 50, 71; values of, 49
Virginians, 32, 95

Waddel, Moses, 33, 34
Wagner, John Harley, 91
Walker, Nancy, 139n21
Walker, William, 105
War of 1812, xxiii
Washington, George, 1, 2, 61
Webster, Daniel, 16
Wells, Jonathan Daniel, 133n10
Wesleyan College, 69
West Feliciana Parish, La., 67, 70
West Florida, 70. *See also* Louisiana
West Point, 86
Westward expansion. *See* Migration
"What's So Funny?" (Morris), 134n33
Whetstone, Pete (fictional character), 51
Whigs: Augustus Baldwin Longstreet and, 26; John Pendleton Kennedy and, 8, 9, 10, 19, 123; Johnson Jones Hooper and, 48, 54, 58, 59; Joseph Glover Baldwin and, 48, 60, 61; newspapers published by, 71; Seargeant S. Prentiss and, 64; Southern humorists and, xxiii
Whitman, Walt, 87
Whitney, Eli, 31
Wigfall, Louis T., 30
Wilde, Oscar, 53
Wilde, Richard Henry, 30

William Mitten (Longstreet), 65, 134n37
William T. Porter and the Spirit of the Times (Yates), 136n7
Willington, S.C., 33
Wilson, Edmund, 108–9, 115
Wilson, John Lyde, 21
Winchester, Va., 60
Winthrop, Robert, 123
Wirt, William, 3–4, 5, 9, 131n4
Women: and class, 43; and dependency, 20; and domestic authority, 118; and evangelical culture, 114; in *Georgia Scenes*, 25, 26, 37, 40, 41, 42, 43–45; and hunting, 68; legal rights of, as widows, 99; and manhood, 7, 85–86; and masquerade culture, 114; in *Odd Leaves*, 85–86, 95, 96–99, 104, 120; and patriarchy, xv, 95; postwar spheres of, 125; roles of, 43; scholarship on, xiv, 134n32; in Simon Suggs stories, 58; in Sut Lovingood stories, 116–22, 120–21; treatment of, during Civil War, 82; and violence, 44; white men and, xvii
Woodcraft (Simms), 43, 44, 126
Woodville, Miss., 69
Woodward, C. Vann, 113
Wyatt-Brown, Bertram, xvii, 19, 97, 99–100, 134n35

Yale, 33, 34
Yankees: John Pendleton Kennedy on, 124; literary depictions of, xvi, 5, 11; and migration, 50, 72, 78; mores of, 19; as synonym for con men, 52; Thomas Bangs Thorpe as, xvi
Yarn-spinners, xiii, 74
Yates, Norris W., 136n7
Yazoo City, Miss., 88, 89
Yeomen, 125–26

NEW PERSPECTIVES ON THE HISTORY OF THE SOUTH

Edited by John David Smith, Charles H. Stone Distinguished Professor of American History, University of North Carolina at Charlotte

"In the Country of the Enemy": The Civil War Reports of a Massachusetts Corporal, edited by William C. Harris (1999)

The Wild East: A Biography of the Great Smoky Mountains, by Margaret L. Brown (2000; first paperback edition, 2001)

Crime, Sexual Violence, and Clemency: Florida's Pardon Board and Penal System in the Progressive Era, by Vivien M. L. Miller (2000)

The New South's New Frontier: A Social History of Economic Development in Southwestern North Carolina, by Stephen Wallace Taylor (2001)

Redefining the Color Line: Black Activism in Little Rock, Arkansas, 1940–1970, by John A. Kirk (2002)

The Southern Dream of a Caribbean Empire, 1854–1861, by Robert E. May (2002)

Forging a Common Bond: Labor and Environmental Activism during the BASF Lockout, by Timothy J. Minchin (2003)

Dixie's Daughters: The United Daughters of the Confederacy and the Preservation of Confederate Culture, by Karen L. Cox (2003)

The Other War of 1812: The Patriot War and the American Invasion of Spanish East Florida, by James G. Cusick (2003)

"Lives Full of Struggle and Triumph": Southern Women, Their Institutions, and Their Communities, edited by Bruce L. Clayton and John A. Salmond (2003)

German-Speaking Officers in the United States Colored Troops, 1863–1867, by Martin W. Öfele (2004)

Southern Struggles: The Southern Labor Movement and the Civil Rights Struggle, by John A. Salmond (2004)

Radio and the Struggle for Civil Rights in the South, by Brian Ward (2004; first paperback edition, 2006)

Luther P. Jackson and a Life for Civil Rights, by Michael Dennis (2004)

Southern Ladies, New Women: Race, Region, and Clubwomen in South Carolina, 1890–1930, by Joan Marie Johnson (2004)

Fighting Against the Odds: A Concise History of Southern Labor Since World War II, by Timothy J. Minchin (2004; first paperback edition, 2006)

"Don't Sleep With Stevens!": The J. P. Stevens Campaign and the Struggle to Organize the South, 1963–1980, by Timothy J. Minchin (2005)

"The Ticket to Freedom": The NAACP and the Struggle for Black Political Integration, by Manfred Berg (2005; first paperback edition, 2007)

"War Governor of the South": North Carolina's Zeb Vance in the Confederacy, by Joe A. Mobley (2005)

Planters' Progress: Modernizing Confederate Georgia, by Chad Morgan (2005)

The Officers of the CSS Shenandoah, by Angus Curry (2006)

The Rosenwald Schools of the American South, by Mary S. Hoffschwelle (2006)
Honor in Command: Lt. Freeman S. Bowley's Civil War Service in the 30th United States Colored Infantry, edited by Keith Wilson (2006)
A Black Congressman in the Age of Jim Crow: South Carolina's George Washington Murray, by John F. Marszalek (2006)
The Spirit and the Shotgun: Armed Resistance and the Struggle for Civil Rights, by Simon Wendt (2007; first paperback edition, 2010)
Making a New South: Race, Leadership, and Community after the Civil War, edited by Paul A. Cimbala and Barton C. Shaw (2007)
From Rights to Economics: The Ongoing Struggle for Black Equality in the U.S. South, by Timothy J. Minchin (2008)
Slavery on Trial: Race, Class, and Criminal Justice in Antebellum Richmond, Virginia, by James M. Campbell (2008; first paperback edition, 2010)
Welfare and Charity in the Antebellum South, by Timothy James Lockley (2008; first paperback edition, 2009)
T. Thomas Fortune the Afro-American Agitator: A Collection of Writings, 1880–1928, by Shawn Leigh Alexander (2008; first paperback edition, 2010)
Francis Butler Simkins: A Life, by James S. Humphreys (2008)
Black Manhood and Community Building in North Carolina, 1900–1930, by Angela Hornsby-Gutting (2009; first paperback edition, 2010)
Counterfeit Gentlemen: Manhood and Humor in the Old South, by John Mayfield (2009; first paperback edition, 2011)
The Southern Mind under Union Rule: The Diary of James Rumley, Beaufort, North Carolina, 1862–1865, edited by Judkin Browning (2009)
The Quarters and the Fields: Slave Families in the Non-Cotton South, by Damian Alan Pargas (2010)
The Door of Hope: Republican Presidents and the First Southern Strategy, 1877-1933, by Edward O. Frantz (2011)
Painting Dixie Red: When, Where, Why, And How The South Became Republican, edited by Glenn Feldman (2011)
After Freedom Summer: How Race Realigned Mississippi Politics, 1965–1986, by Chris Danielson (2011)
Dreams and Nightmares: Martin Luther King Jr., Malcolm X, and the Struggle for Black Equality in America, by Britta W. Nelson (2012)

www.ingramcontent.com/pod-product-compliance
Lightning Source LLC
Chambersburg PA
CBHW032253150426
43195CB00008BA/434